Irish vs. Yankees

Irish vs. Yankees

*A Social History of
the Boston Schools*

JAMES W. SANDERS

OXFORD
UNIVERSITY PRESS

OXFORD
UNIVERSITY PRESS

Oxford University Press is a department of the University of Oxford. It furthers
the University's objective of excellence in research, scholarship, and education
by publishing worldwide. Oxford is a registered trade mark of Oxford University
Press in the UK and certain other countries.

Published in the United States of America by Oxford University Press
198 Madison Avenue, New York, NY 10016, United States of America.

Library of Congress Cataloging-in-Publication Data
Names: Sanders, James W., author.
Title: Irish vs. Yankees : a social history of the Boston schools /
James W. Sanders.
Description: New York, NY : Oxford University Press, [2018] |
Includes bibliographical references and index.
Identifiers: LCCN 2017031673 (print) | LCCN 2017038674 (ebook) |
ISBN 9780190681586 (updf) | ISBN 9780190681593 (epub) |
ISBN 9780190681609 (online component) |
ISBN 9780190681579 (hardback : alk. paper)
Subjects: LCSH: Public schools—Massachusetts—Boston—History. |
Education—Massachusetts—Boston—History. | Education—
Social aspects—Massachusetts—Boston. | Catholic Church—
Education—Massachusetts—Boston—History. |
Catholics—Massachusetts—Boston | Boston (Mass.)—Social conditions.
Classification: LCC LA306.B7 (ebook) | LCC LA306.B7 S33 2018 (print) |
DDC 370.9744/61—dc23
LC record available at https://lccn.loc.gov/2017031673

9 8 7 6 5 4 3 2 1

Printed by Sheridan Books, Inc., United States of America

Contents

Acknowledgments

I wish to acknowledge and thank all the people who have helped me in this endeavor. When I was researching the topic in Boston some forty years ago I was granted generous access to numerous archives, most notably the Archives of the Archdiocese of Boston, where I spent many days and weeks, and those of the Massachusetts Historical Society, but also Boston College as well as those of several Catholic religious communities, in particular the Sisters of Notre Dame and the Sisters of St. Joseph, both of which provided access to archives as well as valuable assistance and advice given by members of their religious communities. I was also granted full access to numerous research libraries including Harvard University and Boston University, where, in particular, I had access to a variety of unpublished PhD dissertations related to my research. I would be remiss if I did not also acknowledge the contributions of the Boston Public Library, which generously provided me with access to decades of Boston School Committee minutes as well as "mountains" of public school records, including school personnel. In every one of the above I was treated with warm acceptance and generous assistance, confirming Boston's reputation as a hotbed of scholarship.

I would like to thank my acquiring editor, Nancy Toff, and editorial assistants, Elda Granata and Elizabeth Vaziri, at Oxford University Press, for guiding me through the complex editing process of this book with welcoming support and great patience. I thank my project manager Prabhu Chinnasamy at Newgen Knowledge Works in India for his impressively efficient organization of the production process, and my copy editor, Wendy Walker, for expertly editing my prose and meticulously identifying oversights. It was truly a wonderful team who rendered my manuscript finally worthy of Oxford University Press.

But most especially I wish to acknowledge the present assistance and encouragement and invaluable contributions of two others. One is my long-time dear friend and now retired head librarian at American University in Washington, D.C., Dr. Patricia Wand. Without her persistent encouragement and even insistence in the recent past that I complete this work even after so many years, as well as her wise advice and active participation in putting together the final pieces, I believe that I might well have abandoned it. The second is my daughter Rachel Lark Sanders, who shares my residence and has not only consistently provided wise and incredibly insightful advice but also contributed all too much of her own valuable time not only to keeping me on track and tending to computer skills that have surpassed me, but also to contributing valuable ideas that would otherwise have escaped me. Indeed, without her personal contributions as well as encouragement in these last years I think that this book would never have been completed. In that sense, I truly consider her my co-author.

Preface

This work is intended to be a social history of the conflict over education in Boston between the so-called native Bostonians, whom I have chosen to call the "Yankees," and the immigrants who flocked into Boston mainly during the nineteenth and early twentieth centuries, of whom the overwhelming majority were Irish. The story of education in Boston during this period of roughly a century was admittedly more than a struggle between the Irish Catholics and the Yankees, and my contention is that this struggle marked a defining aspect of the city's educational history.

Given that the work is intended as a social history, it may appear strange that the chapters are divided according to the tenures of the several Roman Catholic bishops who occupied the Boston episcopal see during these roughly one hundred years. Such a division might suggest that the work is an ecclesiastical rather than a social history. On the contrary, my intention is to establish the fact that each bishop, while representing the official Catholic Church, was in his own unique way very much a part of the social history that was unfolding in Boston. Thus, the first bishop, Jean-Louis Cheverus (who served from 1810 to 1818), was an unassuming Frenchman whose nationality enabled him to benefit from the post-Revolutionary good will that Americans extended to the French, who had helped so much in the Revolution. The second bishop, Benedict Fenwick (who served from 1825 to 1846), was a Southern gentleman of Anglo-Saxon stock, a descendant of the English Catholics who founded Maryland, and a member of the noted but sometimes controversial Jesuit religious order. His pedigree strongly colored his interface both with the Boston Yankees, who admired his learning but not his religious affiliation, and his unlettered Irish flock, who complained that he "did not know the way to the Irish heart."

The third bishop, John Fitzpatrick (who served from 1846 to 1866), was born in Boston of Irish immigrant parents but was sponsored as a youth by proper Bostonians into the renowned Boston Latin School because of his natural abilities. After his return from a Catholic seminary in France, he soared into the upper reaches of Boston society. He became, in a sense, their "window dressing" Irishman, in public acting as one with them, ever careful not to offend, but in private deeply resenting what he considered their arrogance.

The fourth bishop, John Williams (who served from 1866 to 1906) was also born in Boston of Irish immigrant parents but followed a more reclusive path: he associated neither with proper Boston society nor with his Irish compatriots. He left social developments, including schooling, largely to the interplay between the Yankees, who were now fighting a sort of rearguard action to maintain control of "their" city, and the up-and-coming Irish politicians who were emerging from the Irish-dominated local wards and were now staging to take over the city.

The fifth bishop, William O'Connell (who served from 1906 to 1944), was also born in New England of Irish Catholic immigrant parents, and grandly announced at his inauguration ceremony that "the Puritan has passed; the Catholic remains." In many ways he typified the brash Irish usurpers who were taking over the city's political institutions at the same time. Though personally dedicated to providing parochial schooling for all the children of his diocese, he succeeded only modestly because Boston, including its public schools, was now a Catholic-controlled city and its schools posed no threat to Catholic children.

In his own way, each bishop functioned as a key player in the social dynamic that fashioned life in Boston during this fascinating century. Each was a part of those social forces. Thus, the division of the book based on the bishops' tenures would seem to be justified as long as one remembers that these men, though each certainly influential, were far from omnipotent in determining the Roman Catholic response to the educational issues of the day.

***

The gestation period for this book has been considerably—in fact, unusually—longer than most. In fact, it took well over forty years to develop from the germ of an idea to the reality that now lies in front of me. The question that started it all popped into my mind way back in the late 1960s, when I was still doing research at the University of Chicago for my PhD dissertation, which was eventually published in 1977 as *The Education of an Urban Minority: Catholics in Chicago 1833 to 1930*. It was part of the Oxford University Press's "Urban Life in

America" series, edited by my mentor at the University of Chicago, Professor Richard C. Wade.

I still remember that moment, as I was sitting in the University of Chicago library archives reading the transcript of a debate almost a century earlier in the Illinois State Legislature about a petition from Chicago Catholic leaders to provide tax money for their rapidly developing parochial schools. As one legislator delivered an impassioned speech against the petition, he asked a rhetorical question to the effect that "Why can't Catholics in Chicago send their children to public school as the Catholics in Boston do? In Boston, Catholic children attend the public schools." That statement seemed passing strange to me at the time, since I knew that Boston was heavily Irish Catholic, quite militantly so, and presumably not likely to allow its children to attend the public schools that Catholics in the nineteenth century so vehemently railed against as allegedly discriminatory. But I tucked the statement away in memory anyway, intending to check the legislator's contention at a later date.

After finishing my degree and taking a faculty position with the City University of New York, and after being encouraged by my mentors to pursue the line of research that my dissertation had begun, it naturally enough occurred to me that perhaps Boston would be worth investigating, at least to see if it indeed was different from Chicago. Sure enough, a couple of hours looking into old editions of the *Catholic Directory* confirmed that, while there had been Catholic schools in Boston since the 1820s, in comparison to Chicago and other urban dioceses in the East and Midwest, the Boston church's parochial school effort had been minimal, and most Catholic children had gone to public school.

The big question, then, was: Why? What was different about these two cities that might account for the divergence? Fortunately, in 1976, with the generous help of a grant from the National Endowment for the Humanities and a sabbatical from my college, I was able to move my young family to Boston for two years to pursue that question. In 1978 I returned to New York City and my position with the City University of New York, with an entire filing cabinet full of notes and copies of documents gleaned from archives large and small, libraries illustrious and relatively unknown, and from many conversations with scholars as well as school and church functionaries. All of these, taken together, had helped me develop a satisfying and persuasive answer to my fundamental research question: Why did Boston not develop a comprehensive parochial school system? I was ready to write.

That was forty years ago! What happened? Well, I did write much of the book in the handful of years immediately after 1978, using time left over from my teaching and other professorial duties as well as time from being a husband and father of young children. But then, in the mid-1980s, a friend and colleague enticed me into partnering on a small project introducing four "burned-out" public high school teachers to a more creative and, we hoped, renewing approach to teaching called "Discovery Learning." The tiny project worked amazingly well; we applied for and got a federal grant to continue and expand the program; one success led to another, and within four years we were operating on a multimillion-dollar annual budget with more than twenty full-time professional employees. Twenty-five years and some 50 million grant dollars later, I finally retired and began dusting off the old semi-finished Boston manuscript, incorporated data from previously unused notes and files, and researched at least some newer historical records and work that had been produced in the intervening quarter-century. The result is what I present here.

But before proceeding, I think it necessary to elaborate somewhat on my method of presentation. I consider myself a social historian, not a church historian. As a PhD student, I concentrated on American urban and ethnic social history. In writing my previous book on Chicago I tried to avoid not only the boosterism that had characterized most previous scholarship about the Catholic church enterprise in the United States, but also the tendency to write Catholic history from the viewpoint of the Church's hierarchy, based largely on the assumption that Catholic history was determined exclusively by hierarchical decrees and policies that were simply passed down and followed by the faithful masses. My research had convinced me that this had not been the case.

Accordingly, I have tried to explain and interpret events and trends as resulting largely from the interplay of social forces and not just hierarchical decrees. Thus, I had found that development of parochial schooling in Chicago initially gained momentum not from a decision made by the bishop but from German Catholic immigrants who were already familiar with church schools in Germany. Then the Chicago Irish joined the parochial school movement so the Germans would not get ahead of them. Then the later-arriving Poles wanted to outcompete the Germans and Irish, while the later Italian immigrants, who were not accustomed to having to support the Catholic institutions in Italy, did not at first develop even their own parishes, let alone parochial schools. In short, hierarchical decrees were always mediated and their efficacy most often was determined not by the decree itself but by the social forces as well as the individualities at work in the Catholic population, and, for that matter, in the general population as well. Further, the Catholic bishops of Boston differed among themselves with regard to the possibility and desirability of developing a parochial school system. They were not at all homogeneous in their commitment to parochial schools.

I wish to make this point as strongly as possible, especially because the very organization of the present book would seem to undermine the notion that this is a "social" history and not simply a "church" history. In fact, it will be apparent that, though the reigning bishop was indeed always a key player in determining Catholic educational policy, he was by no means the only key player; he was always hugely influenced, and sometimes controlled completely, by the various social forces that impinged on Catholic life in Boston. Nor was every bishop of the same mind with regard to the education of Catholics, and certainly none had the kind of absolute control over the Catholic flock that has often been imagined.

The various bishops were by no means equally involved in the education of Boston Catholics, nor were they equally effective in shaping the direction that education took. Thus, though it might appear at first glance that I have written a "church" history of the education of Boston Catholics, this is in fact meant to be and I hope will be read as a social history, in which Catholics, including their hierarchical leaders, were simply a part of the social fabric that made up Boston and shaped its educational endeavors during the critical formative decades covered by this book.

Irish vs. Yankees

1

Hopeful Beginnings,
1808–1823

On March 4, 1822, after some forty years of concerned discussion, the voters of Boston, by a solid majority, ratified the Massachusetts General Court's proposal to change the town's official status to that of a city. The decision signified more than a mere change in nomenclature. It meant that Boston would now no longer be governed by the informally direct democracy of the town meeting with its will executed by an equally informal board of selectmen. That system of direct democracy had worked quite well for almost two centuries. But now, by decision of Bostonians themselves, a new, more centralized, representative form of government would take its place—an elected mayor and a city council constituted by eight aldermen elected at large and forty-eight councilmen elected by wards.[1]

The decision to change governmental machinery indicated merely that a majority of Boston voters now recognized what some had seen for years past—the need for more effective ways to cope with the new issues that increasingly confronted this growing center of New England population. Boston, after all, counted almost 50,000 inhabitants in 1822, all jammed into the same tiny peninsula roughly three miles long by a mile and a half wide that had comfortably housed only a third of that number just thirty years before.[2] The very growth of population in such a confined space had aroused anxious concern for ways to deal with the welter of issues that had not existed in simpler days—how to dispose of wastes in a sanitary way; how to provide clean and adequate water; how to control the congestion by regulation of buildings, streets, and sidewalks, and through adequate transportation; how to protect the crowded buildings from the ever-present danger of mass conflagration; how to police the growing incidence of drunkenness, vagabondage, assault and battery, and other crimes; how, even, to perhaps relieve the congestion by further expanding the town's geographic limits and its usable space. Not the least of these new concerns—actually the paramount one—was the weighty issue of how to cope with the increasingly heterogeneous composition of Boston's population.

To deal with such weighty and pressing matters, the occasional meetings of citizens at Faneuil Hall would never do. That old and revered system of direct government by the citizens that, among other contributions, had played such a vital role as a forum for promoting the Revolution could not be jettisoned lightly. Before Bostonians could move themselves to the decision of 1822, they had engaged in years of careful consideration, so congenial to the reflective Yankee–Puritan temperament. The decision itself marked a turning point in the dominant Boston mentality, the terminus of a long reflection upon the great river of events that was sweeping what Bostonians considered the "Hub of the Universe" into the modern era.

True, the decision neither initiated the move to modernity nor ushered it in overnight. The Boston of 1822, despite the many changes of the past several decades, still no doubt looked and felt more like the Boston of 1722 than it did like the Boston that was soon to be. Even geographically, the modern Bostonian would hardly recognize the newly designated "city" of 1822. One could still look out to sea from the Common, as well as inland to the rolling, tree-covered hills. Charlestown, Roxbury, Dorchester, Brighton, future sections of Boston, all remained independent country towns. The South End and Back Bay still lay under water. And the city proper joined the mainland only via the narrow neck of land that stretched down what is now Washington Street to Roxbury.

But by the 1820s, with its population growing at twice the rate of the 1790s, and the rate increasing each year, Boston had for some time been struggling to expand its land mass and to establish more viable connections with the surrounding territories—the Charles River bridge to Charlestown in 1785; the West Boston bridge to Cambridge in 1792; the West Cove land fill project west of Charles Street begun in 1803; the annexation of South Boston in 1804; the cutting down of Beacon Hill to half its height begun in 1804, both to create development on the hill and to fill in the large Mill Pond separating the North and West Ends; completion of the Mill Dam, which cut off the Back Bay and connected Boston to Brookline via a highway on top of the dam; and in 1823 the project to fill in the Town Cove that lay at the foot of Faneuil Hall. Though all these projects paled in comparison to the later reclamation of areas like the South End and Back Bay from the sea, they nevertheless handily demonstrated that Boston had engaged itself in the process of rapid physical change.

Social change, too, was now rapidly overtaking Boston's vaunted stability. Despite generations of commercial contact with the most exotic corners of the globe, and despite the broadening effects of its engagement with the other colonies as well as with the colonies' French allies to win independence from England, Boston had remained very much a city unto itself. In view of that, one prominent citizen later nostalgically remembered the Boston of his 1820s youth: "with a population of wellnigh [sic] purely English descent, . . . with ancestral traditions and inspiring memories . . . both by its history and position, the town had what the French call a solidarity, an almost personal conscious-ness, rare anywhere, rare especially in America."[3] And the son of Boston's first great mayor of the 1820s described the city of his youth as "singularly homoge-neous . . . eminently English in its character and appearance, and probably no town of its size in England had a population of such unmixed English descent as the Boston of forty years ago."[4]

Much of what these nostalgic Bostonians remembered was rooted in fact. The city's population *did* still consist overwhelmingly of English stock. And the homogeneous culture, stemming perhaps from the original exclusionary Puritan theology and the founding fathers' conscious desire to build here a harmonious, homogeneous "City on a hill," a "Zion in the Wilderness," did still mark Boston off as unique, with a distinctive character and personal con-sciousness rooted now in long tradition (long at least for America).

On the other hand, such reminiscences also betrayed a wisp of wishful thinking, the vision of a Boston that once had been, as proper Bostonians liked to remember it, but that even well before the 1820s had already been slipping into history. Judged through the spectrum of later years, perhaps, the Boston of the 1820s looked idyllic. But much had changed already then, and Bostonians recognized this when they accepted the fact that their home was no longer a town but a city.

And many must also have recognized that the changes in physical char-acteristics, the newly filled land and bridges and annexations, even the sub-stantial growth in population itself, all taken together were not the only and probably not even the chief reasons for becoming a city. Compared to other centers of population in the fledgling United States at the time, the pace of growth in Boston would have to be considered relatively modest. Boston lacked the industries that were attracting immigrants to other American cities like New York. It didn't have navigable waterways that would make possible trade into the interior, nor did it even have the water power that was beginning to fuel the Industrial Revolution in other New England towns like Lowell, Lawrence, and Fall River. Its earlier wealth had been made on the trade routes to the West Indies and Far East, which had now diminished largely because of English obstruction on the high seas. It was this earlier accumulated wealth that now made possible the physical civic improvements and that was now being turned to financing the development of the new textile industry in the Massachusetts river towns like Lowell and Lawrence and to building up Boston as a financial center. But none of this produced a great need for common labor in Boston itself, except for jobs on the civic improvement projects such as filling land, building bridges, and the like.

Thus, Boston was not situated to attract huge numbers of immigrants as certain other American cities were. The immigrants who came to Boston increasingly came during this period not because they heard of job opportunities but because they could get cheaper passage, sometimes even as ballast on lumber ships returning from Liverpool to the Canadian Maritimes, from which they literally walked down the coast and drifted into Boston.

As a result, while it may have seemed disturbingly gigantic to some old-line citizens, Boston's growth rate remained modest in comparison to some other population centers in the new nation, even though it was admittedly robust enough to create the need for governmental response to expand land availability and provide at least basic social services. All of this contributed to recognition of the need to reorganize the governmental structure from the traditional informal town format, creating instead a city.

But, more fundamentally than that, it was not so much the numbers but the peculiar characteristics of the new immigrants themselves, especially the ethnicity and religious affiliation of the vast majority who arrived in Boston during the early decades of the nineteenth century that began to threaten the very essence of what Boston had always been. This new immigration threatened to destroy the centuries-old sociocultural homogeneity that had so characterized Puritan New England, and in particular, its hub: Boston. The new immigrants were mostly neither Anglo-Saxon nor Protestant, the two foundations on which the Massachusetts Bay Colony, with Boston as its center, had been founded two centuries earlier, and which the descendants of the Puritan founders had striven so mightily to preserve.

But now, the newcomers were not Anglo-Saxon but mostly Irish, and they were not Protestant but mostly Roman Catholic. This flew in the face of what many Bostonians still considered, even after two centuries, essentially Bostonian. The Puritan founders of the Massachusetts Bay Colony had gone to great lengths to ensure that their colony would remain forever as it was at its founding.

But very gradually throughout the eighteenth century, and then with shocking rapidity as the nineteenth century took hold, both the ethnic and religious purity were rapidly fading into the past. In Boston the religious factor predominated, but the ethnic was not far behind; and to many Bostonians the two could not be distinguished. Together, they constituted a disruption that called for a drastic response that could only be possible with the modernized governmental structure that status as a city could provide.

On the religious front Boston's original founders had intended it as a haven for a small, totally homogeneous group of English dissidents bound together by fervent adherence to a very specific form of Christian Protestantism. They had almost immediately passed laws that outlawed the practice of any religion other than their own. In the beginning that meant not just the hated Roman Catholicism but non-Puritan Protestant religions as well. As time wore on, and the colony was gradually exposed to outside influences, the restrictions originally placed on other Protestant bodies were gradually relaxed. By the early 1800s, not only did most Protestant denominations have a foothold in Boston, but its most liberalized expression, Unitarianism, had become the dominant religion at least in influence if not in numbers. Many prominent, old-line Bostonians had gone over to Unitarianism, and almost every one of the town's major church congregations, together with their architecturally notable church buildings, had converted to this liberal form of Protestantism, so liberal that many opponents did not recognize it as even Christian. As the final insult to the Puritan founders, the very institution they had originally founded to educate young men for their ministry, Harvard College, by the early 1800s had been taken over by a majority of Unitarian professors.

Other, more evangelical, more fundamentalist Protestant denominations, too, thrived in Boston by the early 1800s. Most of them sponsored religious newspapers that warred with one another, but especially against the more recently noticeable arrivals, the hated Roman Catholics. While they might differ violently with one another over particulars, all, except the more liberal and accepting Unitarians and to some extent the Episcopalians, who had retained many features of the Roman church, were united in their angry rejection of Roman Catholicism, which was just beginning to emerge as a serious threat as the nineteenth century dawned.

Indeed, it had taken much longer for Roman Catholicism to take root in Massachusetts, largely because of the extreme measures the colony's founders had taken to exclude it. While the founders shunned non-Puritans of any stamp, they positively abominated Roman Catholics. The Royal Patent of 1620 had banned Catholics from the New England colony unless they were willing to take the Oath of Supremacy. As early as 1647 the colony had passed a law outlawing priests, with banishment for the first offense and death for the second. In 1678, when non-Puritan Christians were first formally tolerated in Massachusetts, Papists were explicitly excluded. By 1685, in opposition to the ascendancy of the Catholic James I of England, Bostonians began their long tradition of Pope's Day celebrations, with the annual desecration of the pope's effigy on Boston Common. Under the Royal Charter for Massachusetts in 1692 Catholics were explicitly excluded from all rights, and by 1700 the laws banishing priests were tightened to mandate perpetual imprisonment for the first offense and death upon escape and recapture. Death for the priests does not appear to have been entirely unheard of, for in 1724 there was "great shouting and triumph" in Boston when a French Jesuit's scalp was brought back along with those of twenty-four Indians.[5]

By 1731, when the presence of Irish and French Catholics, attended by a priest, was rumored in Boston, the governor issued a warrant to the sheriff and constable of Suffolk County "to make diligent Enquiry after and search for the said Popish Priest and other Papists of his Faith and Perswasion [sic] and (if need be) in order to apprehend them or any of them, you are Directed and Impowered to break open any Dwelling house, shops, or other Places or apartments, where you shall suspect they or any of them are kept concealed."[6] The zeal for preventing Catholicism from taking root in Boston and its environs was considerably fortified in 1750 when Judge Paul Dudley left a sizeable bequest to Harvard College for a quadrennial lecture "for the detecting and convicting and exposing the Idolatry of the Romish Church."[7] Out of the Dudleian lectures came some of the most colorful anti-Catholic literature of the period.

Anti-Catholicism in Massachusetts had over the years lost some of the theological purity grounded in genuine differences between Puritan and Catholic belief. It had also gotten mixed up in politics and affairs of state, especially efforts to restrain the Catholic French Canadians from proselytizing Indians in Massachusetts territory. But by the 1760s and the annexation of Canada by England, the basis of anti-Catholicism began shifting from fear of French Canada to sentiments supporting the beginnings of revolutionary fervor in America. Thus, the English Crown, both for its friendly toleration of Catholicism in Canada and for its official Anglicanism, which many New Englanders saw as within the papal tradition, increasingly came under attack as soft on Catholicism and even allied with the tradition of papal tyranny. In the Boston celebration of Pope's Day one found by the 1760s the fusion of attacks on papal tyranny with attacks on the tyranny of George III. It was tyranny in all its forms that the New England revolutionaries came to loathe; and for many the prime example, the mother of tyranny at whose breast every tyranny sucked, was the Whore of Babylon herself, the Church of Rome.

Even the younger John Adams fused his opposition to England with his ancestral Puritan loathing for the Church of Rome. The Roman Catholic

Church, argued Adams, had chained human nature "for ages in a cruel, shameful and deplorable servitude to him [the Pope] . . . who, it was foretold, would exalt himself above all that was called God." Civil despotism, thought Adams, had its roots in the canon law of the Church.[8]

With the coming of the American Revolution, though, attitudes toward Roman Catholicism had changed somewhat in Massachusetts, for a variety of political and human reasons. Indeed, in unforeseen and unintended ways the Revolution opened the door for the future of Catholicism in the Puritan state. The colonies, especially the New England ones, now had to cultivate friendship and aid from the Canadians, who were mostly Catholic. They also had to rely on help from Catholic Indians in their territories, who insisted on religious freedom, among other amenities, in exchange. The American government, in an early breach of the wall of separation between church and state, actually paid to supply priests for the Indians. Even more important, Catholic France came to the colonists' aid. During the war, units of the French fleet harbored in Boston, and Bostonians, among other concessions, had to cancel the celebration of Pope's Day for fear of offending the French.

Then too, for some Boston leaders, contact during and immediately after the Revolution with other American colonies where religious toleration had advanced much further came as a cultural shock and surprise. The experience of John Adams serves as perhaps the clearest and most meaningful example. Adams, who had worried seriously about the possibility of papal tyranny in America, met Maryland's Charles Carroll at the Continental Congress of 1774 and found him to be "a very sensible gentleman, a Roman Catholic, and of the first fortune in America."[9] It took several more years, including other acquaintanceships with Catholics and an official stay in France, to more thoroughly dissipate Adam's almost inbred suspicion of Catholicism. But by 1779, when he wrote the draft for a new Massachusetts constitution, the recently liberated Adams wrote into it the guaranteed freedom of worship for all, including Catholics.[10]

Thus, the American Revolution had proved an unexpected boon to Catholics in Massachusetts, in ways that the early New England revolutionaries had never intended. The new state constitution, ratified in 1780, guaranteed freedom of public worship, though in denying to Catholics the right to hold public office and in imposing on them the duty of contributing to the tax support of Protestant ministers only, it did not go as far as Adams intended or Catholics must have hoped.[11] The meaning of genuine equality was to dawn more slowly on the people of Massachusetts, and the removal of first legal and then real barriers to equality would entail a long, step-by-step process, often marked by acrimony and grudging concession.

But at least the first major step had been taken in the new state consti-tution: Catholics were now able to come out of the closet into the full light of day. Most of the Catholics Bostonians saw in the light of day for several years after 1780 were those attending services performed by chaplains of the French fleet still stationed in the harbor until 1782, plus the ministrations by a cou-ple of itinerant French priests who happened briefly into town between 1783 and 1785 to service the small group of French merchants and officials who had collected there in connection with the Franco-American Revolutionary alliance. Gratitude to the French for their assistance in the Revolution helped Bostonians accept these French priests without rancor.

Thus, at the dawn of the nineteenth century Boston had, officially at least, accepted the notion that Catholics would be allowed to live and practice their faith in Boston, though many diehards, especially the militant evangelical Protestants, still protested their presence. For many, the presence of Catholics in Boston was doubly difficult to accept because most of these new Catholics were not even of Anglo-Saxon stock. The few French Catholics in the past had been bad enough, but at least the French had contributed resources and even personnel to the success of the Revolution. But now the Catholics one saw attending Mass as Boston moved into the nineteenth century were predomi-nantly Irish, an ethnicity reviled, and not just because of its religion.

The Irish were not entirely newcomers; they had made a noticeable pres-ence in Boston since at least the 1730s, founding the Charitable Irish Society in 1737.[12] By 1770, there were an estimated 1,368 Irish among the city's 15,220 inhabitants. But almost all of these Irish were Protestants and therefore, though ethnically discordant with the native Bostonians, religiously harmo-nious. The handful of Irish Catholic immigrants who strayed into the town in the 1760s remained inconspicuous until after toleration in 1780. But then, both because of religious toleration and because of possible employment on the several major building projects that had begun to transform the town, Irish immigrants steadily trickled into Boston.

By the founding of the first Catholic parish in 1789 Boston Catholicism was already predominantly Irish. In 1797–98, of ninety-eight Catholic bap-tisms in Boston, only twenty-four were French, and that proportion rapidly decreased in future years. After 1802 the Boston Catholic Church did expe-rience a steady inflow of Yankee converts, from eight to fifteen a year. But these made a marked difference more by reason of their status than their num-bers: increasingly it was the Irish who predominated. By 1820, for example, of 207 baptisms, 28 were adults, mostly Yankee converts, and the rest Irish infants.[13] The growth of the Catholic congregation in Boston from 1800 to 1825, despite the unsteady war years and economic depression in 1807 and after, when many Irish left Boston, was remarkable. Accounts varied, but in 1800 the number of Catholics in Boston appears to have hovered somewhere between 700 and 1,000.[14] By 1820 the number was estimated at over 2,000, and in 1825 at about 5,000.[15] The number of baptisms doubled in the five years after 1820, and the number of parishioners more than doubled, indicating a very rapid spurt. By 1825 Catholics constituted a quite noticeable 8.6 percent of the Boston population. Almost all of this increase was the result of Irish immigration, and a very visible Irish Catholic colony now existed in the North End centering around Broad and Ann Streets.[16]

New England ideas about the Irish had been formed largely through the filter of British traditions about the "wild Irish" of Elizabethan days, and horrifying tales of the Ulster Massacre, enhanced in the post-Revolutionary period by the pro-British sentiments and anti-immigration rhetoric of the Federalists. The Irish were depicted as ignorant, lazy, deceitful, cruel, bellicose, and harddrinking.[17] To staid Yankee Bostonians, the reality often seemed to confirm the expectation. When they could find work, the Irish often accepted wages so low that they displaced more demanding Yankee workmen; when they could not find work, they put a strain on public and private charity alike. Either way, they aroused resentment. Then too, they were already flocking into the Democratic Party, which both promoted further immigration and sided with Ireland in its long struggle against English oppression. Thus, the Irish, though still politically impotent on their own, added some strength to the Democratic Party and aroused Federalist antagonisms.[18] The right to hold public office, finally granted to Catholics in 1820, no doubt further raised anxieties, even though the day when an Irish Catholic could get elected to any public position in Boston still lay in the future.

The Irish were not only Catholic and foreign; they were poor. Already in 1790 a report to the bishop in Baltimore had asserted that "the Catholics are exceedingly few, not above fifty or sixty at most, and these are very poor."[19] In 1796, subscriptions to raise money for a new church produced two gifts of $10, one of $4, two of $3, six of $2, and fifty of $1—not the sign of a very wealthy congregation.[20] The following year the pastor wrote that "we are still reduced here to impotent wishes for a church building, although ours is too small; the means of our faithful not corresponding to their number."[21] The building of a new church finally commenced in April 1800 but had to be suspended in October, with the walls three feet up, for lack of funds.[22] It was completed only in 1802 with aid from Canada, the West Indies, and Mexico, and mostly from some 140 non-Catholics of Boston who alone contributed fully one fifth of the total cost.[23] Indeed, their parish priest neatly characterized the economic status of the Irish Catholics in 1802 when he described the Boston parish as "almost wholly restricted to the class which our Divine Savior would have particularly loved to instruct."[24]

The stagnant economic years beginning with the embargo of 1807 and continuing until after the War of 1812–15, which for a time destroyed Boston's economic prosperity, drove some Irish Catholics out of Boston and reduced many who stayed to even greater poverty. "Many of our poor people have no employment, and all feel the distress of the times," observed their priest; "I really do not know, at present, any of my diocesans, to whom I could apply with a good grace for even ten dollars."[25]

By 1814 the complaint about poverty had become even more strident: "We are in this town very gloomy and poor, our only comfort is to forget home and look abroad," wrote the shepherd of the Boston Catholic flock.[26] Help did come from abroad, but not enough. "Among other obstacles, one which also prevents my doing many other things is the lack of pecuniary means . . . I have received help from my family, but that is all spent."[27] The poverty of the Irish Catholics contributed to the potential for trouble. When employed, it put them in a position of undercutting native labor in their willingness to work for less. When unemployed, it contributed to the stereotype of the lazy, shiftless, drunken Celt.

It was not too surprising, then, that on June 19, 1823, a mob of angry native Bostonians attacked the Irish homes on Ann Street, smashing windows and Irishmen alike. It was a riot of modest dimensions in comparison with some that were to follow during the next two decades, but it did take the mayor and the sheriff to restore order, and it offered a sure indication that all was not entirely well in the social relations of Boston.[28]

In addition to, and fused together with, the hostilities directed toward the Irish by those Boston citizens whose jobs and livelihood were most threatened by the newcomers was the renewal during this period of militant, fundamentalist evangelical Protestantism, which railed against both the threatening emergence of Catholicism and the rise of more liberal Protestantism, especially Unitarianism. Indeed, despite its legalization in the state constitution, the actual acceptance of Catholicism as a religion was by no means universal in Boston or Massachusetts. Through all these years, beginning in the late 1790s, the region experienced a revival of orthodox Protestantism, having its roots mainly in reaction to the rationalism of the eighteenth century and resulting in the bitter controversy between orthodox and liberal Protestants that had led to the great Unitarian schism.

In one sense the internecine strife between orthodox and liberal Protestants that continued throughout this period probably diverted attention from the growth of Catholicism. But in another sense it also provided a base for attack on the Catholic Church from the orthodox camp. In their zeal to defend the purity of Christian belief, the orthodox leveled their guns first at the more influential Unitarians, but then at all others who seemed a threat to orthodoxy. In the effort to return to sixteenth-century Protestantism, they fell back on traditional polemics, including a rebirth of virulent attacks on Catholicism.

This new awakening generated a great spate of new organizations— foreign missionary societies, Sunday School Unions, Societies for the Moral and Religious Instruction of the Poor, tract societies, societies against intemperance, and so forth. Many of these engaged in efforts to counteract the evils of Catholicism, especially by weaning Catholics away from their idolatry.[29] The Boston City Missionary Society, for example, founded in 1816 to promote orthodox Christianity in Boston, gradually adopted a campaign to win Catholic children away from popery.[30] Zeal for revival also produced a rebirth of the religious press. Denominational and missionary magazines began appearing in the Boston area around 1800 and were followed by weekly religious newspapers—the Congregational *Boston Recorder* in 1816, the Baptist *Christian Watchman* in 1819, the Unitarian *Christian Register* in 1821, the Methodist *Zion's Herald* in 1823. All of these, save the liberal Unitarian organ, engaged in diatribes against "Popish intolerance," "Roman Catholic persecutions," "idolatry of Popery," "Roman Catholic superstitions," "Romish deceptions," "perverted Christianity," and the like.[31]

And yet, despite the emergence of a vitriolic anti-Catholic religious press and even the incident of physical violence against the immigrant Irish during this period, the period into the 1820s would have to be considered one of relative peace in comparison to the religious and ethnic warfare that was to rage later in Boston. The big guns were in place but were being held in check, largely by two benevolent forces that, together, contributed significantly to this period of relative calm.

One force was the coterie of well-established, old-line Bostonians, mostly but not exclusively affiliated with the Unitarian and/or Episcopalian churches, who continued to hold out a helping and even welcoming and accommodating hand to the newcomers. In view of what was to occur in just a few years to so drastically unsettle the peace between Protestant and Catholic in Boston, one might wonder how the relationship could have begun in relatively peaceful circumstances that lasted for more than a generation. In truth, the period from the legal toleration of Catholicism at the end of the eighteenth century through the first quarter of the nineteenth century would have to be considered somewhat of a brief honeymoon that already held within it the seeds of later strife.

The honeymoon had probably begun with the good will established when Catholic France contributed to the success of the War for Independence, and when men like John Adams discovered that Catholics like the Carrolls of Maryland were patriots too. In fact, when Bishop John Carroll of Baltimore visited the single Boston Catholic parish with its roughly 120 members in 1791, he was given a warm welcome by the city in recognition of his proved Americanism and his acknowledged status as a gentleman of standing in his own right, and in demonstration of the apparent new openness toward radical religious and cultural diversity in Boston. Bostonians were even more pleased when Carroll settled differences between a couple of French priests with questionable backgrounds and a zealous but autocratic and indiscreet former Congregational minister, John Thayer, who had converted to Catholicism in Europe, become a priest, and returned to evangelize his fellow Bostonians whether they wanted it or not.[32]

And these beginnings of peaceful and even warm relations between Protestant and Catholic in Boston were further enhanced when Carroll finally found a priest properly suited to shepherd the Boston flock. Francis Anthony Matignon, a learned theologian displaced by the French Revolution, able, pious, and genuinely humble, arrived in 1792. Within a year he had healed the French–Irish schism, paid off a debt incurred by his predecessors, and "notably softened hostile prejudice."[33] By 1795, when he sought American citizenship, his application was endorsed by five Protestant ministers.[34] And in 1796 he was joined by a beloved former student and disciple, Father Jean Cheverus, also a refugee from the French Revolution, and also a man of learning, piety, and gentle, humane prudence.

It was Fathers Matignon and Cheverus who together constituted the second force that contributed so much to the maintenance of relative religious and ethnic peace in Boston during this period. These two ably guided the nascent Boston Catholic parish until Matignon's death in 1818 and Cheverus' return to France in 1823. Their enlightened, diplomatic leadership maintained peace among the Catholics themselves, despite the potentially explosive anomaly of a French clergy presiding over a congregation that was predominantly Irish. During these years, when the Catholic Church in New York, Philadelphia, Charleston, and other urban centers was rocked with internal ethnic strife,[35] ethnic peace reigned among Roman Catholics in Boston, and not a single conflict between clergy and laity during this period has ever come to light.

But probably even more significant, Matignon and Cheverus, at first because they benefited from the good will Americans extended toward the French, but increasingly because of the quietly diplomatic way in which they conducted themselves, became quite beloved in Boston. Examples of mutual help and respect were plentiful on all sides. Thus, when Matignon wished to refurbish the congregation's rented church in 1793, $278 was contributed by such prominent Boston Protestants as Thomas Russell Sr., Joseph Coolidge, Samuel Parkman, Theodore Lyman, and Charles Bulfinch.[36] When the parish's first permanent church was constructed in 1803, prominent non-Catholic Bostonians contributed fully one fifth of the cost, with President of the United States John Adams heading the list. The list included such other worthies as Nathan Fellows, Harrison Grey Otis, David Sears, Samuel Tuckerman, Gardiner Greene, Joseph Coolidge, and Theodore Lyman.[37] The church itself, designed in elegant but simple New England style by Boston's leading architect, Charles Bulfinch, could hardly be distinguished from Protestant churches nearby. It seemed to say in form and substance that Catholicism in Boston would blend peacefully, unassumingly, and respectfully into the town's life and culture. Indeed, this was the obvious intent of Matignon and Cheverus.

When the younger and more vigorous Cheverus was made first bishop of the new Boston diocese in 1808, with jurisdiction over all New England, the prospect of a permanent Catholic bishop in Puritan Boston seemed to arouse few fears, except among the more diehard religiously conservative Protestant sects. The quiet, gracious way he conducted himself and exercised leadership assuaged anxieties. The pope in far-off Rome might plan tyrannical coups, but not the gentle Cheverus or his mentor Matignon. Indeed, many were the signs of harmony. When Boston feared invasion during the War of 1812, Cheverus led two hundred parishioners in the digging of fortifications on Dorchester heights. His personal care of the poor, troubled, and destitute of the Catholic flock drew widespread appreciation. By 1817 he could report to Rome that "we are now in this city . . . where a few years ago, the name Catholic Church was, so to speak, infamous, and that of Priest, abhorred, we are now looked on with veneration and friendship, kindly regarded and kindly treated."[38]

Cheverus counted among his true and lifelong friends Josiah Quincy, Boston's most notable early mayor and Federalist leader; Gardiner Greene, the city's wealthiest man; the prominent lawyer and writer Samuel Knapp; and numerous other Boston notables such as Harrison Gray Otis and Francis Parkman Sr. These gentlemen, and others, he saw frequently at the exclusive Anthology Club, the literary society that included the most important of Boston's intellectual, social, and political leaders. He was invariably invited to the most important town functions, including meetings with President Monroe during the latter's visit in 1817. Cheverus was also on good terms with some of the Boston ministry, especially the Unitarian, counting among his friends Edward Everett and the Rev. Mr. Pierce of Brookline.[39]

In truth, the feeling of good will that so encouraged Fathers Matignon and Cheverus did come mainly from a single source—the Unitarians.[40] And even the Unitarian friendship put the Catholic leadership on the horns of a tricky dilemma. Unitarians had proven themselves accepting and liberal, even though they had little use for Catholic doctrine as such. Matignon and Cheverus found themselves attracted to the Unitarians because of both their tolerance for Catholics and their generally warm humanity so akin to their own. Yet the two priests feared and despised Unitarian religious belief.[41] In belief, Catholics stood much closer to the orthodox, but in sentiment much closer to the Unitarians. The problem posed a constant tension—between friendship with the Unitarians as persons and avoidance of what was perceived as insidiously attractive doctrinal heresy. Hence, even while courting the friendship of prominent Unitarians, Matignon and Cheverus privately dissuaded Catholic parents from sending their sons to Harvard College because of the danger to their faith there.[42]

On balance, then, the foundations of religious peace and good will in Boston did not rest on terribly firm ground. But on the whole, largely because of the good will extended toward Catholics by the more liberal Unitarians and to a certain extent by the Episcopalians, both of which were peopled by many of the city's more prominent and better-educated families, relations between Protestant and Catholic in Boston were better during these years than they were to be for a century and more, partly, of course, because Catholics still remained a novel and relatively insignificant minority; partly because the post-Revolutionary spirit of liberality and tolerance still breathed in the land, enhanced in Boston by the humane influence of Unitarianism; but partly also because of these two French expatriates who did so much to smooth over and soften differences.

In many ways, to be sure, the post-Revolutionary period, after such a long history of bigotry, did see the lessening of religious prejudice in Boston. The aid rendered by Catholic France, and Spain too, during the Revolution was long remembered, as was the loyalty of American Catholics themselves. The general enthusiasm for freedom, equality, and tolerance in the spirit of the Bill of Rights heightened the willingness among many to accept all persuasions. The weakening of traditional Calvinism and its harsh rejection of diversity improved the climate for acceptance. And so did the beneficent presence of Fathers Matignon and Cheverus, as living proof that the Catholic Church could not be all bad. Consequently, if the benevolent influence of these French priests coupled with the generosity of the recently ascendant Unitarians and other more accepting religious groups combined to hold off an outbreak of all-out religious warfare in Boston during the first quarter of the nineteenth century, it probably also contributed to largely suppressing the potential ethnic conflict between native Bostonians and the Irish Catholic newcomers, limiting physically violent outbreaks to just the one occurrence during this period on Ann street in 1823.

Already, though, there was one sphere of activity that posed potential long-term trouble. The French clerics with their prominent Yankee converts to Catholicism might go to gracious extremes befriending and being befriended by their prominent Protestant hosts, even while the evangelical press railed powerlessly against the threat of popery. And Protestants of various denominations might attend their respective churches on Sunday while Catholics attended their single parish church, all worshiping the same God according to their own beliefs, neatly avoiding potential conflicts over religious differences. The more benevolent and friendly Protestants might even willingly help the poverty-plagued Catholics build their own church where they could worship separately.

But there was one institution that was expected to bring Protestants and Roman Catholics together under one roof under conditions where differences in religious belief could not be avoided or ignored. This was the school, for both Protestant, regardless of denomination, and Roman Catholic assumed that religion belonged in the school. But whose religion? So, while the issues of religious difference could be politely avoided as long as Protestants and Catholics attended separate churches, it could not be avoided if Protestant and Catholic children attended the same schools.

The potential for disagreement leading to conflict was greatly compounded in Boston by the fact that the Puritan founders of the Massachusetts Bay Colony had from the very beginning made schooling supported at public expense a cornerstone of their social experiment. As early as the 1640s the Puritan fathers had thought it necessary to require a school in every town as insurance against "that Old Deluder Satan" who sought to keep men from knowledge of the Scriptures by keeping them illiterate. Therefore, not only did an organized legal effort to provide schooling come early to Massachusetts, but it came with the clearly defined purpose of explicitly perpetuating those religious values around which the entire society was organized.

Boston itself had actually anticipated the Old Deluder Satan Act by over a decade, hiring a schoolmaster in 1635 and founding the Latin School in 1636. By 1645 Boston had a formal schoolhouse and a house for the schoolmaster, with a permanent endowment of land to support expenditures. By the mid-1640s support for schooling was already one of the town's largest tax expenditures.[43] Accordingly, Boston to this day can boast that publicly supported education in what is now the United States began here. If the next century and a half saw fluctuation in the fortunes of the schools and some changes in their social purposes, it did not see any substantial abandonment of the fundamental belief that schools exist to preserve and promote the well-being of society, and that the well-being of society is founded on religion.

Throughout the eighteenth century Boston maintained a school in each of five sections of town, in addition to the Latin School, and allocated some 16 percent of its total expenditures to their upkeep.[44] While the purely religious and moral purpose of the schools became overlaid with education for economic well-being, reflecting the commercial character and concerns of Boston, that transformation did not seem out of harmony with the original ideal. Prosperity, after all, was a Puritan virtue in itself, and it seemed entirely consonant that the basic textbook, *New England Primer*, should teach that "In Adams Fall we sinned all" as well as "The idle Fool is whipt at school."[45]

Massachusetts, and particularly Boston, had not waited long after nationhood to further upgrade its long tradition of public schooling. In 1789 the state legislature passed the first comprehensive education law in the United States. Though not yet compelling children to attend school, it required every town to support an elementary school, and the larger towns a grammar school as well, and provided that teachers be certified as educationally and morally fit.[46] The concern for educational legislation was prompted no doubt by a variety of convergent factors—the new need for an educated electorate; the need, voiced by Boston's own Noah Webster, to develop a spirit of national patriotism among the new nation's youth; the prospects for commercial expansion; and a nascent concern for public order in a society just beginning to experience the chaos of early urbanization.[47]

Within months of the new state law, Boston, maintaining its reputation as educational leader, determined to go well beyond state requirement in laying the genuine foundations for the nation's first urban school system. Boston provided, for the first time, that girls should be educated at public expense as well as boys, though their school day and school year was to be limited to half that of boys.[48] Under this plan, Boston continued to provide a college preparatory Latin school, plus separate reading and writing schools offering instruction in English grammar, spelling, writing, and arithmetic, open to children from seven to fourteen. Schools were to remain open all year, with uniformly fixed class hours from 7:30 a.m. to 11 a.m. and 2 to 5 p.m. April through October, opening one hour later and closing a half-hour earlier the rest of the year. Students attended either reading or writing school in the morning and the other in the afternoon. Curricula were specified, including the textbooks to be used.[49] To oversee the implementation of all this, and to oversee and set policies in the future, Bostonians set up a separate school committee to replace the selectmen who previously had administered all the town's affairs, including education. The Boston School Committee was elected annually after 1789, one member from each ward.

The creation of a separate school committee, perhaps even more than the precise regulations about schools, curricula, and textbooks laid down in the law, underscored the extreme importance Bostonians placed on their schools, more extreme than ever before. The school committee would be able to oversee the implementation of the law on a day-to-day, year-to-year basis. And the quality of men elected to the very first committee demonstrated its value to Bostonians. The committee included men like Thomas Dawes, a judge, presidential elector, and member of the first Massachusetts state constitutional convention; George R. Minot, municipal court judge and president of the Massachusetts Charitable Society; John Coffin Jones, successful merchant and state senator; and Charles Bulfinch, architect. The addition of several prominent doctors, lawyers, and clergymen accounted for over half the committee.[50]

Under the 1789 act, Boston enjoyed the only real public school system in the new nation—open to the children of all residents and administered democratically through popular election. Boston citizens through their town meeting voted over one fifth of the public tax money for the support of these schools. Nowhere in the new nation, and probably nowhere in the world at the time, had a society placed so much emphasis on and taken so much pride in providing public support for the education of its young. And the public schools of Boston stood ready to enroll and educate the children of these new Catholic immigrants.

But for Catholics, to attend these schools posed a serious dilemma. Both in law and in practice one could find more than sufficient grounds for Catholic apprehension. The control of public education in Boston, as in Massachusetts, was, of course, completely in the hands of Protestants, who frequently warred among themselves over control of the schools but who agreed for the most part on at least a few principles that Catholics were bound to find offensive. The Massachusetts law of 1789, which had begun to rejuvenate public education in the state, required that

It shall be, and it hereby is, made the duty of . . . all . . . Instructors of Youth, to take diligent care, and to exert their best endeavors to impress on the minds of children, and youth, committed to their care and instruction, the principles of piety, justice, and sacred regard to truth, love of their country, humanity, and universal benevolence, sobriety, industry, and frugality, chastity, moderation, and temperance, and those other virtues, which are the ornament of human society, and the basis upon which the Republican Constitution is founded.[51]

The Catholics of Boston could on the surface have found little to quarrel with in this moralistic mandate, save perhaps too much stress on those peculiarly Puritan virtues like sobriety, industry, frugality, and temperance. But the rub came in the fact that the great majority of New Englanders at the time still assumed the inseparability of morality and religion. How could the masters "impress on the minds of children" these great virtues other than in the context of religion, as taught in the Bible and through the supreme example of Jesus? How, indeed, could youth acquire these great virtues except through the saving grace of God, a fundamental belief of all orthodox Christians?

The Boston School Committee, as a pertinent example, within four months of its passage, had further specified the state law by voting "that it be the indispensable duty of the several school-masters, daily to commence the duties of their office by prayer and reading a portion of the sacred Scriptures, at the hour assigned for opening the school in the morning; and close the same in the evening with prayer."[52] Hence, the school committee added prayer and Bible reading as a necessary means of ensuring the virtue of the town's pupils.

Here, no doubt, the Catholic leadership had cause to demur. Whose Bible? Whose prayers? Without question, the Protestant King James Bible and the Protestant version of the Lord's Prayer. At a time when differing translations of the Bible and different forms of the same prayer symbolized fundamental theological, cultural, and political differences and still made blood run hot, a practice that seemed totally inoffensive to Protestants of almost all denominations constituted sectarian teaching for Catholics. Catholics, indeed, considered Bible reading unadorned by the Church's official interpretation to be an openly Protestant exercise in itself. In Catholic belief the Bible belonged to the Church and the Church alone could interpret what it meant, while in classic Protestant belief God spoke directly to the individual through the Bible. Consequently, for Protestants reading the Bible in school without commentary from church authorities seemed a perfectly desirable Christian exercise, while to Catholics it seemed an affront to their fundamental doctrine.

The public school textbooks themselves, even aside from the Bible, gave some ground for Catholic apprehension. The Boston School Committee, aside from enjoining its reading twice a day as a religious exercise, affirmed the Bible as one of its major textbooks. The version, of course, without need to specify, was the King James, which was banned by the Catholic Church. Then too, in some of the other textbooks adopted, Catholics might find offensive passages. *Webster's Speller*, for example, contained six pages of Bible quotes.

In short, the Boston public schools were effectively Protestant public schools. To a degree they taught Protestantism formally, as in the form of prayer and Bible reading and in certain of the textbooks. And, of course, the teachers were all Protestants, as were all the school committee members, many of them even Protestant ministers. Children were expected to pray the Protestant version of the Lord's Prayer and recite the Ten Commandments. They read the Protestant translation of the Bible daily not only as an exercise in reading but as a form of devotion.

Thus, the traditional pervasive Protestantism of the public schools, to which Catholic parents were invited and encouraged to send their children, posed a very serious threat of undermining the peaceful and even friendly relations between the Catholic clerics and Boston's establishment, even the more liberal Unitarians and Episcopalians. Differences of religion could easily enough be avoided when Protestants and Catholics attended separate churches on Sunday, as long as they joined together in saving the city from the English, or promoted and built civic improvement projects, and the like. But the differences could not be avoided when it came to the schooling of the children. While both sides agreed that education should be imbued with religion, they radically differed on the question of *which* religion.

All this the French clerics who guided the fortunes of Boston Catholicism during this period could not in conscience accept. In characteristic fashion, though, they resisted gently, quietly, without fanfare, and without prescription or proscription, but firmly nevertheless, as seen in their concerted efforts over a period of twenty years. Rather than try to change the practices prevalent in the city's public schools, or to publicly protest these practices, they quietly but consistently attempted, though without notable success, to provide their own schooling alternative for Catholic children.

Even before the coming of the French priests, Father John Thayer, the converted New England minister, had informed Bishop John Carroll in 1793 that he wished to introduce into Boston some "religious women, skilled in both English and French, and outstanding examples of holy life . . . to supervise the education of young women."[53] He even bought, with his own money, a three-story school building at Prince Street and Margaret's Lane in the North End and "assigned the property to Father Matignon in trust."[54] The school was never opened, but not because of Matignon's disinterest. Indeed, in 1806 Matignon wrote to Bishop Carroll that only one thing still afflicted his Boston congregation, and that was the absence of a school, which he thought to be "absolutely indispensable."[55] Matignon began a "subscription" to support a school. It netted $573.01 by 1807, enough to make a down payment on a piece of land next to the church.[56]

Meanwhile, Boston Catholics had taken measures to provide a kind of education for at least some of their children, as was entirely common at the time. In 1804 the Holy Cross Church committee decided that "till a house or room can be provided for a school, and till the congregation be able to bear the expense, a small compensation be paid to the young gentleman who now keeps a school, to enable him at least to pay a part of his rent, of at least ten dollars a quarter."[57] The "young gentleman" was John Sinnot, an Irish immigrant with unfulfilled aspirations to become a priest.[58] The subsidy did in effect pay for the schooling of a few Catholic boys. By 1805 the parish committee was also making payment for "the schooling of poor girls at Mrs. Torpey's school." Mrs. Torpey was a member of the parish.[59]

These "schools" enjoyed a shaky existence in the next years. The boys' school lasted under Mr. Sinnot until 1807 and was then revived in 1812 under a Mr. Heaney, "an Irishman, who was also a colored person."[60] A small private Catholic school was also run from about 1812 to 1816 by a semi-invalid Alsatian priest, who then departed.[61] The girls' school ended with the death of Mrs. Torpey in 1806 and was apparently not revived, though for about ten years after 1811 Madame Duplessis, widow of a French navy captain, with her two daughters kept a private school that catered to Catholic girls.[62] These kinds of schools, consisting of a single teacher, were not at all unusual at the time; in fact, the publicly supported schools of Boston often consisted of no more than that. In this case, though, each of the schools, however private and personal, had the support of the Boston Catholic congregation, always in spirit and sometimes monetarily as well.

But, despite the obvious efforts, through these first two decades of the nineteenth century, when Bostonians were building the nucleus of the new nation's first modern public school system, the Catholics failed to establish even one school with a building that belonged to them alone. In 1816 Cheverus complained that "we have not even a school, and we are too poor to establish one."[63]

There were, though, some signs that events might take a more favorable turn. In 1815 Father Thayer died and left $10,764 and other properties explicitly for establishing Catholic schools in Boston. Thayer had also laid the groundwork for bringing a community of nuns to Boston. With this better financial situation, Cheverus began to act. In 1818 he observed to the archbishop of Baltimore that in Boston one finds "free schools for all the children" and added that "we try to teach our children by frequent catechism classes; but schools exclusively for Catholics would be much preferable."[64] By 1919 Cheverus had bought additional property next to the church and by the end of the year had a convent and school built there. In June 1820 a group of four Ursuline nuns arrived from Montreal, and in September the first ever institutionally Catholic school opened in Boston with more than one hundred day pupils, all girls, half attending in the morning and half in the afternoon.[65] This school was apparently a free school for poor Catholic girls, though the Ursulines simultaneously began a more select, tuition-supported academy attended by both Catholic and Protestant girls.[66]

By the early 1820s, then, Boston had a single Catholic school, and one fact was clear: the one hundred or so girls attending the Ursuline school did not constitute any real threat to the viability of the town's public schools. By 1820, as a matter of city policy, public schools were available to all four- to fifteen-year-olds, and enrollments had reached more than 3,800: 1,600 four- to seven-year-olds in the newly authorized (1818) primary schools and more than 2,200 seven- to fifteen-year-olds in the grammar schools.[67] How many of these were Catholic children was not recorded, but, even though schooling was not yet compulsory and many Catholic children of the poor immigrants who had recently entered Boston did not attend any school at all, many did. All but the girls in the Ursuline school must have been attending public school, unless they could afford to be instructed privately, which was still a very common practice in Boston.

The Ursuline school constituted the Catholic school "system." It was hardly more than a token, and the Catholic leadership had meant this tiny girls' school taught by nuns to be much more than this. They had worked and planned for its establishment for over twenty years, striving to raise funds and to secure nuns to teach the children. The record shows that poverty most probably accounted more than anything else for the failure to open additional schools. Wealth among Catholics in Boston at the time was an absent commodity. And, while Protestants might contribute funds for the erection of Catholic churches, they were not about to contribute to Catholic schools when they were already paying substantial taxes (approximately 20 percent of the city's public expenditures) for the support of public schools that stood ready to accept Catholic children, and that enjoyed high esteem built up over two centuries.

Though the French clerics who presided over Boston's Catholics made no effort to secure public support for the parochial schools they were determined to create, at least one Catholic layman, a native Bostonian and convert to Catholicism, did so. In 1806 Dr. Stephen C. Blyth wrote a letter to Harrison Gray Otis, then president of the Massachusetts Senate, requesting legislative approval for a lottery to be run by Catholics as a means of raising money to start a school. Blyth reminded Otis that the law permits approval of lotteries for projects of "public utility." He then went on to argue that a Catholic school would be a "public utility" even though "public schools are numerous and open to youth of all persuasions." Blyth argued that public schools are not truly open to Catholics because "Catholics have an involuntary and afflicting scruple of sending their children to the common schools, where the integrity of their peculiar faith is apt to be shaken by heedlessness or design."[68] In other words, at least according to Blyth, there was, either intentionally or unintentionally, an element of anti-Catholicism in the public schools. Blythe's proposal was not accepted.

Meanwhile, in keeping with its gentle policy, the Boston Catholic leadership made no open protest about the public schools of Boston. It simply voiced its desire, within its own circle, to provide separate Catholic schools for Catholic children. But during these years the effort would have to be judged only marginally successful at best. It made no significant impact on the schooling of the town's Catholic children, nor did it hinder the development of public schooling. If any Bostonian looked amiss at the founding of the Ursuline school, as some did, the objection went unnoticed. Regardless, no one seemed to see in it the portents of a massive Catholic defection from the public schools or the cultural homogeneity inculcated there. Many private schools still existed in Boston anyway, and a large segment of the population still chose them. In fact, of those who went to school at all, almost twice as many attended private schools as attended the public ones.[69] Besides, if the gentle Cheverus was going to teach a few Catholic girls in his own school, no doubt he would see to it that they imbibed essentially those virtues that formed the bedrock of New England society. He had striven, after all, to be like them himself. He was a man who could be trusted.

But the end of this benign beginning was at hand. One cause was the continued influx of impoverished Catholic immigrants from Ireland. Another cause was the fact that around 1820 Cheverus had begun to think of retiring from Boston.[70] The death of his dearest friend, Father Matignon, in 1818, added to health problems, had greatly reduced his desire to live, and his thoughts turned to retirement and preparation for death. Then, too, developments within the American Church had convinced him that his usefulness had neared its end. As late as 1819 four of the five American bishops were French, but the Irish now made up the great majority of Catholics in America, and the hierarchy in Ireland was pressuring Rome to appoint Irish bishops. Cheverus himself, genuinely above nationalism in church affairs, believed passionately that the American hierarchy should be constituted by local men of whatever national ancestry. Then three successive episcopal appointments in 1820—to Charleston, South Carolina; Richmond, Virginia; and Philadelphia—all of Irishmen who had never set foot in America, demonstrated that his view had been rejected by Rome. The future seemed to belong to the Irish.

With a view to withdrawing from Boston, Cheverus did his best to handpick an acceptable successor, Father Taylor. Taylor seemed an ideal choice—a convert from Protestantism but of English descent, well-educated and well-mannered and therefore hopefully acceptable to Bostonians. He also had years of experience in America, several of them in Boston itself. Cheverus spent two years preparing Taylor for the future. Boston, too, seemed ready to accept him, as evidenced in his being invited to offer the official prayer at the opening of the state Supreme Court in 1823.[71]

Meanwhile, news of Cheverus' intentions to resign from Boston had reached France and was greeted first by invitations and then a command in name of the king not to retire but to accept a bishopric in France. Cheverus was at first deterred from leaving Boston by the wishes of his American superior, Archbishop Marechal, and by a groundswell of protest in Boston itself. The latter in particular swayed him. On April 22, 1823, a letter was sent to France protesting Cheverus' removal. It was signed by 226 prominent Bostonians, ranging from Mayor Josiah Quincy to Harrison Gray Otis to Daniel Webster. The list included major bankers, merchants, and the new industrialists like the Lawrences and Lowells. The letter itself was especially significant in the reason it put for keeping Cheverus in Boston:

> The Catholics of this place . . . are generally . . . persons who need not only instruction as to their great duties as Christians, but also advice, consolations, encouragement or correction in their temporal concerns . . . To accomplish objects so important to them, and so necessary to the good order of society, the most commanding confidence is indispensable in their ecclesiastical rulers.[72]

Cheverus himself at first was apparently influenced by this appeal and decided to stay in Boston. But his resolve was broken first by insistence from the French Grand Almoner, the royal official in charge of ecclesiastical affairs, that the king himself wanted Cheverus in France. It was, perhaps, also shaken by the Almoner's terse and entirely accurate penetration of the memorial from Boston. The citizens of Boston, wrote the French official, "look more to public order, which you help to maintain by your virtues, than to the prosperity of the Catholic Church, in which they have no interest."[73] The Almoner had no doubt read the letter from Boston's prominent citizens more accurately and dispassionately than Cheverus had. The letter did stress Cheverus' role in maintaining "the good order of society" and his indispensable value "in our social community," especially in controlling Catholics in need of "encouragement or correction in their temporal concerns." The letter, indeed, sounded typically Bostonian, revealing that same concern for civility that had already put so much energy into the common school movement itself.

Many Bostonians no doubt shared the view expressed by one of them that Cheverus "did more for the peace and order of the city, through the moral means which he employed, than was effected by all the various machinery of the law."[74] In any event, Boston lost Cheverus just at a time when "the good order" of Boston society was about to undergo its severest strains yet. Further, despite Cheverus' warnings about his successor that "a stranger would not succeed there. No one can do anything in a city like Boston, unless he has the support of public opinion," Rome appointed not Cheverus' choice, but a complete stranger.[75]

In hindsight, the first chapter of "modern" Boston Catholic educational history might be considered merely a staging period for what was to come. During this roughly quarter-century the Catholic church took solid though still relatively shallow root in Boston after two centuries of first total proscription, then reluctant tolerance, and finally a time of relatively peaceful though tenuous toleration, thanks in large part to the influence of more liberal elements in the Boston establishment and the quiet, unassuming demeanor of the French clerics who headed the nascent diocese, but also to the fact that the Irish Catholic newcomers still made up less than 10 percent of the city's population.

The Catholic leadership did, though, recognize the areas of almost certain conflict, and particularly the essential objectionable features of the city's publicly supported schools, much revered by the "native" population but offensive to Roman Catholic sensibilities because of their obvious Protestant flavor. Sincere efforts of the Catholic leadership to counteract this objectionable feature of life in Boston by opening their own schools saw only token success during this period, a lack of success that proved to be a dire forecast of the decades ahead even as Roman Catholicism was to emerge from its humble beginnings in Boston to become the city's dominant religion.

2

Laying the Cornerstone, 1825–1846

The departure of Bishop Cheverus from Boston in 1823 occurred at the same time that highly significant changes were starting in Boston itself. One of these was simply the greater availability of educational opportunities for Boston's children, a development that coincided with the arrival of many more Catholic immigrants, mostly destitute Irish families. This development led to very negative changes in the attitudes of Boston natives toward Roman Catholics, particularly the Irish. Due to the arrival of so many new Catholic immigrants, the changes in their attitudes toward the "native" Bostonians, and the arrival of a new Catholic bishop who differed greatly from Bishop Cheverus contributed significantly to a scenario that differed greatly from the relatively peaceful and mutually cooperative atmosphere that characterized Cheverus' tenure.

The years roughly between 1825 and 1845 saw the continuation of a rather mixed array of educational opportunities for children in Boston. There were still many of the private educational enterprises that apparently had always flourished, usually conducted by a single teacher, as well as numerous "charity" schools conducted by religious and/or philanthropic organizations, plus the "Sunday schools" introduced in recent decades by churches that engaged children for the entire day on Sundays to teach not just religion but basic literacy. But because there was still no compulsory schooling law, many children attended no school at all.

The volume of these various educational opportunities declined drastically during the 1820s and after as the longstanding commitment in Massachusetts to public support for education came to fruition, particularly in Boston, through the creation of the new nation's first public school "system." Although there was still no compulsory schooling, the city fathers had evolved, with resolute and prolonged effort and considerable controversy, a nascent but comprehensive educational system financed at public expense and supervised by Boston citizenry. For the first time it included primary schools, actually begun in 1818, for both boys and girls between the ages of four and seven who were not otherwise being educated, with a separate board to implement the program, hire the teachers, and supervise the new schools that were mandated to teach the rudiments of reading, writing, and arithmetic. Second, it included an expanded number of the traditional grammar schools that had existed since Puritan times for youngsters seven to fifteen who could already read and write and were ready to proceed to "higher studies" in grammar, spelling, writing, and arithmetic to add to their basic literacy skills. Finally, for those so inclined and able, usually the sons of Boston's elite, the Boston Latin School accepted boys at least ten years old who had already achieved literacy in English, and provided them with a solid introduction to Greek and Latin.[1]

These public schools were financed by taxpayer dollars and were presided over by an elected school committee. By 1820 there were already 34 primary schools with over 1,600 pupils and a grammar school in each ward with a total of 2,203 scholars. By the late 1820s about 45 percent of Boston's school-aged population attended these primary and grammar schools, and the city was spending almost 20 percent of its budget on public education. However, the program left much to be desired if measured by modern standards: the schools typically consisted of one teacher with an average of sixty-two children in a single, crowded classroom.[2]

Still, though rudimentary, the Boston schools stood out in the entire state of Massachusetts as the exemplar of the public or "common" school movement as it was then called. Massachusetts exemplified for the entire new nation the nascent "Common School Crusade." In 1837 Boston's own Horace Mann would be appointed as Secretary of Education to the Massachusetts Board of Education, the country's first state superintendent of education.

In Boston most assumed that the curricula of all these schools were infused with religion, as they always had been. This included regular reading of the Bible not just as a literacy exercise but also as a devotional one, as well as textbooks that explicitly and implicitly inculcated the traditional virtues and beliefs of Protestant Christianity as well as a consistently Protestant interpretation of European historical events, taught de facto, though not by law, by Protestant teachers and supervised and enforced by a de facto exclusively Protestant School Committee.

This was the educational picture that confronted the Roman Catholic immigrants who settled in Boston during this period. Not only were they faced with already existing publicly supported schools that openly taught the fundamentals of Protestant Christianity, but they were under at least psychological pressure to send their children to them, if they sent them to school at all. Given that the Boston public schools presented a clear challenge to the faith of the Roman Catholic newcomers, one might expect that Boston, even more than other American cities, would witness a concerted counter-effort to provide a Catholic school alternative to the public schools. The fact is, though, that the overall parochial school effort in Boston was much less than would have been expected, and the actual outcome was not very impressive, at least in terms of providing a substantial alternative to the public schools themselves. The major reasons for this "failure" would appear to be several interlocking factors:

1. The nature of the Catholic newcomers themselves, overwhelmingly destitute Irish immigrants with no tradition of schooling in their homeland
2. The background and personal characteristics of the Catholic bishop who presided during this period (from 1825 to 1846)
3. The policies adopted by the Boston establishment that controlled the public schools.

These three factors interacted in unique ways to determine how the education of Boston Catholics evolved during this second quarter of the nineteenth century.

The newcomers to Boston during this period, as they had been for several decades, were overwhelmingly from Roman Catholic Ireland. And they were many indeed. Although earlier historians tend to attribute the great spurt of growth in Boston Catholicism to the Irish famine years after 1846, and to look upon the earlier decades as relatively quiescent and peaceful ones of modest development, Catholic insiders and at least the more astute and concerned native Bostonians of the period experienced the roughly twenty years after 1825 as ones of explosive growth for the Catholic church, fraught with intense group tensions and conflict.[3]

While Boston itself underwent steady growth during these twenty years, with its population roughly doubling, all informed estimates placed the Roman Catholic rate of development far higher. The number of Catholic baptisms alone increased by 500 percent between 1825 and 1846.[4] The Catholic bishop, using a formula based on baptisms, put the number of Catholics in the city in 1825 at 5,000, between 8 and 9 percent of the total population. Ten years later he reported "a most astonishing increase" to 22,000, over 400 percent more than in 1825.[5] By 1845 Boston's first great demographic statistician,

Lemuel Shattuck, in his official Boston city census called explicit attention to the remarkable growth of Catholicism. Shattuck calculated that Catholics numbered 30,000,[6] fully 26.23 percent of the population, and a remarkable 500 percent increase over 1825. Catholicism had become by far Boston's largest single denomination, with the Unitarians at 15.7 percent a distant second, followed by the orthodox (Congregationalists) a poor third at 12.68 percent. "The number of Catholics here given," asserted Shattuck, as if to silence the skeptical, "is greater than has been generally supposed, but it is not, we think, an over estimate, if the facts respecting our population be compared."[7]

Thus, in the twenty years after 1825 Catholics increased in Boston from less than one in every ten to more than one in every four. More ominous still to the traditionally Protestant city, as Shattuck's census report pointed out, the Catholics gave birth at a rate so much higher than the average that "about half of all the children born in the city are of Catholic parents."[8] New England Catholics were disproportionately concentrated in Boston at this time: in 1845 fully half the Catholics in all New England lived in Boston.[9]

This rapid growth of Roman Catholicism set in motion a chain of events that greatly influenced the nature of Boston Catholic life during these twenty years, and, indeed, of the city's life itself. That Roman Catholicism, a religion not that long ago totally proscribed, and more recently cautiously accepted under the benign tutelage of Bishop Cheverus, had emerged in the span of less than twenty years as Boston's largest denomination provided reason enough for the buildup of tensions. But to make matters much worse, the socioeconomic characteristics of the city's burgeoning Catholic population added greatly to the problem.

Only a small part of the remarkable growth could be attributed to the steady and significant trickle of Yankee converts to Catholicism, from thirty to sixty a year according to church records, some of these from prominent families and positions, a fact that made their conversions publicly noteworthy.[10] Also remarkable for their exceptionality rather than their numbers were the handful of Italian seamen, musicians, and businessmen who had settled in Boston by 1845. German Catholics made up a somewhat more sizeable element. By the mid-1830s about three hundred attended the occasional German masses offered at a chapel in the cathedral's basement, and the bishop estimated there were as many as 800 German Catholics in the city.[11] By 1842, after much dissension, and with the financial help of the bishop and the Leopoldine Society in the fatherland, the Germans began constructing Holy Trinity Church in the South End. By 1845 an estimated 2,000 Germans belonged to this parish.[12]

But by far the remarkable population gain resulted from the steady influx from Ireland. Of the ten Catholic parishes in Boston and nearby Charlestown and Roxbury by 1846, all but one was Irish, and even the single German church gave over its basement chapel on Sundays to services for the Irish Catholics in the neighborhood.[13] It was the Irish who set the tone for Catholicism in Boston more than in any other American city. They projected Roman Catholicism's image to the rest of Boston. And already by 1845 Bostonians perceived this image as deeply disturbing, certainly because of its religious symbolism but possibly even more because of its social implications.

Lemuel Shattuck's census neatly characterized the problem in cold numbers and percentages. It established that the influx of Catholics, particularly of the Irish variety, had for the first time brought group-based social pathology to Boston. Social deviance could now be attributed not merely to individuals or even families but to ethnic groups, particularly the Irish. Thus, Shattuck found that by 1845 almost 40 percent of the paupers in the House of Industry were Irish.[14] More than half of those committed to the House of Corrections were of foreign birth, mostly Irish.[15] In the Irish Broad Street area people lived at a density of one to every seven square yards, compared to one to every forty-eight square yards on Yankee-occupied upscale Beacon Street. "A more densely populated locality is scarcely to be found in any country," observed Shattuck. And the density appeared to be increasing rapidly due to both continued immigration and the "prodigious fecundity" that is "a most remarkable characteristic of our foreign population."[16] Despite crushing poverty that severely taxed the ability to support large families, the Irish on Broad Street were producing one baby for every fifteen people every year compared to one in fifty in some other parts of the city.[17] Only the abnormally high infant mortality rate caused by the poverty-ridden congestion itself exercised some control over otherwise unbridled population growth.[18] Adding to the malaise, and despite the laudable progress of the temperance movement among the Irish, Shattuck found hundreds of liquor shops run by Irishmen.

The underlying causes of all this—the pauperism, the crime, the poor health, the congestion, and the drinking—were in large part economic. The signs of wealth among Boston's Catholics were few indeed. The occasional men of means like the Genoese importer Niccolo Reggio and the ready-made clothing manufacturer Andrew Carney were the rare exceptions. The Yankee converts were often of substantial means.[19] German immigrants included a few merchants like Matthias Melchior and Sebastian Kramer and some craftsmen, but relatively few Germans could be found "in good circumstances"; most, though "honest, industrious people" according to their bishop, were entirely "dependent upon their daily labor for their subsistence."[20] Indeed, it took ten years of fundraising and substantial foreign gifts to finance the building of the German Holy Trinity Church.[21]

Among the Irish there was a contingent of carpenters, masons, black-smiths, grocers, bakers, and the numerous tavern keepers who did a brisk business.[22] These were largely the ones who could afford to purchase their own pews in the various churches at up to $150 each,[23] but that constituted half a year's wages for the vast majority of Irish immigrants finding their way into Boston during this period. Most came with no more than $10 in their pockets and with neither the education nor the skills that might have equipped them for jobs more stable and respectable than day labor.[24] Most had tilled the soil in Ireland, not as destitute as those about to deluge New England after the Potato Famine of the late 1840s, but not equipped either to compete in the urban mar-ketplace. Though some shipped directly from Liverpool, most came to Boston during these years via the Canadian Maritime Provinces, to which they got cheap passage directly out of Ireland as ballast in the timber ships. They then walked down the Maine coast or shipped on coastal routes, settling in Boston because of its proximity and because they could afford to go no further.[25]

Unfortunately for many, because Boston lacked the cheap water power that was moving New England into the Industrial Age, it was not primarily a factory town and did not offer opportunity for mass employment in labor-intensive industry. Thus the unskilled Irish often found only irregular employment, usually on a day-to-day basis, in manual labor. They built the railroads that spoked out from Boston during these years to Lowell, Providence, Worcester, Albany, Lynn, Salem, Newburyport, Portsmouth, Fall River, and others. They often found employment within Boston on the public works that continued to transform the city. Their cheap labor made possible such projects as the filling in of South Cove and the widening of the neck connecting Boston to Roxbury that created the new South End.[26] Some worked in the Charlestown Navy Yard, on the wharves, or in the glassworks at Lechmere Point.[27] For most, their twelve to sixteen hours of hard labor on days when work was available put only $1 in their pockets, hardly enough to subsist. This was the typical Boston Catholic parishioner after 1830. In a word, the Catholic Church in Boston was already far on the road to becoming a church of the urban proletariat.

The condition of the Irish Catholic immigrants as they settled in Boston did not sit well with many native Bostonians, and these years were filled with frequent outbreaks of hostility that underlined fundamental dislike of both the ethnicity and the religion of the newcomers. The more peaceful days of the Cheverus era were over.

The great depression of 1837 fell by far most severely on the Catholic popu-lation since they were, as the bishop described the situation, "generally, either poor laborers dependent for their sustenance upon their daily labor, or per-sons hired in factories." They had "no recourse left them" when depression hit and were "seen wandering in quest of employment. Their families reduced to starvation are driven to seek relief in the charity of the faithful."[28] Periods of depression merely accentuated the generally prevalent destitution through all these years, and so did the proliferation of Catholic charitable agencies: the Boston Roman Catholic Hibernian Relief Society in 1826; the Roman Catholic Children's Relief Society in 1829; the Young Catholic's Friend Society in 1835; the St. Vincent DePaul Society in 1838; and relief societies formed in individual parishes.[29] And, as Shattuck had trenchantly noted, the Irish used up a disproportionately large share of tax-supported public relief.

The poverty of the city's Catholics, coupled with other undesirable characteristics, most notably their religion and their ethnicity, grated on the sensibilities of Yankee Boston, most notably the native working class. At almost every point of contact with their new environment, the Irish rubbed them the wrong way. On the labor front, as New England industrialist Amos A. Lawrence put it, "Our lower people hate the Irish because they keep their wages lower."[30] Temperance crusaders and just plain sober Bostonians were offended not only by the hard drinking of the Irish but by the opposition of their leaders to total abstinence legislation. While many Irish Catholic leaders advocated temperance and even total abstinence on a voluntary basis, they argued that "laws are designed to guard the persons of property of the community against direct attacks; not to root out vice from the hearts of men and women."[31] The Irish opposed the legislation of morality, and that offended the Yankee reformers. And the stubborn adherence to Catholicism by the Irish offended many, especially the "Orthodox," but also increasingly groups like the Episcopalians who had grown apprehensive as a result of the Oxford Movement, which was attracting the learned to Catholicism.[32]

The alarming growth of the Catholic Church in Boston coupled with the socioeconomic condition of the largely Irish parishioners greatly exacerbated the centuries-long suspicion and even hatred of Catholicism. The combination led to smoldering tensions periodically erupting into open conflict.[33]

As early as 1826 a quarrel between the Yankee coopers' apprentices and Irish laborers resulted in the raiding of the Irish district around Broad Street for two straight evenings. In 1828 and again in 1832 the Protestants of South Boston took to the streets against the Irish, apparently because the Irish were beginning to move into that district. The year 1834 saw the celebrated burning by an anti-Catholic mob of the Ursuline convent and boarding school in Charlestown, the premier piece of Catholic real estate in all New England at the time, followed by threats to Boston Catholic churches for months after.[34] So intense was the tension that the Irish kept twenty-four-hour guard of their churches and were said to be "wound up to a point where if you go one step further the cord will snap. All are now armed and they keep themselves so."[35] In the years after 1834 insurance on Catholic church property in Boston cost four times the normal rate both because of the ever-present danger of arson and because it was realistically feared that "if the church caught fire, the firemen would make no effort to save it."[36] Violence erupted again on Broad Street in 1837, occasioned by a chance encounter between a volunteer fire company and an Irish funeral procession. By the time the battle ended, twenty-nine Irish homes had been plundered.[37] That same year the Montgomery Guards, an Irish voluntary militia organization of the sort generally popular at the time, were physically attacked by other militia groups because they were accused of being controlled by the pope and made up of "a class of foreigners the most ignorant and degraded among us."[38]

These were not isolated deviations from a normally friendly accommodation between the Yankees and Irish in Boston. Despite the signs of friendship from prominent individuals and even groups such as the Unitarians, the tensions were profound and to be expected. Irish leaders themselves attributed "the principle cause of the persecution which they suffer" to

THEIR RELIGION [sic]. In all the assaults which have been made upon the Irish, their religion has been the chief point of attack. Catholicism has been the slogan cry of attack, whether of midnight incendiaries, or newspapers established for the purpose of banishing Irishmen from our shores, pulling down their houses, pelting their persons, or desecrating the last resting place of their dead![39]

However, the Catholic bishop was probably more accurate in seeing the troubles "as well on account of the poverty of the people as of the prejudices of the anti-Catholics of various denominations whose hatred against us seems to have revived of late and in direct proportion to the increase of our number."[40]

But whether stemming mainly from anti-Catholicism, from prejudice against the Irish, or from an irreducible fusion of the two, there can be no doubt that the Irish themselves, and even notable others, perceived the hostilities during this period as a permanent state. The evidence is overwhelming. In 1834 the bishop complained of a man being beaten in Pond Street "by a gang of ruffians for no other cause but that of being an Irishman and a Catholic."[41] He also contended that the Irish "have been horribly insulted in the public prints which insults they feel most sensibly."[42] After the 1837 riots he complained that

the Yankees have every disposition to do injury to the poor Irish; while they have no redress in law. Their persons have been attacked, their houses pillaged and plundered, Broad Street their principal place of abode, has been made a scene of desolation. Shame! scandal! Altho attacked, they have been the ones hitherto arrested and brought to trial for a riot.[43]

The contention that justice was not administered fairly in Boston was common and continued. As the Irish perceived it, the city peace officers, many of whom, according to The Boston Pilot, were "taken from a class in society whose hatred of the Irish is well known," regularly arrested Irish shop owners for breaking the liquor-selling laws, but not the non-Irish owners of the large public houses: "It is easier to prosecute indigent Irishmen, because their friends are not generally rich and influential."[44] Even some Yankees were profoundly troubled that "Antipathies will pursue the foreigner, sympathies will protect the natives, punishment will be administered with an unequal hand," as the city's (and nation's) most prominent educator, Horace Mann, gloomily analyzed the situation in his journal after the Broad Street riot of 1837.[45] The Irish also complained bitterly that laborers were often subjected to fraud by dishonest contractors who refused to pay them after a day's labor or paid them less than the agreed wage.[46] And even when paid the agreed wage, it was claimed that the amount was unfair. Thus, the city's Catholic newspaper complained that the Irish were employed in building canals and railroads by which their employers became rich and by which "the poor Irishmen [sic] has, in return, a miserable pittance insufficient to procure the comforts of life, and he can lay up nothing for sickness and old age."[47]

Even the public press in Boston was perceived by the Irish as offensive. "No day passes without a recurrence of something to wound their feelings," complained one Irishman in 1834. "The public journals are replete with insinuations, tending to degrade the Irish character. Their religion is scoffed at, their habits and customs ridiculed."[48]

The sense of outrage and alienation was everywhere present among the Boston Irish. In fact, when in 1834 the Catholic layman Patrick Donahoe bought the Boston Catholic newspaper from the bishop, who had founded it and edited it since 1829, he redirected the paper's editorial policy. The bishop had named the paper The Jesuit, a provocative name in itself at the time and obviously indicative of the paper's purpose: to boldly advance the cause of Catholicism. Once in Donahoe's hands, however, the paper's name was changed to The Boston Pilot, and its editorial policy, though still basically Roman Catholic, was redirected almost exclusively at the problem of Irish alienation, particularly after Donahoe took over the editorship in 1839. In his first month as editor Donahoe declared that The Pilot would be "strictly devoted to the rights of adopted citizens; to the exposition of the true relation in which they stand with respect to the native born. The causes of hostility to citizens not natives of the United States, will be frequently and emphatically examined, and particularly those which extend so general and strong an influence against Ireland and her descendants."[49] In following issues he wrote three lengthy editorials about the persecution of the Irish in the United States. And in response to criticism that he was stirring up the embers in a time of relative quiet, Donahoe retorted that the fundamental, abiding condition was one of hostility against the Irish, and that it was best to talk dispassionately about it during what could only be a lull in the storm.

At first *The Pilot*'s tone seemed conciliatory, pleading for time as the healer of wounds. To the Yankee contention that "the Irish retain their old customs when they come to this country," he respectfully admitted that

> this may be partially true. It cannot be expected of a body of emigrants [*sic*] that they should immediately divest themselves of their habits in which they have been brought up from childhood, around which entwine the memory of their mother's smiles and their father's hearthstone. It is expecting too much of any class of men that they should instantly change their own national habit in every particular.[50]

The implication in this early statement was that with time the Irish could be expected to shed their own culture in favor of the native American.

Before long, though, *The Pilot* had shed its conciliatory, Anglo-conformist baggage. By May it was railing against the growing practice among the Irish of changing their names.[51] And by June it had taken an entirely different stance on the complaint that the Irish "do not mingle with the people among whom their lot is cast."[52] The Irish, said Donahoe,

> set the Yankees an example which they would do well to follow, in *MINDING THEIR OWN BUSINESS* [*sic*]. It is truly marvelous and somewhat amusing to hear the most exclusive and illiberal people on the face of the Earth complain that foreigners do not mingle and unite with them. As well might the trapper find fault with the game who will not run into his guns. Do not the Irish know that the embrace of this people is destruction, and that they can mingle with them on no other condition but that of abject servitude. Have they not had abundant evidence that the Yankees only love foreigners as the hunter loves the deer?[53]

Thus, from the recurrent violence against them, from their complaints about injustice in Boston, and from their conscious effort to resist becoming like the Yankees, it becomes clear that the essential Irish experience was truly one of alienation. The evidence also makes clear that the Irish were pulled in two different directions. On the one hand they did wish to gain acceptance, and thus the pressure to adopt the host culture was intense. On the other hand, they resented what they perceived as the arrogance of that host culture, and thus they also felt intense pressure toward separatism. This cultural tug of war had been declared by the 1830s, and it was to last for at least a century.

One might think that, given the intensity and frequency of hostilities with the "native" population, the Irish of these decades would have opted to separate themselves as much as possible, building their own institutions and a way of life independent of mainstream Boston. But, surprisingly, and highly significant for the future of Boston, for the most part this is not what they did. Whether knowingly or unknowingly, whether moved by a belligerent will to win or by a need to belong, during these decades they were encouraged by their own fellow Irishmen who had emerged as their leaders to take on the larger Boston society on its own terms. Rather than retiring into their own separate way of life as a people, they set out to participate fully in the larger society while fiercely retaining their own identity.

In the face of what they perceived as impenetrable obstacles to social and economic acceptance and integration, they focused on the one outlet that could not be denied them, despite the rampant nativism that swept the city and the nation during this period. This was participation in the political process. As early as 1833 the Boston Catholic paper recommended that "all Irishmen in this country get themselves naturalized as soon as they conveniently can. The cost is a mere trifle, the advantages great."[54] Among the advantages, according to the paper, would be respect:

> Let every adult resident Irishman come forward and legally enroll his name for citizenship, in a word, let him become naturalized, and what would be the result? I will tell you. He, that would now point with the finger of scorn at the poor Irishman, with the hod on his shoulder, would then "doff his bonnet," and be the obsequious humble servant on the eve of an election. Should we boldly and proudly take our stand among the citizens of Boston; abuse and insult would cease to ring in our ears; and in a word, we would be respected.[55]

Thus, the Irish very early on grasped the basic principles of American politics, and launched an effort that, beyond their wildest dreams at the time, would eventually lead to a very different Boston, one that in many respects they would control themselves.

When Donahoe took over editorship of *The Pilot* in 1839 he immediately made "the law of naturalization" into a "leading topic" of constant discussion and exhortation.[56] *The Pilot* incessantly urged rapid naturalization, printed information on the process and regulations surrounding it, supported the formation of "Naturalization Associations," and solidly opposed the Whig attempt to lengthen the waiting period for citizenship.[57] By 1843 *The Pilot*, possibly buoyed by Bishop Hughes's recent political success in New York, launched a full-scale "campaign,"

> a movement which will ensure the triumph of justice and religious toleration in this State, reached by the freeman's weapon of redress, the fearless INDEPENDENT BALLOT. Let it be understood that we have no intention of drawing off into a third party. We shall stand on a third ground between the two great divisions of party, and select our friends and denounce our foes in them both.[58]

What Donahoe advocated was what had already been successfully done by Bishop Hughes in New York. True, Donahoe's Boston crusade was still largely rhetoric in the 1840s, since as late as 1845 the Boston Irish immigrants remained highly disorganized and the process of naturalization was just getting under way.[59] The Boston Irish had not yet ever elected anyone to public office in Boston, nor had they even influenced an election. Although it would be some years before the first Irishman would hold a public office in the city, the number of qualified Irish voters increased by 50 percent between 1841 and 1845 alone as a result of the Irish naturalization program. The handwriting was already on the ballot box.

Understandably, the avenue the Irish chose to redress their wrongs served to increase tensions in Boston as natives took alarm at this clear threat to their hegemony. In 1844 the Catholic bishop remarked about the "great excitement in the City against Catholic Foreigners since the election held last Monday in consequence of their supposed partiality to the Democratick [*sic*] ticket."[60] As future events would demonstrate, the alarm was well founded. And, on this point at least, the Irish could already begin to boast that they were not holding themselves aloof from American or Boston life.

It may be that the very early recognition on the part of the Irish lay leaders in Boston that citizenship coupled with determined engagement in the political process would be the route to survival, recognition, and even success in this otherwise hostile city was also instrumental in determining their policies regarding the schooling of the young. In truth, it does appear that the Irish lay leaders, having experienced little opportunity for education in Ireland, did not express much interest in general in the schooling of the young, whether public or parochial. They did not participate in or even pay much attention to the educational revolution that was taking place around them as Boston led the way in the "common school crusade" that created the nation's public school system. But they did not promote parochial schools either, which were being developed elsewhere in American cities to counteract the new public schools. To do that would have taken them in a separatist direction, the opposite of their clear desire to engage in and become a part of the city's public life. Thus, with regard to schooling of the young they followed a decidedly ambiguous and not very engaged course, welcoming from time to time the few parochial schools that came into existence but not urging Catholic youth to seek Catholic education and not opposing the rapidly growing public school system.

The Irish leadership in Boston did recognize the need for education, though it appears to have singled out neither public nor parochial schools as the remedy. Significantly, *The Pilot* launched a fairly intensive examination of the Irish American situation, together with a campaign for its improvement. In the very first editorial on the question the editor argued that

> The Irish in America are a critically situated race; they are numerous, with many virtues and many faults, few of them of a serious nature, the greater number arising from the absence of sufficient education to guide them through the perplexing duties of a new sphere of life, laden as they are with the disadvantages of upholding a libeled birthplace and an unpopular faith.[61]

The Irish, contended *The Pilot*, had grown greatly in numbers, but not in influence. If they wanted to avoid a continuation of prejudice and bad treatment, they would have to "change their tactics and enforce by a higher course of conduct their standing in social and political circles." And the way to do this was through "some schooling, to fit them for the discharge of the many important duties of their new station." "Irish immigrants must educate," contended *The Pilot*, "or they must sink."[62]

Thus, *The Pilot* recognized lack of education as a major weakness in the Irish American situation. The lack it attributed partially to a phenomenon afflicting Catholics in general:

> In every Catholic community, needing education, there is unfortunately a too great propensity for more physical enjoyments, such as balls, raffles, etc. etc. This is a natural consequence of the misapplication of that contentment which our holy religion gives to

the minds of its professors. We would not, in any harmless particular, abridge the pleasures of the people—but their precious hours should at least be divided between culture and relaxation.[63]

More fundamentally, though, it correctly attributed Irish lack of concern for education to the English penal code, which had produced generations of illiterate Irishmen.[64] No group required education more, argued The Pilot, "than Irish immigrants, whose education has been prevented, at its natural season, by the results of an infernal penal code."[65]

Surprisingly, however, this impassioned plea for education was not followed up by a crusade for either public or parochial schooling. It did result for a time in an attempt to provide "adult" education in the evening for teenaged youth who worked during the day, but this effort seems to have been short-lived, largely because it was taken over by well-meaning Yankees who failed to live up to the expectation that the program would also include developing pride in the students' Irish heritage. The sequel made it clear that The Pilot's main concern was not the children of the Irish immigrants, but the immigrants themselves. The Pilot's analysis of the Irish situation led to a crusade not for either parochial or public schooling but for adult education. "How are we, who work for fourteen or sixteen hours per day, with scanty means and many depending on us" to gain an education, asked the editor? The answer was through some form of adult education during "the long, precious, dark evenings, when the mind, if not fed, will wander in childish fancies, or become steeped in inebriation, or lost in frivolous conversations."[66]

At first The Pilot advocated Mutual Irish Clubs with dues of perhaps 25 cents per week to buy newspapers, periodicals, and books, but the idea quickly picked up strong support from unexpected sources. In less than six months an adult education program had been launched by the Boston Repeal Association of the Friends of Ireland, headed by J. W. James, who was apparently not Irish and who "had been for many years a member of the city government, and the Massachusetts Board of Education."[67] The idea elicited strong support from Yankee notables, among them men like James, S. B. Emerson, Gideon Thayer, the Rev. Charles T. Barnard, H. B. C. Green, the Rev. Amos Smith, Dr. Walter Channing, G. W. Snelling, Dr. John D. Fisher, and J. T. Tower.[68] They formed the Friends of Adult Education, and The Pilot exhorted Irish immigrants to participate: "Let us not deceive ourselves as to our actual condition—we are but 'hewers of wood and drawers of water."[69] The Pilot saw adult education not only as the road to "make immigrants more wealthy and independent," but as a general panacea. Adult education will "lessen prejudice," insisted The Pilot; it "will stop the objection that naturalized citizens are ignorant voters; will give the laborer more respect in the eyes of employers; will safeguard constitutional government;" and will make immigrants "even more American than they are now."[70] All this was to be done in complete independence of the official Church, though *The Pilot* expressed hope for "the private cooperation of all denominations, more particularly of the priesthood."[71]

The program had as its primary purpose reading, writing, and arithmetic for boys eighteen and older and girls sixteen and older; the classes were taught on three nights a week, with the academic basics supplemented by lectures, adapted to the laboring class, on food, clothing, fresh air and ventilation, basic morals, political economy, human physiology applied to health, first aid, natural philosophy, and municipal law.[72] This program at first seemed highly successful, attracting over two hundred students just as a start.[73] But, despite frequent editorials in *The Pilot* supporting what was now called the Boston Institute for the Education of Adults, and despite constant exhortations that "Irish immigrants must educate, or they must sink," the program did not prosper for long.[74] Within a year *The Pilot* had to admit that "it has not advanced with great rapidity."[75]

Just why the adult program faltered was never explained. Its attractiveness for the Irish might well have diminished because its direction was rather quickly coopted by Yankees, however well-meaning. Indeed, when *The Pilot* first proposed the idea, it advocated a very different curricular orientation from what developed. "This schooling should be of two kinds—Prospective and Retrospective," argued the editor.[76] By prospective he meant relating to America, its history, constitution, and so forth; by retrospective he meant relating to Ireland: "Without more or less of these kinds of knowledge, no Irishman can be a good American citizen."[77] In learning about Ireland the Irish would "learn about ourselves, of our national feelings, our tastes, our capabilities, and our desires. The more proud of his native country an Emigrant may feel, the more likely he is to become a good citizen."[78] Thus, the program as first envisaged was to serve a kind of bicultural purpose that would enable immigrants to function in America while at the same time developing their own consciousness as Irish. In addition, *The Pilot* at first insisted that the program should be "truly and purely Catholic"[79] as a means of preserving the immigrant's faith in the face of New England prejudice.[80]

Instead, once the Yankee "directors" had taken over and implemented the program, the curriculum included neither Irish history and culture nor Catholicism, but subjects much more attuned to the Puritan ethic and the desire to preserve social order and stability. The Irish immigrants may well have experienced alienation from all this.

But of more importance here is the fact that the only educational crusade undertaken by the Irish Catholic lay leadership of the day was one for adult education. The editor seemed more concerned about the present generation of adults than about the future generation of children. Before the initiative was usurped by "native" Bostonians, this campaign for adult education fit nicely into the fundamental thrust to enter immediately into the political process. With regard to the education of children, *The Pilot* was for the most part silent, although the editor must have known that many Catholic children who went to school at all attended public schools.

Thus, the Irish lay leadership, at least as expressed by *The Pilot*, seems to have been only minimally concerned about basic schooling for children, whether public or parochial. *The Pilot* did not comment at all on the several conflicts, particularly one in 1843, between their bishop and the Boston School Committee over alleged anti-Catholicism in the public schools. On the one hand the Boston Irish lay leadership seems to have welcomed parochial schools, at least judging from the written record, but without ever advocating them as a matter of policy. The Catholic newspaper regularly reported on the few parochial schools that existed and their activities and public exhibitions, and supported them in various ways.[81] In 1832 it welcomed the Sisters of Charity as "much wanted in this city,"[82] though the Sisters of Charity were more engaged in charitable works than in education, and the welcome may have had more to do with these. In 1838, after a visit to the parochial school in Worcester, the editor expressed hope "that public spirit enough may be found in Worcester to place the school on a permanent and sure foundation. Let the parents of those children remember that a good education is the best legacy they can give them in this world, next to being well instructed in their religious faith."[83] And again in 1840 *The Pilot* stated that "It gratifies us to learn that the spirited congregation of St. Mary's are about to establish a Catholic Free School."[84] *The Pilot* approved the plan in effect in Lowell where separate schools were conducted for the Irish Catholics by teachers of their choice at public expense, but praise for the Lowell plan focused exclusively on the liberality of the town's citizens and not on the benefits of a separate education for the Irish.[85]

Never during these more than two decades did *The Pilot* take up the issue of parochial education as a matter of policy or principle, nor did it ever urge parents not to send their children to the public schools. This was simply never discussed, as if it did not exist as an issue at all. When Bishop John Hughes engaged the city and state of New York in a battle over the right of parochial schools to share in tax funds, *The Pilot* rooted heartily for Hughes,[86] though this may simply have reflected its admiration for Hughes as its esteemed hero in the Catholic immigrant struggle for recognition. But in all its extensive coverage of the controversy in New York, *The Pilot* never once applied the issue to Boston. It made no reference to the need for parochial schools or their right to a share of tax funds in Boston, perhaps knowing that such a "right" would not even be considered in Boston.

The behavior of the Irish lay leadership with regard to educational issues during this period suggests that they were oblivious to or uninterested in the public school revolution that swirled around them. *The Pilot* never engaged in any of the lively and critical contemporary debates over public school issues; in fact it never even mentioned them. For example, it did not even comment on the fact that in 1837 Massachusetts was the first state to appoint a secretary (superintendent) of education, Horace Mann, nor did it ever comment or report on Mann's tireless crusade for the public or common school as the "equalizer of the conditions of man." In 1842 it announced "an Oration which will be delivered by the honorable Horace Mann" at the Fourth of July celebration on Boston Common, but after the celebration, though devoting over a column to the procession of the Catholic temperance societies as "the grand feature of the day's proceedings," it had no comment on Mann's address or its contents.[87] The silence merely typified *The Pilot*'s almost total lack of involvement in or even awareness of public school affairs.

As for the official Catholic Church leadership in Boston during this second quarter of the nineteenth century, the education of Catholic children was a very serious issue, characterized essentially by a desire to provide Catholic education for Catholic children but in reality by the failure to develop a significant Catholic alternative to the public schools. This anomaly had several sources but was most intricately tied up in the personality and convictions of Benedict Joseph Fenwick, the man who became the Catholic bishop of Boston in 1825.

At first glance Rome could not have chosen a man better suited to preside over Boston Catholicism's rapid growth amid both severe economic restrictions and recurrent outbreaks of hostility. Fenwick came to Boston at the age of forty-three possessed of great learning, immense practical ability, experience well beyond his age, and robust, energetic good health. He had worked as a priest for years in New York, learning first-hand the ABCs of parish, college, and orphanage building. He was a member of the renowned Jesuit order and had served two terms as president of its Georgetown College in Maryland. When a schism threatened to render the Diocese of Charleston, he was sent in as troubleshooter. His reputation for learning, able management, and holiness had spread throughout the American Catholic Church. For ten years prior to 1825 he had been spoken of and recommended as certain episcopal material. Perhaps even more important than all these accomplishments, Fenwick was directly descended from the English Catholics who had founded the colony of Maryland. He was of English descent and seemed the kind of man whose ability, experience, and impeccable lineage could easily match the challenge now arising for the Catholic Church in Boston and New England. In most respects he was.[88]

Fenwick moved in on the Boston diocese with characteristic energy and self-confidence. His first actions were entirely indicative of the decisive, innovative, rational, often ingenious, if autocratic, administrative style by which he would supervise every detail of Boston Catholic affairs for the next twenty years. In 1825 Fenwick did not really have much in the way of institutions to take over. The only real parish in all of Boston was his own Cathedral of the Holy Cross, with an estimated 300 Catholics who should be parishioners.[89] In addition, there was a small chapel of St. Augustine in South Boston, built by his predecessor mainly to bury the dead in the adjoining cemetery. In the whole of New England, which then comprised the Boston Diocese, there were only seven other churches—one in Salem, one in New Bedford, one in Claremont, New Hampshire, and four in Maine, including two Indian churches. More depressing still, there were only three priests in the entire territory, only one of them in Boston.[90] In addition there were four nuns, members of the esteemed Ursuline religious order, whom Bishop Cheverus had brought from Montreal in 1820 to run a school next to the cathedral. They lived in the heart of Boston, educating some one hundred poor girls in the basics as well as a handful of more fortunate Catholic and Protestant girls in a more exclusive "academy" atmosphere.[91] This was the extent of Catholic schooling in Boston when Fenwick arrived.

The conditions for the simple exercise of Catholic worship for the growing mass of Irish immigrants, which was much more basic to the Church's welfare, were even more desperate. His greatest initial effort went into meeting this need. In addition to doubling the size of their cathedral, Catholics in Boston proper added six new parishes to the one already existing, two more in territory later to be annexed, and seven in nearby suburbs. (Two were built in the North End, 1836 and 1843; two in the newly expanding South End, 1836 and 1844; another in East Boston, 1844; one in Charlestown, 1829; and another in Roxbury, 1845.) No sooner had St. Mary's parish in Charlestown opened in 1829 than the bishop observed: "there are Catholics enough to fill yet two more churches."[92]

After establishing new churches in the North and South Ends in 1836, he again remarked that "so rapid is the increase of Catholics that I find new congregations rising up where two years ago I little expected anything.[93] After complaining in 1842 of "the great crowd of people unable to get into any of the Catholic Churches,"[94] he saw to the building of five more in the next three years. Even then, the Boston Catholic newspaper complained that "in Boston we are sadly off for want of churches. There is not half enough room for the people."[95] Many were said on a Sunday morning to be found "kneeling on the stone steps" outside the churches and "following in prayer the progress of the Mass inside."[96]

The new bishop, though, quickly assessing the immediate situation, also determined on a more far-reaching course of action. First, he saw the greatest need as that for more priests. Because he was averse to tapping the only quick source, the foreign market, he looked for a way to begin raising up an American-trained clergy. Second, upon visiting the Ursuline convent next to the cathedral, he was horrified at the cramped living conditions and the sisters' inability to take fresh air except on the public streets. "Health has long since taken leave of the house," he noted in his diary.[97] He resolved to provide them with quarters more suitable to their calling. Third, the cathedral could no longer accommodate the burgeoning number of parishioners; something had to be done to alleviate the squeeze.

Fenwick's simultaneous solution to all three problems revealed a practical genius for neat, economical solutions to seemingly complex issues. He determined first to move the nuns into a proper domicile in the country where they could thrive physically and spiritually and develop the kind of exclusive convent boarding school for which they were noted.[98] He therefore bought a ten-acre farm across the Charles River in the western part of Charlestown near Bunker Hill.[99] By 1829 he had enlarged this to twenty-four acres and built an elegant three-story brick structure housing the sisters and over sixty boarders. The sisters financed this development with the $800 Fenwick paid them for their Boston property next to the cathedral.[100] For Fenwick this was a highly prized institution, and he visited it often and watched its progress with great pride.[101] He made the sisters' former Boston property into his own residence, with room for several young men whom he intended to recruit to study for the priesthood—an incipient seminary under his own roof. He simultaneously determined to raise and enlarge the cathedral, both to provide room for the bulging congregation and to provide space for "ample classrooms in the basement for boys' and girls' schools."[102] The basement he fitted out as a large chapel for extra Sunday Masses, with folding doors to close off the sanctuary during the week when the rest of the space was used as a school. The school was to serve a dual purpose: first the obvious one of providing education for the Catholic youth of Boston and second the practical one of helping defray the expenses of the seminarians, who would simultaneously study for the priesthood and pay their way by teaching in the school.[103]

Thus, with just a few bold moves and a minimal expenditure Fenwick had greatly enlarged the cathedral's capacity, laid the groundwork for a clerical seminary, provided space for a parish school, and established a proper, upscale convent school in a choice Charlestown location. These early actions typified the approach that allowed the bishop to cope successfully and economically with the rapid transition to urban Catholicism in Boston, even though the scale of development remained small enough to enable a man of Fenwick's ability to exert personal supervision.

He exercised close control over almost every detail. When constructing the Charlestown convent he let all the contracts, everything from the building of a fence to the installation of a slate roof.[104] As new churches rapidly became needed in Boston and elsewhere, he hunted for the site, bought the property, arranged the financing, and supervised the construction.[105] By the end of his reign he had seen to the erection of fifteen new parishes and churches in and around Boston, not to mention the many throughout New England.

He seemed ever on the move, not just in Boston but in the whole of New England, over which his bishopric held jurisdiction. In the early years he traveled by coach and coastal packet or braved winter blizzards through Franconia Notch, then increasingly on the new railroads to Worcester or Lowell or wherever to seek a site for a new church or to settle a dispute.[106] In 1833 he bought half a township in the backwoods of Maine, determined to colonize it with Catholic Irishmen.[107] By 1842 he had settled over three hundred there, having chosen the settlers from among the "industrious poor," sold the plots to them on favorable terms, supervised the clearing of the land, experimented to select the right crops, built sawmills, erected a church and a large school building originally intended as a diocesan seminary, and paid for it all.[108] Wherever he saw the need, he moved boldly ahead. On one occasion, after borrowing more money than seemed possible at the time to repay, he said of himself, "It is well for me that I have so much courage. This enables me still to sleep soundly, spite of this new and great debt."[109] This characterized Benedict Fenwick—courageous self-confidence, together with unusual business acumen. Always the debts got paid.

At the same time, he was not only a builder; his supervision of the flock's spiritual development received at least equally detailed attention. Not satisfied with the quality of music used in the parish churches, he compiled and published his own sacred hymnal. Not happy with the catechetical books used in the religious instruction of the young, he translated one from the French that he liked better.[110] Concerned to defend and explain the Catholic faith, in 1830 he published five different books to help accomplish that objective.[111] To counteract the anti-Catholic press of the period, in 1829 he founded the first weekly Catholic newspaper in the United States, named it provocatively *The Jesuit*, and edited it during the formative years.

With regard to education for his Catholic flock this enterprising churchman did not settle for providing an "elite" education for the more privileged girls attracted to the upscale Ursuline convent school. Fenwick began as early as 1827 to develop what was to become an unusually complete program of catechetical instruction. His enthusiasm for this endeavor no doubt stemmed at least partially from fear of the Sunday school campaign launched by Protestants during the 1820s, which he viewed as aimed at Catholic children "for the purpose of making Proselytes to their respective tenets."[112] The Protestant Sunday school movement in Boston provided a constant irritant during the 1820s and 1830s. Protestant Sunday schoolers were accused of "kidnapping Catholic children in town and country."[113] On one occasion a Protestant Sunday school teacher in Boston was accused of enticing into his school two Catholic children whom he found "violating the fourth commandment" at the head of Theatre Alley. Fenwick's newspaper indignantly warned such teachers to "let our children alone and not to interfere with them, as they pass through the streets,"[114] and the Catholic clergy were told to put "Catholics on their guard against the Calvinists and others who are going about the town in quest of Catholic children."[115]

Fenwick's dedication to building up his own Sunday school program extended beyond mere competition with Protestants. As soon as he had enlarged the cathedral in 1827, he opened a Sunday school in the two large basement rooms. It was more than a Sunday school: on Sunday the children met from 9 to 10:30 a.m. and then went as a group to Mass, prefected by Fenwick's seminarians, who stationed "themselves in front, to observe their conduct during Mass, in order to correct afterwards any ill behavior."[116] The children then returned on Sunday afternoon for another session followed by attendance at Vespers, a rather full day of religious instruction and exercise, which included, as was the practice in Protestant Sunday schools throughout Boston, instruction in the 3R's for children not otherwise being so instructed. In addition, Fenwick's classes met twice during the week, on Wednesday and Saturday afternoons.[117] Despite the obvious rigors of the program, the number of pupils in the cathedral school swelled to 400 within the first month.[118]

At first the bishop's seminarians taught the Sunday school, but by 1832 Fenwick had secured the Sisters of Charity to take over instruction of the girls.[119] By 1833, dissatisfied with the large classes required for a handful of seminarians and sisters, Fenwick also began recruiting lay catechists, which made it possible to divide the children "into small classes and giving each to an individual to instruct."[120] By 1835, partly to help implement the strategy of small classes and partly to deal with the fact that many poor children, apparently because they were not properly clothed, were not attending Sunday school, Fenwick formed the Young Catholics Friend Society. As the preamble to its constitution stated, "beholding, with feelings of deepest regret, many poor children, belonging to the Congregation of the Holy Cross, prevented by indigence and other causes from receiving suitable instructions in their holy religion, the Catholic Young Men of the city of Boston, to remedy this evil," formed the society.[121] The society first provided clothing for poor boys and brought them to Sunday school, and by 1836 took over the cathedral Sunday school itself. [122] In 1836 a reporter for *The Pilot* found the school flourishing, chiefly filled by "the most indigent portion of the Catholic community,"[123] but numbering some eight hundred to nine hundred boys and girls in classes of about ten per instructor.[124]

As the number of churches and Catholic congregations increased, the catechetical program expanded proportionately. Fenwick made sure that space was provided in each new church for Sunday school instruction and commanded his priests that "Catechisms of the children must be duly attended to by you on Wednesday and Saturday p.m., as well as before Mass and Vespers on Sundays. This is highly important for the welfare of the rising generation."[125] By the early 1840s St. Mary's church in Charlestown had at least five hundred in its Sunday school.[126]

The bishop typically supervised the several Sunday schools in close detail, visiting frequently, hearing the children's recitations, finding them "very deficient" on one occasion or praising them "for their diligence" on another,[127] or professing himself "greatly pleased with the order and regularity prevailing as well with the proficiency of the children" on still another.[128] When needed, his sermons included appeals "in behalf of the poor children of the Congregation with the view of procuring them winter clothing to enable them to go to church and catechism."[129]

He acted in every respect as "superintendent" of Sunday schools, hearing, for example, "the complaints made by the teachers against some of the Boys for misbehavior in the Chapel, and writing and scratching on the wall."[130] On the fun side, he promoted and attended annual outings of the Sunday school scholars and their numerous teachers, marching with banners flying from the cathedral to the railroad station for picnics to Needham or Dedham or other outlying towns. By 1846 over two hundred boys attended the outing.[131]

The Sunday school program received Fenwick's devoted attention and appears as one of his major concerns. In the only recorded occasion on which he deliberately included Boston officialdom in Catholic affairs, "by special invitation" Fenwick invited the mayor to visit "the Chapel and the children male and female when assembled in it for catechism."[132] The bishop expressed delight that the mayor was "well pleased at the good order maintained" in the school. It appears that both in Fenwick's eyes and as viewed by Bostonians generally, the catechetical program constituted the chief Catholic educational endeavor in Boston. Shattuck's census of 1845, while failing to mention the existence of any other Catholic schools, noted the presence of seven Sunday schools with 246 teachers and 4,100 pupils.[133]

Though nowhere explicitly stated, even in the Constitutions of the Young Catholics Friend Society, as was common and even assumed in Sunday schools of the time, the schools also taught children basic literacy. Thus, in 1836 *The Pilot* boasted that of about 240 boys observed in the Holy Cross Sunday school, "not more than 18 or 20 were unable to read."[134] And in 1838 the Young Catholics Friend Society Report boasted that of all the boys taught by them, there was "not one boy over seven years of age but can read and study the catechism. The same can be said of the school under the charge of the pious and amiable Sisters of Charity."[135] This would help explain why the classes met four times a week.

It appears that this system of Sunday schools came into existence just at the time when the recently established public primary schools were largely replacing the literacy functions of the Protestant Sunday schools. What part the Catholic Sunday schools may have played in this is not clear—that is, whether they assumed the primary school function for many Catholic children. There is no record to indicate whether the robust Catholic Sunday school program kept the children out of the newly developing public primary schools, but probably to a considerable extent they did.[136]

At the same time, however, Bishop Fenwick did not shy away from an attempt to directly compete with Boston's rapidly developing public school system, though this proved to be far less successful. He seems to have seen this effort as less critical and therefore it received less of his attention. Typically, though, after moving the Ursuline nuns to their more exclusive "finishing" school status in Charlestown, which was his top priority, he turned to providing a basic schooling for children of his cathedral parish in the heart of Boston. He at first resorted to "one or more mistresses elected from the Congregation" to teach the girls, and instituted a small school for boys taught by his seminarians that imparted the "ordinary branches," including English, reading, writing, grammar, arithmetic, geography, and history as well as optional Latin "as an introduction to those who feel disposed to study for the Church."[137] The girls' school taught the same subjects as well as plain sewing, bead work, and other such skills.[138] Though these schools were meant for those "in the most moderate circumstances,"[139] they were not entirely free: each charged an $8 annual fee to help support the seminarians in their studies and the matrons in their living.[140] The bishop viewed these two schools as antidotes to the city's public schools so parents "may not be obliged, as heretofore, to send their children to the Town schools, where the masters are all Protestants and where they are obliged to mix with children whose habits they contract to their very great detriment."[141]

Neither the girls' nor the boys' school enjoyed an entirely unruffled existence, though. The girls' school, depending as it did on the availability of a "proper matron," suffered from impermanence and also from having to charge tuition, which excluded some potentially worthy pupils.[142] For this reason in 1832 Fenwick, "anxious to have a poor school established upon a proper and permanent basis," wrote to the Sisters of Charity at Emmetsburg, Pennsylvania, requesting four sisters to run the school and also to open a much-needed orphanage.[143] He got three quarters of what he wanted when the congregation offered him three sisters. Elated, he set about with typical thoroughness to prepare a proper place for them. He formed an "Association of Ladies" in the parish to raise money for the sisters' travel, to rent a house on Hamilton Street off Fort Hill, and to buy furniture as well as books for the school. Some 296 ladies contributed $227.82 within two months. Fenwick supervised the furnishing and painting of the house, welcomed the sisters on their arrival, and expressed himself "highly pleased with the Sisters of Charity."[144] "How many innocent souls will be sheltered from the contagious influence of the streets through the maternal care of the Sisters of Charity!" exulted the Bishop's newspaper. "How many of these children will be rescued from the road to ruin, into which some may have been partially led by bad example, or the sectarian prejudices, which many of them have hitherto been but too frequently obliged to hear."[145]

The bishop was determined to keep this a free school, and the more than two hundred five- to twelve-year-old girls who registered the first year and thereafter paid no tuition whatever. Funds to support the sisters continued to be raised by collections among the faithful. An annual contribution of one dollar earned the title of Benefactor, and two dollars bought full membership in the Roman Catholic Female Charitable Society, which Fenwick organized to care for the school's financial needs. The first subscription attracted 418 donors.[146] The funds from this organization were supplemented by charity fairs and special collections in later years as funds got tighter and the sisters' operation became more expensive, especially with the addition and growth of an orphanage, which took up an ever-greater portion of the sisters' energy and financial resources.[147]

Fenwick, with his remarkable energies and keen interest in the support of Catholic education in Boston, continued to observe, cooperate with, and supervise the sisters' activities. Four times between 1832 and 1846 he moved them into larger and more expensive quarters, each time attending to every detail.[148] He devoted equally interested attention to the children in the school. Thus, in 1834 he organized an outing for the roughly three hundred little girls attending the school, mostly from "the poorest portion of the community."[149] The pupils, accompanied by the sisters, marched two by two from the school on Hamilton Street to Dorchester Heights, clad in their little uniforms and carrying with them "provisions for the day," and making "truly a splendid spectacle to the citizens of Boston."[150] Fenwick customarily attended these outings, on at least one occasion accompanied by his two foremost protégés, John Fitzpatrick and John Williams, both future bishops of Boston.[151]

The boys' school, which had been named St. Aloysius, did not fare as well. Enrollment fluctuated between sixty and eighty boys. At least until 1833 the teachers were seminarians living and studying in Fenwick's house.[152] The boys do not seem to have applied themselves seriously. Fenwick "heard many complaints from the Masters in relation to their general idleness"[153] and on examination he found that the young scholars "did not acquit themselves as well as on former occasions," and was forced to reprimand them "in strong terms."[154] Examination the following year found the boys "generally defective on the score of Arithmetic."[155] For undisclosed reasons—possibly ineffective teaching or a decline in the number of available seminarian teachers because he was beginning to send them away to schools in other dioceses—sometime in the mid-1830s the boys' school was taken over by a Mr. Rogers. This did not end the troubles, because in 1837 Fenwick had to dismiss Rogers for unspecified "misconduct." Later the same year, with enrollment down to twenty, examination again found the boys "deficient in reading and spelling," and by 1839 St. Aloysius closed altogether.

The fate of St. Aloysius seems to have closely typified most of the attempts during Bishop Fenwick's reign to found parochial schools as an alternative to the public schools. He tried to provide a school in every parish, but the net result was not impressive. In the face of daunting obstacles, he probably did not consider parish schools to be the most important antidote to the public schools that were covering the city. Every new church was built with a schoolroom, either at the back or in the basement, fitted both for Sunday school instruction and for a day school. Thus, St. Mary's in Charlestown (1829) was equipped with "spacious schoolrooms back." St. Mary's in the North End (1834) was built with "a sufficiently elevated basement story" for a school.[156] And St. Patrick's in the South End (1834) also had a "basement story which is intended as a schoolroom."[157]

At some of these churches parochial schools came into existence "under the direction of prudent masters and mistresses," at least for a time. St. Mary's in 1832 had a school with one master and fifty-four girls and thirty-three boys.[158] When Fenwick visited it he found that "the female children generally acquit themselves well, but the Boys badly." Two years later tragedy struck the school: a lightning bolt killed "three of the Boys on the spot and disabled two or three of the Girls."[159] In 1840 St. Mary's opened a free school.[160] When Fenwick visited it in 1842 he found that "the children seem in general to have acquitted themselves well,"[161] despite the fact that some three hundred boys and girls attended, all apparently taught by just two teachers. These schools, plus one that existed at Lechmere Point for a time[162] and probably others in the basements of Boston's newer churches, struggled in vain to survive.

None of these schools still existed when Bishop Fenwick died in 1846. Their shaky dependence on available and affordable lay teachers accounts for a substantial part of the explanation. Of all the Boston parochial schools so energetically begun by Bishop Fenwick, besides the Sisters of Charity Free School in the cathedral parish, only one still existed at the end of his reign: the one founded by the Germans of Holy Trinity parish in 1844. It had been opened simultaneously with the formal establishment of the parish itself and was to become the oldest continuously existing parochial school in New England. Fenwick, typically, had insisted on a spacious basement in Holy Trinity so "the children of the Germans might assemble in it for the purpose of receiving instruction."[163] The Germans eagerly endorsed this idea, as they did in other dioceses throughout the United States; when a permanent German pastor was assigned to the new church in 1844, he immediately started a school where "naturally, the German language was given a place in the curriculum."[164]

This, then, was the extent of parochial schooling as a direct antidote to the public schools in Boston by 1846:

> Sunday schools, apparently in every parish, which taught the rudiments of literacy in addition to religion
>
> The Sisters of Charity school for girls in the cathedral parish, with about three hundred female pupils
>
> The German school with an undetermined but small enrollment of boys and girls
>
> A small parochial school in St. Mary's, a central city parish that had been taken over by the Jesuits.

There were also apparently a few private schools run by Catholics and with a Catholic orientation. For example, when Miss Stephens was displaced from the cathedral school in 1832 by the coming of the Sisters of Charity, she opened a school of her own offering the academic subjects in the morning and sewing, painting, and so forth in the afternoon. And in 1843 a Mrs. Jane Walsh opened a boarding school for Catholic children in Charlestown neck.[165]

Though Bishop Fenwick by all his words and especially by his actions left no doubt that he believed in Catholic education both in general and specifically in Boston, where Catholic immigrants had faced so much antagonism, he left the diocese with a smaller proportion of Catholic children in Catholic schools than he had found it. In 1825 the single school run by the Ursulines next to the cathedral had educated about 1.4 percent of the total public and Catholic school combined enrollment in Boston. In 1846 the two Catholic parochial schools educated about 2.8 percent of the combined total. But even this minor gain was deceptive, since the Catholic proportion of the Boston population had gone from 8.6 percent to 26.2 percent during the same period. In reality, then, the Catholic parochial schools had substantially lost ground to the public in terms of the proportion of Catholic children they educated. Statistically, they could not even reasonably be considered in competition.

No doubt this had not been Bishop Fenwick's intent. On the other hand, the fact that Fenwick, a man of almost unbounded energy and outstanding ability, did not succeed in establishing a parochial school system to counteract the public schools that the Irish children were attending suggests that other factors deterred him from creating a viable parochial school enterprise.

One important factor was that the Irish lay leadership in Boston did not launch any effort to promote parochial schools for the hordes of Irish immigrant youngsters. They seem to have been more concerned about the education of immigrant adults to prepare them for citizenship and improve their employment opportunities. Little attention was paid, at least in the press, to the education of children. The Irish leadership seemed hardly aware of the public "common school" crusade. And they are not on record as having advocated schooling for the children, or even objecting to the anti-Catholicism in the public schools. The Irish Catholic press did not cover a controversy in 1843 over the bishop's objections to public school textbooks.

This silence reflected the general lack of interest in schooling by the Irish lay leadership. It was also related to the fact that Bishop Fenwick and the Irish Catholics of Boston did not get along. The Irish leadership, and many of their followers, did not support him in virtually any of his enterprises, not just education. On the contrary, they became radically alienated from him and progressively less inclined to support his initiatives. What he accomplished beyond the provision of churches and basic religious services he had to accomplish largely on his own.

Even before he arrived in Boston, Irish Bostonians were expressing their displeasure. No sooner had Fenwick been appointed to Boston than John England, the bishop of Charleston, wrote to Rome that the Irish were not accepting his appointment readily.[166] Their initial reaction developed into a permanent attitude. Fenwick's problems with the Irish stemmed from several sources, the most noteworthy being that he was neither an Irishman nor an immigrant. He descended directly from those Northumberland English Catholics who had settled in seventeenth-century Maryland.[167] Born to secure if not great wealth, broadly educated first by tutors at home, then at Georgetown College, then by the Jesuit order of which he became a member, then by his own immense curiosity and self-direction, Fenwick was by birth a gentleman, by education a scholar, and by blood and culture an Anglo-Saxon. Though wedded to his constituents by bonds of common faith, he differed from them profoundly in ethnicity, culture, and personal orientation. These differences appear to have caused continual strain.

During his first several years in Boston Fenwick demonstrated, at least privately, a certain distaste for the Irish. He always left the city on St. Patrick's Day, which they celebrated with extravagant, speech-filled dinners and parades. Thus, in 1828 he retired to the Charlestown convent on March 17 "to avoid being present at the dinner given by the St. Patrick's Society;" in 1831 he informed his brother that "this being St. Patrick's Day, in the morning I have run away from Boston to avoid a great dinner party. I have hidden myself in my little Cottage [at the Ursuline convent]."[168] Fenwick did by the late 1830s begin to participate, if not in the secular celebration of St. Patrick's Day, at least in its spiritual side—not always with happy results. In 1843, while celebrating St. Patrick's Day Mass at the cathedral, a parade "with drum and fife" passed by. Many in his congregation, torn between their attention to the Mass and their curiosity to "behold the spectacle," gave way to the latter and flocked to the cathedral door to see the parade, which the bishop did not appreciate at all.[169]

Fenwick developed a keen sympathy for the Irish as he witnessed their sufferings, both from poverty and persecution. Thus, he lightened the Lenten fasts, lamented the high death rate, condemned the anti-Irish insults in the press, expressed outrage at the outbreaks of violence and the unequal administration of justice, and even helped to mobilize the Irish defense.[170] But even in these expressions of sympathy and solidarity, one always detected the element of paternalism. Fenwick felt for the Irish as an outsider; he could never be one of them.

Much in the way Fenwick conducted his affairs, however justified and even correct, did not endear him to the Irish. He became very early "more and more convinced of the impropriety of ever admitting lay members of the church to any participation in the government of even the temporals of the church."[171] On occasion he did refer decisions to the laity, particularly the choice of property for churches,[172] but these were exceptions to a generally autocratic administration. The very energetic genius with which he handled the rapid institutional development of the diocese tended to alienate the laity, since it was all done by Fenwick.

The bishop sought, though without final success, to fill his diocese with native-born priests rather than Irish immigrants. He was influential in formulating a policy adopted by the American hierarchy of recommending only native-born priests for vacant episcopal sees.[173] This, too, did not endear him to the Irish immigrants, even though he was unable to carry out his desire simply because the need for priests was too great and the supply of native-born clergy too small. Of the eighty-three new priests admitted to the Diocese of Boston between 1831 and 1846, sixty were born in Ireland, and most of the rest had Irish-born parents.[174]

Fenwick's view of how the clergy should relate to the people did not appear to please the familial, gregarious spirit of the Irish. He attempted to establish a strictly professional relationship between his clergy and the people, admonishing the clergy to "pay and receive but few visits, the fewer the better. Invite as seldom as possible people of the world to dine with you."[175] Among the clergy and some lay friends outside the diocese Fenwick enjoyed a reputation for warm humanity and great good humor. But this more genial side he apparently rarely if ever showed to those in his spiritual charge, except perhaps to the children, whose outings he regularly attended. No one could ever accuse him of a failure to build churches, to preach, to administer the sacraments, to produce Catholic books and Catholic music, but these activities apparently constituted his entire relationship with the Catholic people of Boston.

Fenwick's Southern, aristocratic background, too, seems to have put him out of tune with Irish sentiments. Fundamental distinctions between wealth and poverty he appears to have accepted as a given, and these distinctions sometimes received obnoxious expression in his running of the diocesan temporal affairs. Thus, in the beginning he took it as a given that money should be raised for new churches by the selling of pews, with the best-located pews going to the highest bidders. As a result, the wealthiest parishioners got the "orchestra" seats while the poorest were left with standing room only or were relegated to basement chapels. Thus, at the cathedral "such poor people as cannot find seats in the cathedral above"[176] attended Mass in the basement. In the North End the wealthier attended St. Mary's, where the pews were owned, and the poor went to the "Free Church" nearby, which had been financed solely by donations and where no one owned a pew.

In churches where the poor and the better-off attended church together the bishop sometimes had to settle disputes over "property" rights, which he did with a curious brand of aristocratic justice. In Charlestown's St. Mary's church a dispute arose in 1830 over the right of non-pew owners to stand in the aisles during Mass. The wealthier pew owners objected to the resulting congestion. Fenwick solved the dispute with a quaint piece of logic by ruling that, while the pew owners had an absolute right to occupy the pews they owned, the poor also had an absolute right to occupy the space in the aisle while they stood on it. Thus, he concluded, "it follows that the rights of all are equal so far as relates to the property of the Church."[177] Such administration of justice could hardly have pleased the city's teeming poor Irish Catholics.

There was a more fundamental element in the way he administered the diocese that ultimately led to open hostility with a very sizeable faction. This happened in 1842 over Fenwick's settlement of a quarrel among parishioners over which of two priests should be pastor of St. Mary's church in the North End.[178] Less important is the nature of the dispute than the nature of the attack it prompted against Fenwick. It was signed by a large number of Boston Catholics and received prominent attention in the public press. The bishop was accused on a variety of counts, most of which came down to two issues.

The first accusation had to do with financial matters. The objections to Fenwick's handling of financial affairs started with the familiar church pew issue but did not stop there. Fenwick had promoted the sale of pews at St. Mary's, it was correctly asserted, to the extent that over 100 of the 160 pews were owned by "a number of stockholders as their private property," while hundreds who contributed to building the church "cannot even get a seat."[179] Fenwick had indeed sold most of the pews.[180] The church, they argued, was fast becoming a private society "where every man who does not own a pew or a seat will be looked upon as an intruder."[181] This was despite the fact, the accusation continued, that the non-pew holders had contributed most of the money to build the church in the first place:

> How often have you seen posses about the north end of this city, for the last four years, screwing money out of you. Who subscribed to the fund to build the parochial house? Pewholders? No. The laboring men on railroads were hunted for it, and often obliged to give the only dollar they cleared during a broken month towards it. And yet the church is now the property of a number of stockholders while thousands have no place to go to adore their God on the Sabbath.[182]

Adding to the bitterness, the complainants alleged that not only were the poor supporting most of the church and getting not even the use of a pew in return, but much of the parish's money was being siphoned off for other purposes. Fully $16,000 was said to have been collected beyond the church debt and the priests' salaries, and yet parishioners were being told that more debt remained. The bishop kept all financial records, so no one could prove what supposedly everyone knew. Thus, not only did the malcontents object to the obnoxious distinctions between pew holders and non-pew holders, but they resented Fenwick's monopolistic control of all funds and even implied their misuse.

Another issue that aroused the discontent ran deeper still. At a parish meeting it had been alleged, as quoted in *The Boston Daily Mail*, "HE [*sic*] has no sympathy with the Irish Catholics; he does not know the way to their hearts; their happiness is with him only a secondary consideration."[183] Here was the nub of the matter. Significantly, Fenwick's response to the charge, also quoted in *The Daily Mail*, while in one sense exonerating him, in another sense underscores the gulf that separated him from the Irish. "My accusers pretend that I am an enemy to the Irish!" he mocked. "I am an enemy to the Irish, I who have reared up more Irish young men and who are now in the different colleges of Canada and the United States at my expense, and even in a seminary in France, more young men from Ireland than any other bishop of the United States."[184] The allegations had been made publicly at a parish meeting, and Fenwick's letter was in answer to them. (They later were printed in *The Daily Mail*.)

Fenwick was speaking the truth. He had been carefully providing, at great personal cost, for an American-trained clergy of Irish descent. Even as the Irish hostility swirled about him, he was preparing two young Irishmen who would succeed him as bishops of Boston for over half a century. Perhaps no sounder proof of his concern for the Irish could have been asked for, and yet this was a very long-range policy. It was rational indeed, but aloof.

So too was Fenwick's much-maligned handling of finances. He kept financial matters entirely to himself, but there is no evidence that he skimmed funds out of St. Mary's or anywhere else for his personal gain. On the contrary, he spent his fortune building up the Boston Catholic Church. He did take funds out of St. Mary's—but not for himself, for other church enterprises he deemed of higher priority. He would have seen nothing wrong with this, since he viewed the entire Catholic enterprise as a whole, not as a collection of separate entities either spiritually or financially. He was ever buying, borrowing, collecting, and paying in the continual effort to make institutional development keep pace with population growth and emerging need. He might well have "taken from Peter to pay Paul" in the process.

This is the tragedy in Fenwick's relationship with the Boston Irish. He thought he was doing the best for them, and he sacrificed his wealth and probably his health in the process. But his manner was too autocratic, too patronizing, and perhaps too rational. He did not know the way to their hearts.

This was clear from other evidence as well. Once *The Boston Pilot* was taken over and edited by Donahoe in 1839 and dedicated to "the rights of adopted citizens,"[185] there is little mention of Fenwick or his works. Instead, the Irish bishop of New York, John Hughes, became the new hero. "It is well for the Church," commented *The Pilot*, referring to Hughes, "that when the immortal [bishop] England departed from the American Hierarchy, he left behind him one so able to take his impregnable position."[186] On one of the few occasions *The Pilot* said anything about Fenwick, it called obviously annoyed attention to the fact that "Our Bishop" had administered the sacrament of confirmation in Frederick, Maryland.[187] And when Fenwick died in 1846, though *The Pilot's* coverage was polite and even complimentary, referring to the deceased as "our venerable and beloved bishop," it was also distant and hardly exuberant in its praise.[188] Obituaries in the regular Boston press were more laudatory than those in *The Pilot*.[189] The editor was criticized by one of Fenwick's admirers for giving such short shrift to the bishop's obsequies, to which *The Pilot* replied that fuller coverage had been "unavoidably crowded out last week," hardly an admission of guilt and certainly an affirmation that in *The Pilot's* eyes the death of the city's Catholic bishop did not merit prime coverage.[190] Probably Bishop Hughes of New York put the matter most accurately in the eulogy he delivered at Fenwick's funeral: "whilst alive perhaps [he] was not sufficiently esteemed."[191]

In short, the rocky relationship between the Irish and Bishop Fenwick did not bode well for expectations that his policies would be endorsed, including his efforts to build a parochial school system as well as his efforts to secure the rights of Catholic children in the public schools. The Irish leadership itself seemed more concerned about providing adult education for Irish immigrants, and Irish immigrants were coming to Boston without any schooling tradition in their homeland because of centuries of enforced educational deprivation. This probably largely accounts for the absence of any parochial school enthusiasm on the part of the Irish in general. They simply sent their children to the local public schools—if they sent them at all.

However, even had the Boston Irish Catholics fallen solidly in line with Bishop Fenwick and his enterprises, it is not likely that his most favored enterprise would have been the creation of a comprehensive parochial school system, even though that was obviously a part of the plan. Fenwick had not experienced any such parochial school effort during his years growing up and beginning his career in the South, where the children of the upper classes attended private schools and the common folk were left to Sunday school catechetical instruction and such rudimentary academic learning as accompanied it. In Boston, even though he did make sincere efforts to counteract the new "common school crusade" by establishing parochial schools and by removing offensive practices from the public schools, this was a movement essentially foreign to him. His greatest efforts went into the development of "elite" and "higher" education.

The first example was his action, almost immediately after arriving in Boston, to transform the Ursuline convent school from a downtown free day school for a few dozen "children of the poor" into an exclusive boarding "finishing" school in semi-rural Charlestown, charging $125 yearly plus extras.[192] His great personal involvement in its development and management underscores his educational priorities. While the common Catholic children of Boston were running the streets or attending the local public schools, Fenwick was erecting a fine boarding school for what he called the "better class" of girls in what was then a suburban setting. And even after the Ursuline school was destroyed by an angry mob and the nuns returned to Canada, he continued efforts to revive it in another location. The very next year he was busily trying to recruit "a small colony of nuns" from the Convent of the Visitation in Georgetown to "supply the place of the absent Ursulines" and provide a school for "the higher class of Catholics" who were at the time "obliged either to send their children out of the State for education, or confide them to the care of Protestants to the great danger of their souls."[193] And after that effort fell through, another year later he was back negotiating, unsuccessfully, the return of the Ursulines from Quebec to supply a "religious house of education for the better class of young females."[194]

He could never move on beyond the travesty of the mob's destruction of his prize accomplishment in Boston, the Ursuline convent school. Over the next twenty years he continuously demanded public restitution for the destruction, always without success.

Fenwick's penchant for the more exclusive form of Catholic education and at a higher level than that of the common school can be seen with greater clarity in his herculean efforts to establish higher education for Catholic males in his diocese. These attempts took even higher priority than the Ursuline convent school, and they were considerably more successful. They also even more profoundly militated against the growth of a parochial school system. These efforts often fused his desire to provide for the education of young men for the priesthood with a proclivity to favor higher education for males in general.

One of the bishop's preoccupations during his twenty years in Boston was the understandable and no doubt essential effort to establish a seminary for the training of priests for the diocese. But in addition, he was determined to establish a college that would provide a Catholic alternative to the prestigious Protestant colleges already existing in New England, which, as a well-educated man, he much admired. Though in theory these two objectives differed, in reality they could often not be easily distinguished because Fenwick also thought of the college as a seed-bed for priestly vocations, and in the various shapes his efforts took the seminary and the college were envisioned as embodied in a single institution.

Fenwick's desire for a proper seminary as a means of training a native clergy educated on a par with the New England Protestant ministry appears from the beginning. Within the first year of his arrival in Boston he had "determined to put all his savings apart to carry into effect this laudable and necessary object."[195] Speaking of his "extreme desire to have clergymen," he decided that he would "live more frugally" as a means of raising money for the seminary.[196] After first housing a handful of seminarians in his residence and educating them himself, in 1832 he bought property with a large house on it next to the cathedral, borrowing money to finance the enterprise. It was "intended as a Seminary for Ecclesiastics to educate young men for the Church."[197] The school accepted young men "sufficiently well instructed to commence the Latin language" and included a course of studies identical with that of a "regular college," but it accepted only those intending to become clergymen. It was essentially a secondary school.[198]

The need for "professors" to implement his educational goals had been apparent to Fenwick from the beginning. Though he did educate a solid number of future Boston clergy himself, the task was impossible on a large enough scale, and he set out almost immediately to persuade the Jesuit superiors to found a Jesuit institution that would serve both as seminary for future priests and a college for boys in the Boston diocese. As early as 1826 he asked the Jesuit superior to "purchase a lot on one of the beautiful hills around Boston and build a College on it."[199] In the following years he attempted without success to raise money in Europe for this project.[200] At times it seemed the failure would be permanent, and at one point in 1831 he even seemed resigned to the possibility that "I shall prepare the way, shall even dig the foundations, if I cannot do more. My successor will build upon them."[201] But by 1838 he was after the Jesuits again, this time to locate a seminary and college at the colony he had established in Maine. He built the building and set aside two hundred acres as an endowment, plus the proceeds from a sawmill and gristmill. But the more urban-oriented Jesuits found the backwoods of Maine too out of the way, and nothing came of the offer.[202] The dauntless bishop, protesting that "I cannot do any longer without a respectable house of education in the Diocese,"[203] then turned to Worcester as a possible location. Here one of his protégés, the Rev. James Fitton, had already opened an academy on a sixty-acre property that he was willing to turn over, and Fenwick felt the proximity to Boston might attract the Jesuits.[204]

By 1843 he was urgently pushing the Worcester location on the Jesuit superiors, who again resisted, this time arguing that they did not want a boarding school where twenty Jesuits would be needed to educate 150 students as compared to 1,000 in a day school.[205] Fenwick did not see the matter that way, first because he viewed the school as primarily a training ground for future priests who needed seclusion, but also because in general he wanted a place where boys could be removed from "the seduction of the streets and the dissipation and distraction of large cities." He was also looking for the kind of boys who would stick out a long period of schooling, not the kind attracted by a day school, coming mostly from "the lower order of society, whose parents are extremely poor" and who would have to go to work as soon as possible. But the enterprising Fenwick, seizing the opportunity wherever he saw it, now proposed the desirability of *both* a day college in Boston and a resident college in Worcester "to which the elite of the City schools must ultimately be sent to finish studies."[206] The Jesuits did agree to take over the institution at Worcester if it were made to meet their specifications. That meant the expenditure of some $2,500, which Fenwick gladly provided, mostly from his savings.[207] In June 1843 he exuberantly laid the cornerstone, and by November the College of the Holy Cross opened in Worcester with twelve students. In the next few years before his death Fenwick made frequent trips there to observe the fruits of his long efforts.[208]

Nor did he forget the possibility of a second college in Boston itself. By the beginning of 1845 he was proposing

> to select in a central part of this city a lot of land sufficiently large to erect upon it a house for the accommodation of five or six Fathers of the Society of Jesus [Jesuits]—adjoining to this house, a church capable of containing one thousand persons—and adjoining to this church, large school rooms capable of holding from four to six hundred scholars; the whole to be served and superintended by the fathers.

The fathers would be supported by "the rent of the pews of the church so as to leave the school free for all." The school would provide instruction "in the various branches of a sound and solid education, including the Latin and Greek Languages."[209]

Fenwick did not live to see its actual founding, but his efforts had not only resulted in the opening of Holy Cross in Worcester but sowed the seeds of what was to become under his successor Boston College. He not only worked strenuously during these twenty years in Boston to create Catholic higher education in this Athens of America, but he also spent most of his personal financial resources doing it.

The long-term wisdom of Bishop Fenwick's determination to provide higher education for Boston Catholics, though not appreciated by them at the time and probably not understood by Fenwick himself, would later be validated with a vengeance, even in its profound effects on the basic education of all Boston's children. But in the 1820s, 1830s, and 1840s, when both financial and human resources were desperately scarce, the emphasis on initiating higher education took away any possibility of building a significant parochial school enterprise that might compete with the public schools.

In short, Bishop Fenwick's educational priorities, given the limited resources at his disposal, coupled with the lack of interest of Irish leaders and the actual hostility of many parishioners, led almost inevitably away from the successful development of a vital parochial school system. That he concentrated on providing for the higher education of the clergy made perfect sense, since such a policy was essential for the long-range development of the diocese. But beyond that, his priorities were seriously debatable at the time. For the cost of the exclusive Ursuline convent school, for example, he could have built eight primary schools at the prevailing public school rate of expenditure for new schools.[210] And the resources he committed to establishing the foundations of Catholic higher education for men dwarfed what could have gone into parochial schools that would have competed with the public schools.

The same applied to his great efforts at founding Holy Cross. The $25,000, mostly of his own money, spent on the college could have provided for the education of large numbers of Boston children. Instead he chose to try to develop an institution of higher learning that would be attended by Catholic boys from all over the United States and that, he hoped, would rival Harvard College in excellence and would establish Catholicism's academic credentials in the rarified New England academic atmosphere. Here, his concern to provide an educated clergy merged with the predilection for higher education. He hoped that at Holy Cross, under the benign influence of the Jesuit fathers, the best among Catholic youth would join the ranks of the educated Catholic ministry so badly needed in New England. He considered Holy Cross to be his chief legacy to the Boston diocese.[211]

Even when he got around to promoting a permanent institution for the education of boys in Boston itself, it was not a modest parochial school in each parish that he singled out as the great priority, but a "college," again run by the Jesuit fathers, complete with a classical curriculum. Nothing better reveals the curious inability of this otherwise shrewd and capable man to grasp the nature of Boston's common school revolution than his plans for what was to become Boston College. He wrote in 1845 to the Congregation for the Propagation of the Faith:

What we desire most now, and what will ultimately be of the greatest benefit to the Catholic cause, is to provide means for the education of the thousands of Catholic children who are now running wild in the streets of Boston, and who have no other schools to resort to than the Protestant schools already established, and for the support of which our Catholic parents are equally taxed with others. Unless some remedy be applied to this evil and applied soon, it will be needless to erect any more churches.

Given this clear perception of the Boston public schools as the immediate danger, one would assume his proposed remedy to be an alternative system of parochial schools. Instead, Fenwick then went on to outline his plan for what would become Boston College. As the antidote to Boston public schools, he advocated a Jesuit college![212]

Fenwick's strategy proved to be much shrewder than he could have anticipated or even imagined. Within hardly more than sixty years Boston College graduates would take over the principalships of the city's most prestigious public schools, including Boston Latin, and Boston College faculty would control the public school curriculum. Boston College for all practical purposes would run the Boston public schools.

But Fenwick's behavior at the time suggests that, despite his extraordinary talents, he did not fully grasp the significance of the fundamental educational revolution taking place around him that was rapidly sweeping the nation towards universal, public-supported mass education. Like the Irish lay leadership and The Pilot under Donahoe, Fenwick did not engage in the lively contemporary debates about the creation of a public school system for all children, especially in Boston and Massachusetts where the Honorable Horace Mann crusaded for public education and where critical public debates even about religion in public education were taking place.[213]

At the same time, Bishop Fenwick was very much aware that the great majority of Irish children who were going to school in Boston were attending public schools, and he did not ignore this fact. Even while he resolutely followed the convictions that led him to labor mightily to create elite and higher education possibilities for Catholics in Boston, he did not forget the common Catholic folk. He succeeded in creating and sustaining a catechetical program for the common folk of which he was proud enough to show off to the Boston establishment.

More than that, he kept a close eye on what was transpiring in the public schools, which most of his charges attended. And he took it upon himself to see that Catholic children in these schools were being treated without prejudice and that their religious faith was not being undermined. He did not suffer from feelings of inferiority to the Bostonians who managed the city's schools. Though professing a different religion, the bishop was acutely aware that, as a well-educated native-born American, descended from the same ethnic stock, possessing all the accouterments of the gentleman and scholar, deeply versed not only in the philosophy and theology of his profession but also in literature, history, music, and language, he stood on at least equal footing with the best that Boston had to offer. Though he greatly admired the intellectual and cultural development he found in Boston, he was not cowed by the weight of Yankee tradition.[214] And he let it be known that he expected, even demanded, that his Catholic children be treated equally and properly in the city schools.

The bishop was well aware that thousands of Catholic children were attending the public schools. On one occasion he estimated that two thousand Catholic boys were in attendance. However, given the obvious lack of interest on the part of the Irish Catholic leadership on the one hand, and the general lack of funds and his priority for higher and elite education on the other hand, the bishop could not and would not do anything to provide an adequate alternative parochial school opportunity for those pupils. Instead, he demanded accommodations to Catholic interests in the public schools, and he did not shrink from intruding into public school affairs to achieve that goal.

The most illustrative and most public instance of this intervention took place in 1843, after Bishop Fenwick addressed a letter to Mayor Martin Brimmer, ex officio member of the Boston School Committee, complaining about anti-Catholic bias in public school textbooks. He singled out Worcester's *Elements of History*, claiming that

> after having attentively perused its pages I unhesitatingly say that it is not such a Book as should be put into the hands of children of any Denomination of Christians who are desirous of being correctly instructed in history and much less into the hands of the Catholic youth of this city, whose religious tenets it unsparingly assails, whose morality, as taught by their church, it takes every opportunity to impugn, and whose best men it everywhere holds up as superstitious and ignorant.

Fenwick also charged that "several other schoolbooks are liable to the same objections," and he concluded with a polite, but thinly veiled though most probably unenforceable, threat: "We have at this present moment many thousands of children frequenting the public schools who will have, much to our regret, to be withdrawn from them in the event of the evil here complained of not being immediately remedied."[215]

Fenwick sent a much lengthier, twenty-eight-page letter directly to the School Committee, detailing his objections to both Worcester's *History* and other books used in the schools.[216] The matter was referred to the committee on books.[217] Exactly one month later the book committee reported back, but apparently their recommendation was not accepted and the matter was referred back again.[218] Another month later the subcommittee submitted its final report. The report stated unequivocally that "Your committee have a high opinion of Worcester's Elements of History. If there were none but the children of Protestants in our schools, we should never have been called upon to inquire into its fitness as a textbook." After several other hostile statements that "we should reject with indignation the idea of presenting garbled statements of facts, or of suppressing truths which ought to be told in an historical work," the committee did grudgingly admit that

> the allegations against it amount to little more than this, that it treats the points at issue between Catholics and Protestants in a Protestant spirit. To this charge your committee think that it is justly liable. Expressions are used in some places respecting individuals of the Roman Catholic faith, and the doctrines and institutions of that denomination which seem to your committee to conflict with the provisions of the statute [referring to the Revised Statutes of the State of Massachusetts (1835) which mandated that textbooks may not "favor any particular religious sect or tenet"].[219]

Thus, admitting that the book probably violated the law, the committee recommended that the chapter on ecclesiastical history be entirely dropped from the text as well as several other passages. The committee had already consulted with the text's author, Mr. Worcester. Worcester had admitted that "he had no expectation, when he prepared it, that it would be used as a textbook in the instruction of Catholic children." And he was now quite willing to make it "better adapted to our schools, if the changes required were such as he could make conscientiously."[220]

On the next day the Boston School Committee adopted the subcommittee's recommendation and instructed Worcester to make the necessary changes.[221] Through the mayor it also advised Bishop Fenwick of its action, with a copy of the resolution.[222] Worcester began work on a revised edition of his textbook, but it did not appear until 1850, four years after Fenwick's death. The revision added more balance to the conflicting ways that Protestants and Catholics interpreted various historical events. For example, earlier editions had described the English monarch Queen Mary as "a woman whose bigotry, moroseness, tyranny, and cruelty, procured for her the title 'Bloody' Mary restored the Catholic religion, and commenced an unrelenting persecution against the Protestants."[223] The revised edition, after again depicting her cruel persecution of Protestants, added that

> her character is painted by Protestant writers in the darkest colors; but it may be remarked, by way of apology for her, that the treatment which both she and her mother had received from those who rejected the papal supremacy was calculated to inflame her prejudices; that she was under the influence of evil counsellors; and that she lived in an age when the principles of religious toleration were not practiced by either Catholics or Protestants.[224]

Fenwick was apparently somewhat mollified by the School Committee's show of conciliation, and he made no move to remove Catholic children from the schools even though none of the other texts he had complained about had been changed, and even though the Protestant King James Bible continued to be read in the classrooms. That he settled for such a partial victory might be explained by the fact that it was simply the best he could do. He did not have the resources to launch a campaign for parochial schools; besides, that would have undermined his preferred efforts to introduce Catholic higher education into Boston. In addition, he could not count on the city's Irish Catholics to support such an effort; *The Pilot* had not even mentioned the controversy. In reality, the bishop's best allies, if one can call them that, were probably the reasonably fair-minded Boston notables who sat on the School Committee and who respected this Southern gentleman who shared many of their ideals, if not their religion, and who were at least willing to make the compromises necessary to keep the Catholic children coming to public school.

The School Committee during these years, as the city itself, was still run not by politicians or aspiring politicians but by "proper" citizens. They seem to have recognized Fenwick's personal stature and in general acted with civility, making as many compromises as were necessary to keep a relative peace. Of the twenty-four committee members when Fenwick made his petition, four were listed among the wealthiest men in Boston; five were prominent Court Street lawyers; four were doctors; and seven were ministers of religion.[225] No Catholic had as yet served on the committee, but the settlement of the 1843 controversy was the first of several crucial compromises the Protestant Yankees were to make in the nineteenth century that went far toward keeping Catholic children in public school. Each time, as in 1843, they were faced with the threat that Catholic children would be removed en masse, and each time they made just enough concession to avert the threat.

The Worcester book incident probably describes as well as any the situation regarding Boston's public schools during this period. The schools were indeed essentially Protestant-oriented schools, though presided over by a School Committee made up principally of gentlemen representing the Boston establishment, men who were grounded in Boston tradition but who prided themselves in being fair-minded with regard to treatment of the newcomers. They were willing to make concessions when necessary to satisfy what they considered the legitimate complaints of this new Catholic population.

The natural representatives of the newcomers themselves, the men who stood out as the leaders of the Irish immigrants in Boston, remained silent when a contentious issue over the education of their children arose. *The Pilot* uttered not a single word about the 1843 textbook controversy, nor about any other incident regarding the treatment of their children in the public schools. *The Pilot* appears to have been unbothered by issues having to do with the city's public schools or the attendance of their children in them. It was only Bishop Fenwick, by himself, who took on the Boston establishment when he perceived real or imagined religious discrimination in the public schools. He remained profoundly dissatisfied by all this. Two years later in a letter to Rome he was still calling the public schools "Protestant schools entirely under Protestant teachers" in which the books are "teeming with the abuse of Catholics, and with slander against their religion. The minds of our youth are poisoned in their infancy by the books they read in these schools," he lamented.[226]

Yet, he did not, as he had threatened, remove Catholic children from the public schools, nor did he make further formal protest. By his own admission thousands of Catholic boys and girls still attended the public schools of Boston.[227] Between 1830 and 1843, while the school-aged population of Boston increased by 47 percent, the public school population increased by 114 percent. "This result establishes the gratifying fact," boasted the Boston School Committee, "that a much larger proportion than formerly of the children of our City avail themselves of the advantages of our public schools."[228] The largest single group accounting for this astounding increase was the children of Irish immigrants.

The figures suggest that, in addition to the fact that the Boston Irish leadership did not promote parochial schools, Bishop Fenwick, while totally dedicated to protecting the faith of his charges, on the educational front was willing to settle for what seemed practical. Though it bothered him profoundly, in comparison with his dedication to creating Catholic higher education in Boston, the public schooling of ordinary Catholic children did not appear to him as a matter of life and death, and he settled for continued efforts to provide catechetical instruction for the mass of Boston Catholic children.

In reality, in some ways Bishop Fenwick, even while differing from them radically on religious matters, fared better with the Boston establishment than he did with his own mostly Irish constituents. Just as he, even if grudgingly, respected their culture and learning even though they were "heretiks," as he referred to all Protestants, they recognized and paid due respect to this Southern, though "Jesuitical," gentleman. When he lay dying in the hot summer of 1846 in his chambers next to the cathedral on Franklin Street, the city authorities ordered the street passing his house sealed off to allow the prelate more quiet in his last hours. And when he died on the morning of August 11 the bells of the nearby Unitarian Federal Street church tolled to honor his passing.[229] In contrast, *The Pilot* excused its omission of an adequate obituary for Bishop Fenwick by claiming that fuller coverage had been "unavoidably crowded out last week."[230]

At the time of Bishop Fenwick's death in 1846, the Boston Catholic parochial school system consisted of three schools: one in the cathedral parish, one in the central city (St. Mary's parish, which had been taken over by Fenwick's own religious order, the Jesuits), and one founded by Boston's lone German Catholic parish. There existed a well-organized catechetical program for the rest of the Catholic children, who attended the public schools if they attended school at all. The public schools continued to be conducted with a Protestant flavor, though some of the most offensive practices and teachings had been removed through Fenwick's efforts and the cooperation of fair-minded Yankee gentlemen who presided over the School Committee. In nearby Worcester, Holy Cross, Fenwick's dream of a rival to Harvard, had been established for Catholic young men. And in Boston plans had been laid for the creation of Boston College, which would effectively "Catholicize" the Boston public schools in little more than half a century. Meanwhile, the Irish leadership remained essentially on the educational sidelines.[231]

3

Peace at Almost Any Price, 1846–1866

In 1846, the year that Bishop Benedict Fenwick died, leaving the Boston diocese to a successor, blight destroyed the potato crop in Ireland and spread famine throughout the land. Poor crops in the succeeding years and the failure of British authorities to seek an adequate remedy forced hordes of Irishmen off the land and discouraged countless others from continuing the depressing struggle to survive in Ireland. The emigration to the United States that had already been substantial for decades now turned into a mass exodus. The consequences were momentous both for the Catholic Church in Boston and for the city as a whole.[1]

Boston, which for years had been absorbing a sizeable 4,000 to 5,000 Irish immigrants a year, was now inundated by over 37,000 in 1847 alone, causing Edward Everett Hale to label the new immigration "the most remarkable social phenomenon of our time."[2] In the decade after 1846 arrivals in Boston from Ireland averaged six times what they had been in the early 1840s.[3] Many did not remain in Boston, but some observers noted that it was the more fit who tended to move on. By 1850 the foreign population had increased by 26,117, mostly Irish, over what it had been in 1845. Foreign-born people made up 45.7 percent of the city's total population, and half of the children between ages five and fifteen were foreign or the children of foreign-born residents.[4] By 1855, 29 percent of the Boston population had been born in Ireland, and 19 percent of the inhabitants in the suburbs of Brighton, Cambridge, Charlestown, Somerville, West Cambridge, Brookline, Dorchester, Roxbury, West Roxbury, Chelsea, North Chelsea, and Winthrop were Irish immigrants, most of them laborers and domestics.[5] In Roxbury alone the number of foreign-born residents, mostly Irish, almost doubled between 1845 and 1850, when it made up 43 percent of the population.[6] While new arrivals declined substantially after the mid-1850s, as late as 1865, 45 percent of the children born in Boston had both parents born in Ireland. If one added children of mixed Irish parentage and children of second-generation Irish, over half of Boston births were of Irish origin.[7]

While the majority of pre-Famine Irish immigrants had been poor, the newcomers arrived not just totally destitute, but many were seriously ill and suffering from malnutrition. Few had occupational skills, and Boston in the 1840s was not a city with enough work for all the unskilled laborers who suddenly found themselves dumped there.[8] By 1850, in a city that counted ninety-two distinct occupations, 71 percent of the Irish workers were employed in only three of these categories: manual labor, domestic help, and ready-made clothing. Sixty-four percent of the Irish who were employed worked as either day laborers or domestic servants. The Irish made up 82 percent of the city's day laborers and 72 percent of its domestics. In contrast, though they made up 33 percent of the total workforce, they represented less than 5 percent of the professionals.[9] In 1850 the average day laborer in Boston, which was the occupation of the large majority of Irish males, made a dollar a day, or $295 a year if he was lucky enough to work regularly, while the estimated minimal living expenses for a family of four would have been at least $540.[10]

Underemployed and poorly paid, the Irish could ill afford decent housing. While, as Lemuel Shattuck's census of 1845 had amply documented, the pre-Famine Irish were living in conditions over five times more congested than the Yankees,[11] their plight paled in comparison to what now took place. The new Irish immigrants crowded into the North End and Fort Hill district and along the waterfront. Former mansions as well as warehouses were subdivided into tiny apartments where families of nine or ten people subsisted in single rooms less than twelve feet square. Shanties were thrown up on every available piece of unused ground, while other newcomers crowded into dingy basements, some of which were flooded at high tide. So poorly clothed were many of the children that a separate hall for Sunday school was rented on Broad Street because their "ragged condition prevents them from attending the exercises in the chapel of the Cathedral."[12] Little wonder that illness and disease spread throughout these districts, and mortality rates shot up. There were yearly outbreaks of smallpox, and in 1849 there was an epidemic of cholera.[13] In 1845 Shattuck had reported mortality among the Irish at twice the rate elsewhere in the city; now it was much worse.[14]

Given their desperate condition, many turned to drink to ease the pain, which in turn resulted in brawling, petty theft, and other forms of social deviance. By 1848 assaults on police officers had increased 400 percent in Boston, and aggravated assaults with weapons were up by 465 percent. Though Irish crime tended to be of the less serious variety, it was so widespread that many Bostonians came to identify the new immigrants with criminality. Even in the years after the Great Famine, which brought a continued onslaught of poor Irish, the crime statistics did not diminish. Throughout the 1850s and into the early 1860s, although state prison rates for serious crimes like murder, rape, arson, armed robbery, and the like among the Irish were not above normal, half the inmates in the House of Correction had been born in Ireland. In 1858 the House of Industry on Deer Island, which included paupers as well as criminals, counted 68 percent born in Ireland. And as late as 1864 the Irish-born made up 76 percent of the arrests and detentions made by the Boston police, which probably also reflected a police prejudice against the Irish.[15] Indeed, the Catholic *Boston Pilot* often complained that "The constables and watchmen in this city will arrest an Irishman for the most trivial offence, while the big native rogues and rioters escape with impunity."[16] This perception only contributed to the Irish sense of alienation in the city.

The pathology included the children of the Irish immigrants. In 1847 Boston attorney and educator Edward G. Loring announced in dismay that "Our foreign population furnishes altogether, the largest proportion of children, left to the moral infection of the streets, . . . and those children, furnish five sevenths of our juvenile convicts."[17] And the same year School Committeeman George B. Emerson described the Irish youth as "most of the time quarrelling and gambling. They are beggars, male and female, strolling from street to street, through lanes, byways and alleys, practicing the elementary lessons of pilfering, lying, deception and theft. They are the loafers on wharves and in stables, spending their time in idleness, profanity, and in all the modes of juvenile vice."[18] In 1852, urging a more concerted Sunday school effort, *The Pilot* complained of the hordes of Irish boys who "associate together on Sundays, about the wharves and other places, where they pass their time in idleness and vice, corrupting one another and indulging in all the evil propensities of their nature." It urged concerned adults "in their walks about Broad Street, Fort-Hill, and the South Cove" to "observe the children they meet, let them but stop and listen to their language and notice there their ways; let them reflect that these children are our own."[19]

Boston and Massachusetts authorities as well as ordinary citizens rose to the challenge in a variety of ways. During the height of the potato blight non-Irish Bostonians had sent over eight thousand tons of food to prevent starvation in Ireland, and for some this seemed the best way to deal with the problem[20]—that is, alleviate the situation in Ireland so the Irish would stay where they were, on the "old sod." As Edward Everett put it, "It behooves us to keep Ireland from starving."[21] But that strategy at best momentarily held back the tide. To deal with the large numbers of sick arrivals who posed a threat to the city's general health, in 1847 Boston established a quarantine station on Deer Island in Boston harbor where all newcomers would be screened and the contagiously ill detained or sent away. By 1848 extensive hospital facilities had been established there. In South Boston, where "City Lands" had been set aside, a whole complex of facilities was erected, including houses of correction and reformation to cope with the surge in numbers of criminals, an alms-house to harbor the most destitute, and a lunatic asylum.

This sudden presence of so many and such undesirable newcomers in their midst caused some Bostonians to give up and get out. By 1852 an official city report commented that

> While our foreign population is rapidly augmenting, our native population is in a greater ratio diminishing . . . Many streets formerly occupied by some of our wealthiest and most respectable citizens are now wholly surrendered to foreigners . . . Many citizens of Boston are erecting houses in the neighboring cities and villages, and increasing the taxable property in these places from the profits of business transacted within our limits.[22]

Thus, the Potato Famine had caused the first suburban flight as early as the 1850s with its attendant problems, including the transfer of wealth from the city.

If the Irish could not be kept in Ireland, some Bostonians decided upon a different strategy: encourage the Irish to move westward.[23] The westward movement was aided by the fact that it became known in other parts of the country that Boston had become a labor reservoir. Ads constantly appeared in Boston papers for workers needed elsewhere, and many Irishmen shipped out to labor camps, some returning to Boston between jobs.[24] Some evidence suggests that the more able-bodied and daring tended to move out of Boston, where they saw little opportunity. They left behind, in the opinion of poli-tician and educator Edward Everett, "the infirm and especially the chronic paupers."[25]

The vast pool of cheap labor provided opportunities for Yankees of the more entrepreneurial stripe. In the decades before the Great Famine immi-gration, Irish labor had fueled the city's first great land fill projects and, in the words of *The Pilot*, "dug, and hewed, and tunneled and leveled" a network of railroads into existence.[26] But industrialization, which had been spearheaded by the mechanization of textile production and which had already done much to transform the New England economy (though financed largely by Boston money), had taken place outside the city in places like Lowell and Lawrence where abundant waterpower drove the mills. But now the Boston industrialists began to manufacture in Boston itself. For example, between 1845 and 1850 the number employed in ready-made clothing factories in Boston more than tripled, while by 1856 eight thousand women were sewing in their homes for one manufacturer alone. By the Civil War Boston had taken over from New York as the center of the factory manufacture of ready-made clothing in the United States. The Boston shipbuilding industry employed fourteen times as many men in 1855 as it had in 1845. The casting of iron, copper, and brass and the manufacture of pianos, organs, furniture, shoes, sewing machines, glass, and numerous other items increased many times over.[27] Between 1845 and 1865 the number of industrial employees in Boston more than quadrupled.

It was the abundant supply of cheap Irish labor that "achieved the transition from the earlier commercial to the later industrial organization of the city." Before the arrival of the Irish, the "rigid labor supply had made industrialization impossible,"[28] but now "the Irish energized all aspects of industrial development in Boston by holding out to investors magnificent opportunities for profits from cheap labor costs."[29] While the Irish, in making industrialization possible, indirectly displaced the artisans, such as tailors and shoemakers, who had formerly manufactured products by hand, they directly displaced native unskilled laborers because they were willing to work for less. Despite the great industrial growth, immigration kept the labor supply greater than the demand, wages remained low, and unemployment was "endemic to the economic system."[30] Nor did the large numbers of Irish laborers employed in the city building public works fare any better. While their presence made possible the continued reclamation of land from the sea that had begun earlier, and the laying of the city's infrastructure, it was done largely at their expense. Workers laying the city's water mains, for example, were paid 75 cents a day, even less than in private industry.[31]

The underemployment and underpayment of their husbands and fathers drove large numbers of Irish women into the workforce to supplement the family income. By 1865, more women than men were employed in Boston.[32] The influx of women into the workforce also transformed life for many Yankee households. Large numbers of Yankees now found that, at the greatly lowered wages, they could afford maids and servant girls.

Thus, the arrival of the Irish greatly enhanced the Boston industrialist's opportunity for profit and the homeowner's opportunity for leisure, but at the expense of near slavery for the Irish. Some even thought that the Irish had become to the North what Black slaves were to the South. Prominent Bostonian Edward Everett remarked in an 1851 letter: "Now if our Southern People could make up their minds to send their slaves back to Africa, this over whelming immigration which has reached 250,000 per annum, would afford the ready means of filling the vacuum."[33]

But if Boston industrialists and their wives were offering employment to the Irish men and women, during the long hours these poor immigrants toiled at work their children went untended. A large part of the great educational effort expended by the people of Massachusetts from the early nineteenth century on was prompted by and directed at the immigrants, and this effort gained unprecedented impetus from the Famine Irish. As the great champion of the effort, Horace Mann, had put it in his 1845 annual report as State Secretary of Education, "a foreign people . . . cannot be transformed into the full stature of American citizens, merely by a voyage across the Atlantic . . . They remain unfitted, until they have become morally acclimated to our institutions."[34]

That the public schools of Boston were meant to assimilate the children of immigrants in the sense of making them conform to the standards set by the host society was confirmed again and again in the history of nineteenth-century Boston public education. According to *The New Englander* in 1855, the public schools were "a policy of insurance for our republican and protestant institutions . . . These schools draw in the children of alien parentage with others, and assimilate them to the native born."[35] When a group of German immigrants, for instance, petitioned the Boston School Committee in 1851 for "the formation of a public school for German children in the Southern section of the City," the Committee responded that, instead of a separate school, "it is the English language that the Germans must know, and it is important that they should begin as early as possible to learn the national characteristics and the peculiar development in human nature of those with whom they are to be associated in life." The request was denied, and the German children who attended public school continued to learn about, and presumably try to imitate, "the peculiar development in human nature" that native Bostonians thought they had achieved.[36] The much more numerous Irish children were expected to do the same.

Boston's willingness to provide education for the newcomers was heavily tinged, if not primarily motivated, by an instinct for self-preservation. As the Boston School Committee bluntly put it, "Our rich men submit to this taxation not as a matter of mere benevolence, not for the personal advantage of those educated, but for the general benefit thereby to the whole land."[37] The *American Journal of Education* stated that "the simple question is, do the wealthy or well educated prefer to be ruled by ignorance, and the corruptions which follow in its train, rather than to pay the expense of universal education? Do they value a tithe of their income more than property and life?"[38] When the School Committee adopted a recommendation in 1854 to provide schools for foreign-language-speaking adults, it did so "to enable them to get employment, . . . thereby diminishing the danger of their becoming the victims of vice and pauperism."[39] To Governor Edward Everett it was "this peaceful army of twenty-seven thousand children . . . waging the great war against the legion hosts of ignorance, vice, and anarchy . . . with the spelling book, the grammar, and the Bible" that would ensure civil order in the commonwealth.[40]

Self-interest emerged particularly clearly in the debates over the question of compulsory schooling around mid-century, tinged as usual with thinly veiled skepticism about the newcomers' ability to assimilate. Warned the School Committee in 1850:

> If we let them run wild, we shall feel the effects ten years hence, in the insecurity of property, in the records of our criminal courts, in the expenses of our houses of punishment, and in our taxes for pauperism . . . We must open the doors of our school houses and invite and compel them to come in. . . . In our Schools they must receive moral and religious teaching, powerful enough if possible to keep them in the right path amid the moral darkness which is their daily and domestic walk . . . Unless we can reclaim this population in their childhood by moral means, we must control them by force, or support them as paupers, at a maturer period of life.[41]

The School Committee had stated the same sentiment more succinctly in 1841: "Unless they are made inmates of our schools, many of them will become inmates of our prisons."[42]

The public school rhetoric of these years often contained insinuations or even outright assertions that the Irish wallowed in "moral darkness," depravity, cultural and possibly even hereditary inferiority. As early as 1833 the editor of the *American Annals of Education* had observed that "European immigration is not now, as formerly, from the best classes of the community. On the contrary, the government and individuals of foreign countries are employing our country as a convenient receptacle for the most ignorant, and too often the most vicious of their subjects."[43] In an official Boston School Committee report in 1846 Edmund G. Loring wrote that "It is a matter of daily remark, that immigration is constantly countervailing the Puritan leaven of our people, and reducing the scale of public morality and public intelligence." Loring hoped, though, that the situation could be "corrected by our schools."[44] According to Joseph Whightman, the contemporary historian of the Boston primary school, "plain sewing" was introduced as a "necessity" into these schools once they had filled up with "a class of children from the lowest ranks of society, where home education was unknown, and whose moral as well as intellectual faculties must be developed by our teachers."[45] By the late 1840s the School Committee became preoccupied with finding "the best method of securing, to all the pupils of our grammar schools, that *moral instruction*, which is required by the Constitution and laws of this Commonwealth."[46]

The alleged depravity fed into the compulsory schooling movement that had been building momentum ever since the 1820s when Boston school authorities had decided to take action to prevent the spread of a newly emerged plague, that of children roaming the streets with nothing to do. In 1826 the School Committee had appointed a truant officer whose duty it was to see that these vagrant children either went to school, found a job, or went to the House of Reformation. In 1836, motivated in part by the desire to reduce child labor, a regulation had been enacted that required that children could only be employed if they had attended school for at least three months that year. Though this law lacked adequate enforcement provisions, it at least gave an indication that the city fathers were getting more serious about school attendance.

A decade later, in 1847, faced by the tidal wave of Potato Famine immigration, newly elected mayor Josiah Quincy Jr. appointed a committee to study the truancy problem, which reported on the "mischief caused by habits of truancy" in the city. The mayor was alarmed that "hundreds of children of both sexes, are daily kept from school to support their parents, often in idleness and drunkenness, by pilfering about the wharves or by some other profitable form of vice, and are regularly educated for the brothel and the dram-shop, for the poorhouse and the jail."[47] Committees were periodically appointed to devise better ways of "securing the steady attendance in our public schools" of the children not attending school.[48] Among the recommendations were truant officers "whose duty it should be to look up children within the ages of eight and sixteen, who do not attend school; and to use all proper measures to induce them to attend."[49]

In 1852 a compulsory schooling law was passed that required a minimum of three months of schooling each year for eight- to fourteen-year-olds, with at least six weeks in succession.[50] But the law did not sweep all the children off the street immediately, and the School Committee continued to plead that "Those children should be brought within the jurisdiction of the Public Schools, from whom, through their vagrant habits, our property is most in danger."[51]

The Boston school authorities went to unprecedented lengths to make schooling for the newcomers more feasible. For example, while textbooks had never been provided as a part of public education in Boston, in September 1847 the School Committee began studying the advisability of providing free books "so as to render our common schools more completely free schools."[52] The reality was that many of the new children could not afford to buy their own textbooks.

And all the efforts produced results. By 1849, 48 percent of the children in the city's primary schools were of foreign parentage, with the proportion climbing each year. Three years later it had jumped to 57 percent.[53] An effort by an English visitor in 1852 to ascertain the exact number of Roman Catholic children in the public schools produced a rough estimate from the authorities that over a third of all the school children were of that faith.[54] According to one study, by 1850 school attendance in Boston, at least at some time during the year, had reached surprisingly high levels, with little difference between children of varied social class backgrounds until the teen years. Thus, while 88.9 percent of children aged six to twelve whose fathers were artisans attended school at some time during 1850, 85 percent of children whose fathers were unskilled or unemployed did so, a lower but nevertheless very high rate of attendance for the mid-nineteenth century. Only for older children, aged thirteen to sixteen, did more appreciable differences emerge, 58 percent enrollment for children of professionals versus 39 and 34 percent for children of the unskilled and the unemployed respectively.[55]

This suggests that a high proportion of the Irish children, who made up the largest portion of the lower class in Boston, attended school. The same study found that while 90 percent of the native-born children aged six to twelve attended school, 84 percent of the first- and second-generation Irish did so, a lower but still very high percentage. Only when it came to "higher" education did the Irish lag significantly behind, with 34 percent of the Irish versus 55 percent of the natives still in school between the ages of thirteen and sixteen. Still, for over a third of the Irish children to still be attending school at this age in 1850 was remarkable. Further, the statistics showed that the second-generation Irish children were 83 percent more likely to be in school from ages thirteen to sixteen than those born in Ireland.

Thus, the Yankees could rejoice that their schools were increasingly enticing the Irish not only to attend but to stay in school. The price was high. Between 1820 and 1865, Boston spent annually almost one fifth of its revenues on public education. Not everyone agreed, but the majority of Boston citizenry considered this a price worth paying.[56]

Because of the growing residential segregation in the city, many of the schools had a much higher percentage of immigrant children than the average. In the seventh ward, for example, more than three quarters of the children between the ages of five and fifteen were the offspring of immigrants or immigrants themselves in 1850. In wards one, three, four, nine, and twelve the proportion ranged from 52 to 62 percent.[57] In one school a class of fifty girls had only one "American," in the Endicott School in the North End forty-five of fifty boys in the class next to graduation were Irish, and in the Boylston School on Fort Hill fifty-two of fifty-eight scholars were immigrants.[58] In many of the schools with heavy Irish enrollments the School Committee found much to be desired. It described the Boylston School as "disturbed" and complained of the children's "personal appearance." At the Endicott School, "many of the children being Irish, their attendance is irregular and not long enough for much improvement. They receive little or no attention at home, and are often kept from school, as well by the requirements of the church, as by parental command for household purposes."[59] Despite the limited results here and there, the Boston establishment's monumental efforts to get the children of Irish Catholics into the public schools, where they could be forged into proper, law-abiding, productive citizens, were, as the statistics show, hugely successful overall.

For the most part an alternative Catholic parochial school system, which did not materialize to any significant degree during the tenures of Bishops Cheverus and Fenwick, did not develop over the next twenty years either, despite the huge growth of the Catholic populace resulting from the Famine. Among the urban Catholic dioceses of the United States Boston began to stand out for the absence of anything resembling a parochial school system. There seem to have been several reasons for this. First, the pressure from the "host" society for the newcomers to acculturate through the public schools may have been simply too much to resist. Second, the penury of the new immigrants made the financing of an educational alternative to the public schools unlikely.

Even before the Potato Famine immigration, Irish lay leadership in Boston had not paid much attention to the development of Catholic schools. They had not begun a tradition of alternative schooling, and the only schools that had come into existence had been the energetic work of Bishop Fenwick. His successor, John Fitzpatrick made no move to take up the parochial school crusade that was already well under way in other urban American dioceses and that Fenwick had attempted to initiate. It may well have been the new Catholic bishop of Boston who was the defining reason that a serious parochial alternative to the public schools did not develop in Boston.

To all appearances Fitzpatrick was the ideal choice to take on the demanding and delicate position as Roman Catholic bishop of Boston. He was a man of proven intelligence, apparently enhanced by a commanding presence that, it was said, marked him as a person born to rule.[60] But far more important,

Fitzpatrick's roots sank deep both into the Boston Irish community and into the more rarified world of Yankee Boston. He had not only been born in Boston, but as a youth he had been sponsored into the upper reaches of Boston society. He was a rarity for mid-nineteenth-century Boston, an assimilated Irishman.

Fitzpatrick was born in 1812 of Irish immigrant parents.[61] His father was a tailor with his own business in the days before "ready-mades" took over the clothing industry. He was apparently relatively successful, though the family continued to live in the Irish immigrant section of town, including for a time at its core on Broad Street. John would have been eleven when the anti-Irish Ann Street riot took place nearby and fourteen when a similar riot raged for three days on Broad Street, with native mobs, inflamed by the threat of losing their jobs to Irish immigrants who would work for less and by the rising tide of anti-Catholicism sweeping the Eastern cities, smashing windows, yelling insults, and daring the Irish to come out and fight.[62] No direct record remains of the effect, if any, on the young boy, though one can imagine that at least some residual impression might have lasted into adulthood, especially considering that his father remained active in Irish affairs, rising to the presidency of the Charitable Irish Society in Boston.

Young Fitzpatrick was being exposed to other influences that were to profoundly affect the course of his life. One was his attendance at the public schools, first the Mason Street School (known later as the Adams School), then the School for Mutual Instruction (Boston's "Monitorial" school, in which to save money the older, more advanced children instructed the less advanced), and then the Boylston School. In 1826 he was chosen as one of fifty entrants to the prestigious Boston Latin School. In all these schools he distinguished himself with various honors, including the coveted Franklin medals. Particularly at Boston Latin, the youth was introduced not just to the intricacies of Latin, Greek, algebra, and the like, but also to that other Boston world so foreign to the Irish inhabitants of Broad Street. Boston Latin, ever since its founding in the 1630s, had served Boston's best families to prepare their sons for entry into Harvard College and cultured life among the town's first citizens.

Among Fitzpatrick's contemporaries at Boston Latin were the offspring of Boston's elite families such at the Appletons, Abbots, Cabots, Hancocks, Lawrences, Lincolns, Lorings, Parkers, Parkmans, Peabodys, Tuckermans, and others. Many were to emerge as prominent local and national citizens, some even as household names. Wendel Phillips, the famous abolitionist orator, graduated at the end of Fitzpatrick's first year; Charles Sumner, future abolitionist senator from Massachusetts, graduated the year before. Henry Ward Beecher, son of nativist Lyman Beecher, and future reformer and prominent minister, sat in the same classrooms with the future Catholic bishop. His schoolmates included two future mayors of Boston, a future U.S. Secretary of State, a U.S. Attorney General, a distinguished Harvard professor, historians, editors, men of letters such as Edward Everett Hale, and prominent businessmen such as George Cabot.[63] Fitzpatrick's years in the Boston public schools had a lasting and profound effect on his future. However, while most of his Boston Latin classmates went on to enter Harvard, he set off in a direction totally foreign to them.

While growing up, Fitzpatrick had experienced life on the immigrant Irish streets and wharves of Boston as well as in the Yankee-fied classrooms of the city's best public schools. His parents had exposed him to another influence that was to prove decisive in determining the direction of his life. His father had been a prominent member of Boston's first Roman Catholic congregation and was on familiar terms with both Father Matignon and Bishop Cheverus, and then after 1825 with Bishop Fenwick. It was apparently shortly after Fenwick's arrival in Boston that the thirteen-year-old Fitzgerald confided to the bishop that he wished to study for the priesthood. From that time on it appears that Fenwick took Fitzpatrick under his episcopal wing, even while the boy was still completing his studies at Boston Latin School.[64]

Once he graduated from Boston Latin, Fitzpatrick was sent by Bishop Fenwick to study for the priesthood at the College of St. Sulpice in Montreal for the next eight years, and then in 1837 to the Sulpician seminary in Paris. At both he distinguished himself with scholastic honors and a strong personal reputation. He was ordained in Paris in 1840 and immediately returned to become Fenwick's assistant at the cathedral in Boston. The aging bishop, who had apparently not only paid for the young man's education but had insisted that it be the best available and even longer than was necessary, lost no time in capitalizing on his investment.

From the very first Fitzpatrick was often used to do the troubleshooting that Fenwick himself had done in earlier years. He was sent into the North End's faction-ridden St. Mary's parish in 1842 and restored order. In Cambridge the same year he started a new parish in another troubled congregation. In 1843 it was off to Providence on a similar mission. When the brilliant but erratic Orestes Brownson approached Fenwick about converting to Catholicism, after preliminary interviews the bishop turned him over to Fitzpatrick for instruction, a striking act of confidence in the young priest fresh out of the seminary, especially considering Brownson's standing in the American literary and scholarly community. Other responsible assignments as well as the fact that he was repeatedly asked to accompany the bishop on important visitations leave little doubt that Fenwick had very early singled him out for special consideration.

Although Fenwick had earlier apparently fastened on a Canadian priest as his successor,[65] Fitzpatrick proved able and ready far beyond his years. By 1843, at the Fifth Provincial Council of Baltimore, the bishop made two significant requests for the diocese of Boston. One was that the states of Rhode Island and Connecticut be split off as a separate diocese; the other was that Fitzpatrick be made coadjutor to the Diocese of Boston with right of succession. Both requests were granted.[66]

At Fenwick's death two years later in 1846 Fitzpatrick, just thirty-four years of age, smoothly switched into the driver's seat with hardly a hesitation.[67] It appeared that the Roman Catholic diocese of Boston could hardly have been better situated to benefit from its new leadership. Its young bishop, in addition to the immense advantage of youthful energy, possessed impeccable intellectual and personal credentials, as had been repeatedly recognized throughout his scholastic career. He enjoyed the advantage of the best ecclesiastical training available at the time. And he had been painstakingly groomed for the position by his immediate predecessor. Unlike his predecessor, however, he not only shared the same ethnic origins as the overwhelming majority of his flock, but he had grown up among them on the streets of Boston. Bishop Fitzpatrick had not only participated in the Boston Yankee world through its heralded public schools, especially Boston Latin, but had apparently been accepted by it.

In 1837 Fitzpatrick had been singled out as the prime example of the wonders that could result when the child of Irish immigrants came under the beneficent influence of the Boston public schools. While stopping off in Boston after completing his ecclesiastical studies in Montreal and before departing for further studies in Paris, Fitzpatrick had attended a reunion of Boston Latin School alumni at Faneuil Hall. There, in the presence of Governor Edward Everett, Mayor Samuel Eliot, President Josiah Quincy of Harvard College, and many other prominent Bostonians, Fitzpatrick was praised in a formal, public introduction to the entire assemblage as "a young man, a native of Boston, of Irish parentage, and a Roman Catholic. He has been educated in our schools and is a medal scholar of more than one of them." After citing the fact that young Fitzpatrick had just graduated with highest honors from a college in Montreal and was on his way to "perfect his education" in France, the speaker, Major Benjamin Russell, concluded that "Boston and her schools may be proud of such a man and such a scholar."[68] Perhaps it was this occasion, and Fitzpatrick himself, that Everett had in mind years later when he remarked in a letter to the Duchess of Argyle that while "spirits are as cheap with us as most other things, and this is a temptation which poor Pat finds it hard to resist . . . the children are sent to our free schools, and the second generation comes out greatly elevated."[69] In any event, it was clear that the new Catholic bishop of Boston was regarded in the city's best circles as their window-dressing Irishman.

The courtship between the Boston establishment and Fitzpatrick continued throughout his tenure as bishop. Some might say, and some apparently said at the time, that Fitzpatrick in many ways had been coopted by Boston's Brahmins to the detriment of Boston Catholicism, and even to the detriment of his own well-being. In 1846 the bishop was invited by renowned surgeon John Collins Warren to become a charter member of the Society of Mutual Improvement, an exclusive social circle that held weekly meetings "for social and scientific conversation" and later became variously known as the Warren Club and the Thursday Evening Club. As the only Roman Catholic member he associated with the most cultivated of Boston society, and throughout his episcopacy attended meetings in their fashionable homes.[70]

All his life he maintained friendships begun at Boston Latin School. Through his former classmate George Cabot he became friends with the entire Cabot family, frequently visiting their home at Nahant in the summer. According to the reminiscences of George's nephew, Henry Cabot Lodge, "He was known to every one as 'Bishop John,' and was a most excellent man, very popular and greatly beloved . . . Bishop John was not only very kind to me, but the best of companions, genial, affectionate, and sympathetic."[71]

In addition Fitzpatrick enjoyed the acquaintance and apparently the genuine friendship of other notable Bostonians, including Senator Charles Sumner, who at one point he tried to persuade to run for president[72]; Chief Justice of the Massachusetts Supreme Court, Lemuel Shaw; famous defense attorney Rufus Choate; the leading real estate conveyancer in Boston, Nathaniel Bowditch; historian Francis Parkman; industrialist Amos A. Lawrence; Charles and Nathan Hale, publishers of *The Boston Advertiser*; and various Boston mayors, including Benjamin Seaver, who requested Fitzpatrick's presence at his deathbed.[73] When Joseph Wightman published his history of the Boston primary schools, he sent an inscribed copy to Bishop Fitzpatrick.[74] And when Richard Henry Dana set out for his *Two Years Before the Mast* journey he went with a letter of introduction, in Latin, from Fitzpatrick.[75]

In 1862, when for health reasons he had to leave Boston and travel to Europe, Fitzpatrick was asked by the Lincoln administration to help the Union cause while there by serving at the American embassy in Catholic Belgium, which he did for several months.[76] Finally, probably at least in part because of his personal service to the Union cause and also in behalf of "the Irish who have offered themselves freely for the army," in 1861 he was granted the highest honor Yankee Boston could bestow, an honorary degree from Harvard.[77] In 1862 he was elected to the American Academy of Arts and Sciences.

A biographer lists as one of his two distinguishing characteristics "his ability to hold the respect and the friendship of many influential persons not of his own faith."[78] After his death one of his fellow bishops, remarking on the presence at the funeral of both the governor and mayor, reflected that "He was evidently much loved and respected by those outside of the Church and they were proud of him as a 'Boston boy'."[79]

To all appearances, Fitzpatrick and the Boston establishment made a perfect fit, and the fit seemed to promise benefit both to Boston and to the Catholic Church in Boston, especially as he took the helm in the midst of the Potato Famine immigration. But appearances can be deceiving. One source of the deception was probably the fact that Fitzpatrick's apparent absorption into Boston's mainstream and his identification with it, rather than making it easier for him to gain concessions to and support for Catholic interests that he would like to espouse, actually seems to have made it more difficult. To oppose public policies because they offended Catholics would sometimes have been to offend the very people who had befriended him. In contrast to Bishop Fenwick, who considered himself at least the equal of the best that Boston had to offer, and not at all beholden to them for anything, Fitzpatrick seemed at crucial times even apologetic for daring to oppose or even question decisions made by the City Council or the various official bodies that controlled affairs, such as the public School Committee. Again and again he offered very weak, apologetic, always deferential objections to offensive public policies. It may well have been that the bishop could not bring himself to oppose the numerous prominent and influential Bostonians who had sponsored him into their inner circle, though there is no record that any of them ever explicitly attempted to influence his actions.

In addition to his deferential posture regarding public policies in Boston, Fitzpatrick consistently showed timidity in the face of financial challenges. Unlike Fenwick, who boasted about his courage in the face of financial difficulties, Fitzpatrick characteristically chose not to meet these difficulties at all. For example, wherever possible, he avoided building new churches, instead buying used church buildings on the cheap as their Protestant congregants abandoned neighborhoods being "invaded" by Catholic immigrants. While this probably made financial sense, it does not appear to have been a practice that pleased his Irish Catholic parishioners. Of much greater consequence, using the excuse of financial hardship, he chose not to establish Catholic charitable institutions or even to recruit nuns or brothers to establish them. He instead relied on the charities conducted by the city for the sick, the destitute, the orphans, and the like. There is no record that he was ever instrumental in founding a single such institution, nor of soliciting orders of priests or brothers or nuns to do so, though in several instances these were recruited by local pastors or well-meaning lay people.

Often Fitzpatrick's policy, or lack thereof, motivated by financial fears, resulted in consequences that were much less than desirable for Catholic interests. Just one example was the hospital on Deer Island founded by the city for Irish immigrants who were already ill upon arrival. The bishop first exulted that "The whole conduct of the authorities and citizens in general has been characterized by much kinship and good feeling, and although the immense numbers of destitute creatures who arrive daily are really a burden there is no expression of complaint." But then just a week later he learned that his priests had been denied access to the Catholic immigrants there. His personal appeal to the mayor, who was an acquaintance, won a concession to allow priests not free access but to visit twice a week. The bishop accepted the concession.[80] Just ten days later Fitzpatrick learned that the same situation had emerged at the Almshouse in South Boston: priests were not being allowed entry. Again, the mayor promised to do something "if possible."[81]

What emerged in Boston was what appeared to Catholics as a coherent policy of using public institutions to separate Catholic immigrants and their children from their faith. This problem of the Protestant influence in Boston charitable institutions continued throughout the Fitzpatrick years, erupting periodically into a major issue but smoldering always beneath the surface.[82] Through it all Fitzpatrick publicly maintained a deferential, non-belligerent posture, and he did nothing to develop a countervailing network of Catholic institutions, though other individuals and organizations did take action and to some degree filled the vacuum.

One can hardly escape the impression that Fitzpatrick was overwhelmed by the weight of his responsibilities, and also that, despite his apparent reception into the rarified air of Yankee Boston society, he never felt quite at home there, at least not enough to speak out forcefully when he disagreed, and certainly not enough to take contrary action. In addition, he appears to have been so coopted by his sponsors that he could not bring himself to openly oppose them, even though in private, in his diary, or to a fellow Catholic dignitary, he sometimes vented his true feelings. It was this constant tension between his public face and true inner feelings that may, as at least one student of the Fitzpatrick era has suggested, have led to the severe hypertension that plagued his tenure as bishop, which often rendered him unable to work, and eventually led to a premature death at age 54.[83]

The first recorded indication of this radical dichotomy between the outer appearance of integration with proper Boston and the inner experience of alienation came in 1838 when he was still studying for the priesthood in France, the year after he had been gloriously toasted at the Boston Latin School reunion. An angry letter to his sister and confidant, Eleanor, reveals with crystal clarity how he actually felt about at least some of his Yankee sponsors. Commenting on the public insult and vilification of an Irish militia regiment at a recent Boston celebration, he complained,

> It is another example of the base spirit of New Englanders, *Vile* narrow-minded scoundrels . . . They'll drawl long speeches about liberality and toleration and about the freedom of their institutions. [But] it would be hard to find a people more void of honest principles and of every sentiment becoming an honorable man and yet they have the insupportable vanity to look upon themselves as the first nation on earth. Spitefulest of wretches. I'll not stir up my bile by thinking of them any longer.[84]

His white-hot anger was directed not at the rabble who snubbed the Irish militia or perpetrated riots, but at the makers of speeches and preachers of toleration, the representatives of the dignitaries who were sponsoring his acculturation and whose companionship he had already begun to cultivate and would continue to nourish for the rest of his life. There is no record that on this occasion, or any other when he felt legitimate Catholic interests had been offended or denied, he made more than a half-hearted, muted, and always apologetic and conciliatory protest.

It appears that Fitzpatrick had chosen, either with deliberation or perhaps subconsciously early on, possibly while still attending public school, certainly before he returned to Boston from his seminary training, not only not to "stir up" his bile against the Yankees, but to suppress it, at least publicly in his dealings with them. To all outward appearances he succeeded perfectly. One detects no indication in anything that was written of him by his Yankee friends that they had any inkling of this inner dissatisfaction. As bishop, though he was in conscience forced from time to time to protest against what he saw as injustice perpetrated on his Catholic flock and its enterprises, his protests and complaints were always made in a patient, nonthreatening, respectful manner, always appealing to what he apparently saw as the Yankees' Achilles heel: their desire to be thought of as fair-minded. But in the process he often failed to achieve what he perceived as justice for legitimate Catholic interests.

The advice he gave to the bishop of Cincinnati, John B. Purcell, in 1859 typifies his public approach to the Yankees. Fitzpatrick had invited Purcell to dedicate the cornerstone for a new church on Bunker Hill in Charlestown, a significant and potentially explosive event given the past intense hostilities there, such as the burning of the nearby Ursuline convent and school, as well as the location's historical significance. Numerous important local dignitaries were to attend. The Cincinnati bishop had asked Fitzpatrick for suggestions on what to say at the dedication. Bishop Fitzpatrick replied, "Nothing works upon them so effectively as a show of confidence in their sense of justice," and he advised the use of a little "soft soap"[85] to keep them happy.

This appears to have been Fitzpatrick's consistent strategy: always patient and long-suffering, always respectful, always counseling against violence, always conciliatory, ever ready to apply a little "soft soap" to soothe the Yankees.[86] This strategy, with its dichotomy between outward behavior and inner feeling, Fitzpatrick was to repeat again and again.

Even in the face of open hostility, he consistently counseled long-suffering patience. For example, in 1847, to deal with a threatening demonstration of the Native American Party on Fort Hill, he sent "several priests through the streets inhabited by Irish Catholics to advise and exhort them." The priests were told to have them "remain in their houses and suffer the procession to pass unnoticed."[87] During the Hannah Corcoran disturbances in 1853 he called off the Lenten services to keep the Irish at home and off the streets.[88] When rumors spread that anti-Catholic rabble-rouser "Angel Guardian" Orr's followers were planning to burn Catholic churches and attack the Irish, he appealed through *The Pilot* to Catholics:

> We earnestly beseech every good Catholic of Boston to consider himself as specially bound, not only to keep the peace himself, but to employ, under the direction of the clergy, all honest means to keep these few thoughtless Catholics out of the way when the know-nothings [sic] make their appearance ... If they come before your very door to insult you, take no notice of them, and trust to the laws for protection.[89]

When a Know Nothing crowd, thinking that the papal visitor Monsignor Bedini was inside, demonstrated outside his own home, Fitzpatrick remained quietly inside and then wrote a public letter affirming his pleasure that out of a city with 300,000 inhabitants the bigots had been able to produce fewer than 200 demonstrators. In response to the complaint voiced by others that the authorities had not broken up the demonstration even though it took place at night, he remarked, characteristically, that "Upon this point I have neither complaint to make nor defence to offer."[90]

Fitzpatrick, though Irish, had shed all outward association with the Irish subculture and did not wish to flaunt or even promote a sense of Irish pride and identity in Boston. Unlike his father, who headed the Charitable Irish Society, the son behaved much more like his immediate episcopal predecessor, shunning the Irish feasts and even absenting himself from Boston to avoid them. "I hate such national manifestations," he declared.[91]

Given that Fitzpatrick had been coopted into Yankee Boston from an early age, and that he had obviously accepted the fact that he had been "adopted," despite privately expressed disdain for his Yankee sponsors, it was not surprising that he did little or nothing that might offend them. He gained a reputation among more militant Catholics, both in Boston and in the Catholic Church generally, as well as among some non-Catholic observers, for what was perceived as a lack of courage coupled with a lack of energy. For example, the visiting Englishman Lord Acton, though very much taken by him personally, astutely noted a negative characteristic: "He is not such a good man of business as Dr. Hughes," observed Acton. "Perhaps he is even wanting in energy."[92]

Comments about Fitzpatrick's lack of energy seem to have been common as his tenure in Boston wore on, which seems surprising given the fact that Bishop Fenwick, a man of seeming boundless energy himself, obviously chose him as successor in good part because of what seemed his potential for energetic action. This raises once again the interesting speculation that as time went on the inner tensions of pleasing his Yankee sponsors versus the demands of doing what was best for his Catholic flock may have sapped his resolve. In any case, there is no doubt that his conduct in office revealed a lack of boldness and a distinct timidity in the face of the monumental challenges his position entailed.

Evaluations from within the Church were often quite negative, and not very forgiving. Archbishop Hughes in New York, who aggressively took on all opponents of the Church, seems to have been less than enamored of his more diplomatic or possibly timid colleague in Boston, though he stopped short of condemning him.[93] The Apostolic Delegate from Rome, Monsignor Bedini, who considered Hughes the outstanding American prelate, especially for the mighty battle he had fought in the early 1840s to gain tax support for parochial schools in New York, found the Boston bishop's failure even to suggest such a possibility in Massachusetts a sign of weakness and timidity.[94] Bedini had spent fifteen days in Boston, which he considered "the most distinguished city of the American Union." Fitzpatrick, too, he considered distinguished, "a man of outstanding talents, authoritative presence, and distinguished orator." However, the Italian prelate went on to observe that the bishop of Boston, despite his oratorical skills, "speaks too infrequently" and "he lacks certain external qualities and a zeal for action."[95] This was the kind of behavior that might have inspired the remark from still another of his episcopal colleagues, the highly respected Bishop John Lancaster Spalding of Peoria, that the bishop of Boston was "remarkably diffident," a surprising judgment about one who from early on had apparently been identified as a person born to rule.[96]

The absence of a "zeal for action" surfaced from other sources, too, particularly with regard to Fitzpatrick's passivity in the face of anti-Catholicism. On one occasion after a mob threatened the cathedral, the prominent convert Orestes Brownson's daughter Sarah wrote that "indignation runs riot through the city. The Bishop does nothing."[97]

But it was with regard to the lack of effort to develop a parochial school system that Fitzpatrick's timidity in the face of the Boston establishment probably had the most telling negative impact on Catholic educational development in Boston. Added to the already well-established lack of interest in developing parochial schools exhibited by Irish lay leaders in previous diocesan administrations, plus the extreme poverty of the newest Irish immigrants of the Fitzpatrick era, plus the all-out crusade on the part of the Boston establishment to enroll the new Irish immigrants in the public schools through compulsory education laws, Fitzpatrick's personal refusal to develop parochial schools, based ostensibly on his conviction that they could not be afforded, came close to providing the death knell to any possible parochial school movement in Boston during his tenure. However, a phenomenon often alluded to as the "schoolmen," local pastors who worked essentially on their own initiative, did begin to emerge during Fitzpatrick's tenure.

On at least several occasions Fitzpatrick asserted that parochial schools would be preferable, though he always added that for financial reasons they were not possible. He sometimes also affirmed that he did not view the public schools as a serious threat to the faith of Catholic children, a view possibly bolstered by his own successful experience in the Boston public schools. One interchange he had with a British visitor is probably a good example of his true feelings about having parochial schools in Boston. In 1851 he entertained the Honorable Edward Twisleton, a member of the British Parliament who was visiting the United States to study the common school system and stopped in to ask Fitzpatrick his opinion. Fitzpatrick confided to Twisleton that the public schools "are to a Catholic very defective but still under the present circumstances they are the best we can have."[98]

The prominent convert to Catholicism, Orestes Brownson, who spoke with him often, informed Archbishop Hughes in New York that "The Bishop says that to send our children to the public schools is the best thing we can do, but not the best he could wish." Though Brownson did not explain further, he presumably referred to Fitzpatrick's conviction that parochial schools could not be afforded.[99] Brownson did not advocate parochial schools because he believed that the Irish were so culturally deprived that they would do better if they were exposed to New England culture. The Rev. Augustus Thebaud, a Jesuit who had served as president of Fordham in New York City and who knew Fitzpatrick well, similarly explained that "though he acknowledged that Catholic parochial schools were better, still he thought that as long as we could not have one of them in each parish we might avail ourselves of the help offered us by the state . . . He thought that there was no great danger for the children of Catholics if they frequented the public schools of New England."[100]

To parochial school advocates, his affirmations that parochial schools could not be afforded were further evidence of his timidity in the face of challenging situations. No doubt the comment made by Archbishop Purcell of Cincinnati to Archbishop Blanc of New Orleans in 1859—that Fitzpatrick was "not sound on the school question"—stated the conviction held by many of Fitzpatrick's contemporaries in the hierarchy.[101]

There were also signs of discontent within the diocese over the lack of a parochial school effort. It is difficult to determine to what extent a variety of letters from priests and laypeople protesting Fitzpatrick's behavior reflected the usual presence of a few malcontents or whether these were but the tip of an iceberg. Even assuming the protests simply reflected a fringe element in the diocese, however, the nature of the complaints is revealing. For example, in 1858 a group of Catholic laypeople, headed by a J. Toland, complained directly to the pope that the diocese for some years has not been "everything that could be desired. This is partly owing to the tepidity and want of vigor in our bishop." After recounting his failure to control money-grabbing priests, exorbitant fees in the Catholic cemeteries, and other specifics, the letter devotes its most detailed and passionate complaint to the school question. Decrying the absence of parochial schools in Boston, the Toland letter claimed that

> Our whole Catholic community would generously support these schools, and it is solely owing to the noncompliance of our bishop and his native born priests that they have not been in operation long ago. In the Diocese of New York under the care of B Hughes and mostly in every other large city in America, every Catholic church has its free school attached and the system works admirably. We are wholly dependant [sic] for our children's education on those godless publick schools belonging to the state and under the whole control of Protestant teachers whose instructions are to use every cunning to poison the minds of their Catholic pupils and induce them to abandon the faith of their parents.[102]

An 1863 letter from an anonymous "Sacerdos Dei Altissimi" (priest of the most high God) complained to Rome that Fitzpatrick "nihil agit ad promovendum relgionis bonum" (does nothing to promote the good of religion) and singled out his failure to open parochial schools.[103] The same year another anonymous priest protested that Fitzpatrick glorified himself as an example of what the public schools produce, and "Accordingly, except for a few places, nothing is done by the Bishop and his followers, who approve of those schools, to erect truly Catholic schools in the Diocese of Boston."[104] In 1865, in a protest to Rome about the American bishops, a New York Catholic singled out Bishop Fitzpatrick as being excessively interested in money and lacking zeal and piety.[105]

Fitzpatrick's behavior on the "school question" as well as his accustomed "don't rock the boat" policy came under the most acute stress in 1859 during and immediately after what came to be called the Eliot School case, which for several weeks rocked Boston and brought into clearest focus the dilemma that faced the Protestant Yankees as well as the Catholic newcomers, and in particular Fitzpatrick. The Eliot School case also illustrates the dichotomy between Fitzpatrick's public stance regarding the Yankees and the intense feelings he harbored privately.

The Eliot School case presented all the elements of high drama. The Eliot School, on North Bennett Street in the heart of the North End, accommodated about eight hundred boys, roughly six hundred of them Irish Catholics from St. Mary's parish. The principal, Mr. Samuel Mason, had apparently handled the religious issue with deference to Catholic sensibilities, not forcing Catholic boys to read from the King James version of the Bible, and even allowing them to read the Commandments and the Lord's Prayer from their own catechisms. But for some reason that has never come to light, perhaps under pressure from the School Committee member Micah Dyer, who was known to be a Know Nothing and whose special jurisdiction included the Eliot School, on Monday morning, March 7, 1859, the teacher of one class, a Miss Shepard, ordered the boys, each separately, to recite the Ten Commandments, and insisted that it be from the King James translation. One boy, Thomas J. Whall (or Wall), who had not quite reached his tenth birthday, refused, saying that his father had forbidden it. The matter was referred to the principal, Mason, who in turn consulted School Committee representative Dyer, who ordered that no boy should be allowed in the school who refused to obey the regulations. During the ensuing week Whall's father, who was apparently an illiterate stevedore, visited the school several times, consulting with Mason. An agreement was finally worked out that Mr. Whall thought, apparently incorrectly, exonerated his son from reciting the Protestant version, and it was agreed that the boy would return to school on Monday, March 14.

Meanwhile, one of the priests at St. Mary's parish, a Swiss Jesuit named Bernardin F. Wiget, intruded himself into the affair when he instructed the boys on Sunday, March 13, not to recite the Protestant version.[106] Wiget had just a few months earlier opened the parish's first boys' school, which to that date had attracted only about thirty young scholars, and he may have hoped that the issue would drive more of the boys into his school.[107] Before school on Monday the boys met and agreed that none of them would recite the Protestant version, motivated at least in part, according to one Catholic source, by the hope that they would be put out of school and enjoy a holiday.

When class convened on that fateful Monday, March 14, Miss Shepard began by asking each boy to recite the Ten Commandments. In other classes of the school the same demand was made. Everywhere the Catholic boys refused to use the Protestant version. The school now had not just one recalcitrant boy but a full-scale revolt on its hands. A School Committee member who was in the building at the time, a Mr. Hazelton, was asked to intervene.[108] Because of the previous week's incident, Hazelton assumed young Whall was the ringleader of this revolt, and he concentrated on getting Whall to conform. When the boy staunchly refused, Hazelton turned him over to Mr. McClaurin F. Cook, another teacher in the school and apparently a disciplinarian. Cook, deciding to use force, beat Whall on the hands with a rattan for approximately a half-hour until the boy yielded and repeated the Commandments in the Protestant version. His hands were bruised and bleeding and later required medical attention.

The beating only seemed to harden many of the other boys in their resolve. Several hundred left school rather than conform, a situation that continued throughout the week. On the following Monday the boys returned to school, but, perhaps counseled to do so by Father Wiget, brought with them their Catholic catechisms, prepared to recite the Commandments in the Catholic version. They were again dismissed from school, and the situation had developed into an ugly standoff.

The drama, which had already become front-page news in all of Boston, was heightened when Whall's parents filed suit against Cook for malicious assault on their son. The drama now shifted to the Boston courts. The local papers recounted every detail of the legal arguments advanced by the contesting attorneys in the case, Whall's contending that the boy was merely exercising the religious freedom guaranteed by the state constitution as well as obeying parental authority, Cook's arguing that the teacher was merely trying to enforce the law. After some days of deliberation, the judge chose to look at the matter more narrowly as a case of a teacher exercising his authority to enforce the legitimate education law of the state. Cook was exonerated.

The large-scale defection of Catholics from the public schools that might have been expected as a result of this affront did not materialize. That it did not was no doubt due to the behavior of the leadership on both sides, and constitutes a far more significant, even if not as interesting, aspect of the Eliot School affair. Bishop Fitzpatrick, constituting the Catholic leadership, played his predictable role in his approach to Yankee Boston, trying to defuse the situation publicly while privately venting his anger. First, he urged Catholic parents to send their children back to the public schools they had been attending. Second, the gravity and notoriety of the case forced him to abandon his preferred public silence. In a public letter to the Boston School Committee, speaking in the third person, he explained that although "It has been supposed that, because he was silent, he was satisfied with the state of our public schools. This is not so." Fitzpatrick went on to explain that his previous silence was due to his judgment that speaking out would only give rise to "angry passions" and "violent acts" and would only cause "much strife, but very little good."[109] Now, however, the Eliot crisis forced him to speak out "with a spirit of conciliation, and with a true disposition to promote good will and charity amongst all classes of citizens." While he clearly outlined the objections that Catholics had to the "enforced use of the Protestant version of the Bible . . . The enforced learning and reciting of the Ten Commandments in their Protestant forms . . . [and] The enforced union in chanting the Lord's Prayer and other religious chants," he prefaced all this with the hope "that it will not be regarded as an act of presumption or obtrusiveness, on his part to offer some few remarks upon the subject." Referring to his "personal knowledge" of several School Committee members, he made a pointed effort of "disavowing the slightest thought of imputing to the gentlemen who framed the school regulations any design to disregard the rights or feelings of Catholics."[110] Thus, Fitzpatrick showed himself once again reluctant to take a confrontational stand, preferring deference to belligerence, "soft soap" to hard line, though he did lay out in the letter, clearly and affirmatively, the substantive Catholic objections to the religious practices in the public schools.

What Fitzpatrick confided to his diary was quite another matter. On the day after Whall's beating, he noted that "much excitement has been created throughout the city this week in relation to treatment of Catholic pupils in the common schools" and cited specifically the boy who "was severely and even cruelly beaten and then expelled from school with a great number of others who followed his example." Fitzpatrick reflected on the fact that, because of the compulsory schooling law, if they did not return to school they

can be taken from their parents and sent to a penal institution at Westboro College the reform school. There they may be kept until

21 years old cut off from all catholic instruction. At the same time it is impossible to open catholic schools. To buy lots and erect buildings for this purpose would cost at least half a million dollars, and then the annual expense for the support of such schools would be, at the lowest estimate 30 or 40 thousand dollars. Already we find it almost impossible to provide churches for the hundreds of thousands of poor people whom the last ten years have sent to our shores. The provision of schools is then plainly impossible. No redress can be expected by petition to the authorities for the state is ruled by a vast majority of persecuting bigots . . . The only alternative at present seems to be that the children, under open protest, submit to the tyranny exercised over them, but at the same time to loathe and detest its enactments.[111]

The entire tone and content of Fitzpatrick's entry into his diary, calling the authorities "persecuting bigots," radically contrasts with the tone and content of his letter to the School Committee and constitutes yet another instance of the gulf between his public and private behavior in his dealings with Yankee Boston. Publicly he appeared the friend of public education and expressed faith in its leaders' willingness to deal with Catholic interests reasonably. Privately he indicated that he resorted to public education as the least desirable but only possible alternative and that he had no faith whatever in the willingness of the "persecuting bigots" who ran the state to deal with Catholics fairly. The contrast is startling.[112]

Fitzpatrick in this instance may have sold the Yankee spirit of fairness somewhat short. Although in the heat of the Whall affair itself, most closed ranks around the teacher Cook and the law as it existed and many expressed amazement that Catholics should have any complaint about the vaunted Boston public schools, it also became widely accepted that in the longer run something would have to be done to satisfy the Catholic complaints.[113]

The School Committee, though its members voiced divergent opinions, adopted a basically conciliatory approach. Preliminary discussion of Fitzpatrick's letter to the Committee indicated unanimity that the Committee should separate consideration of the Eliot School case from consideration of the basic Catholic complaints that lay behind them. It was agreed that the Committee must back the school authorities in their handling of the Eliot School situation. They created a special committee to investigate the more fundamental Catholic complaints, but its mission was indefinitely postponed until a little "masterly inactivity" had cooled things off.[114] By May of the following year a motion was introduced to solve the problem by having the teacher alone read all texts of a religious nature. This was narrowly defeated, the chief argument against it being that the issue was still too close and that some of the Catholic boys in the Eliot School were still being rebellious.

After the "masterly inactivity," it was the state legislature that finally settled the matter in 1862 by revising the law of 1855, retaining the compulsory Bible reading but requiring "no scholar to read from any particular version, whose parents or guardian shall declare that he has conscientious scruples against allowing him to read therefrom."[115] Thus, though still "officially" Protestant, the public schools were somewhat more acceptable to Catholics, and Fitzpatrick could afford to ignore his critics by continuing his refusal to launch a parochial school crusade.

A few Catholics, dissatisfied with what still appeared to be an affront to their faith in the Eliot School affair, took action. They did not accept what they considered to be the bishop's overly timid stance. For example, *O'Neill's Irish Pictorial*, an Irish-oriented Catholic newspaper published in Boston that enjoyed considerable popularity at the time, used the Eliot School incident to urge the building of parochial schools, using the Catholics of Lawrence as a model to imitate: "The die is cast. The sooner our people BUILD SCHOOLS FOR THEMSELVES [sic] the better."[116] And one Catholic school at least did appear to benefit, at least briefly, from the Eliot affair: Father Wiget's school for boys in St. Mary's parish. According to *The Boston Journal*, after the Whall incident many of the boys at the Eliot School sought certificates to transfer to this school, but the principal would not give them.[117] According to Whall's later recollection, about three hundred boys did transfer to Wiget's school after the incident, but their attendance there must have been temporary, since the school did not endure very long; Father Wiget was transferred, presumably by Bishop Fitzpatrick, to another position, a probable sign that the bishop, in typical timid fashion, did not want to make the Eliot School affair a cause for an outbreak of parochial school activity.

More significant for the future, Father John Haskins, a well-known Yankee convert to Catholicism who during the Eliot School controversy had counseled Catholics to send their children back to the public schools, and who was still preaching several weeks later that there had been "no intention of bigotry on the part of the School Committee," nevertheless dealt much more aggressively with the underlying issue by running for a seat on the very School Committee that had decided against Whall. In the fall of 1859 he was elected as the first Catholic ever to sit on that august body.[118] Although his one vote amounted to but a token Catholic voice, it nevertheless symbolized that in the future the Catholics of Boston would seek to fulfill their educational goals in the public schools rather than in the parochial.

Many Yankees no doubt had mixed feelings about this and would have preferred Catholic participation in public school without representation. There was even some talk of challenging the legitimacy of Haskins' election from the First Ward.[119] Then, too, some wondered whether the compromises necessary to keep Catholics in the public schools were worth the price. As Yankee industrialist Amos Lawrence put the issue in the heat of the Eliot School affair, "If Protestant Christianity is to be abandoned in our public educational system, we shall convert the schools of the Puritans into heathen temples, or what is next to that."[120] But in the end, token Catholic representation on the School Committee as well as some compromise on Protestant practices in the schools was a price that had to be paid in Boston to prevent Catholic defection from the public schools.

Some on the Catholic side, who, not satisfied with what appeared to them a token concession by the Yankees on the school question, continued to advocate parochial schools. They were led by a number of local Catholic pastors who do not appear to have been organized into a group but who came to be identified, then and later, as the "schoolmen." It was probably the schoolmen who undermined Fitzpatrick's argument that parochial schools could not be afforded. Probably the most significant of these at the time, as well as what he produced for the future, was the Jesuit Father John McElroy, who had come to Boston with the intention of realizing his friend and classmate Bishop Fenwick's dream of opening a Catholic college in the city. But to do so he needed a beachhead, and therefore, at Fitzpatrick's urging, in 1847 he became the pastor of previously conflict-ridden St. Mary's parish in the North End,[121] with the understanding that he would also establish a college.[122]

McElroy's primary educational goal was the college, and he met with much opposition. For example, at one point after he had purchased property on "North Square" *The Boston Daily Evening Transcript* reflected that

> these buildings occupy the precise spot, upon which the second church of Boston was erected in 1650 . . . What would our fathers say could they but know the use that is to be made hereafter of the ground, which they for so many years considered "holy!" That the spot, upon which the celebrated Mathers, Increase and Cotton, had preached for so many years and where they had denounced with so much vehemence, the various working and devices of the Devil, . . . should be devoted to such a purpose as the education of *Catholic* children![123]

In the end, McElroy gave up on the North End and instead was able to open the college on Harrison Street in the South End, thus realizing Fenwick's dream.

In this effort to establish Catholic "higher" education in Boston he had the active, though private, support of Bishop Fitzpatrick.

Like his deceased friend Bishop Fenwick, McElroy could hardly have foreseen the long-term consequences for the education of Boston's children that would result from Boston College's founding, nor could Bishop Fitzpatrick—nor, for that matter could the opponents of Roman Catholicism's inroads into Boston affairs. Fitzpatrick apparently did not realize either that after founding Boston College Father McElroy would become a powerful agent for Catholic education at the parochial elementary school level in Boston. All the while McElroy had worked to establish Boston College, he also labored to provide parochial schooling for the children of St. Mary's parish. There was one false start: the Sisters of Charity opened a school in the parish for six months in 1849 but had to be relieved because "with one exception they were by no means qualified to teach even the common English branches." But before the end of the year he had secured some Sisters of Notre Dame from Cincinnati, where he had good connections.[124] By February 1850 he was telling the bishop of Cincinnati, who had assisted in the recruitment, that the sisters were educating 250 of "my poor Irish girls" as well as conducting a night school "for our good servant girls, numbering now 120," who were learning to read, write, sing, and study their catechism. "We can have in the spring 400 girls," concluded McElroy, "if we had room for them."[125] By 1853 there were over seven hundred children in this school, with nine sisters and more on the way.[126] The enterprise was then transferred to a larger building bought from the Boston School Committee, which had used it as a public school.[127]

The introduction of the Sisters of Notre Dame into McElroy's St. Mary's parish very quickly became a boon to Catholic schooling beyond this parish, and the sisters developed into an independent educational force, developing their own internal leadership and multiplying and fanning out into other parishes in and out of Boston.[128] In 1853 they opened a boarding school for girls in Roxbury,[129] and in 1854 a parochial school for girls in St. Joseph's parish in the West End. In 1859 they moved into a "new and substantial" building on Lancaster Street in the North End, an enterprise that the bishop attributed to "the zeal, courage and enterprise of Sister Mary Alphonsus the Superior." Sister Mary Alphonsus, a native of Belgium and a "woman of rare capacity," had raised the money herself.[130] From their house on Lancaster Street the sisters served other parishes too, including one opened in 1859 in Holy Redeemer parish across the Charles River, to which they commuted each day, and a second opened there a year later.[131] In less than a year they had four hundred pupils in this school and were seeking additional sisters to staff it.[132] In 1860 they opened a parochial school for girls in Saints Peter and Paul's parish, and three years later in Gate of Heaven parish, both in South Boston.[133] By 1864 they had built a large convent and opened a select academy for girls on Berkeley Street, "surrounded by the most costly private dwellings of our citizens" in the prestigious new Back Bay.[134] As the sisters' educational enterprises prospered, they attracted recruits to the order.[135] In just ten years after their arrival the sisters had seventy members teaching and working in the diocese.[136]

Thus, both the efforts of Father McElroy and then those of the offshoot from his efforts, the Sisters of Notre Dame, appear to support the contention that in Boston there was a serious desire among at least some Catholics for parochial schools, and that "where there was a will there was a way." McElroy seems to have had relatively little trouble getting financial support from his parishioners, even though, given the parish's location, they were among the poorest in the diocese. Yet, in one Sunday collection in 1852 he raised $1,954 for the school.[137]

Although the Sisters of Notre Dame's enterprise in Boston came about solely because of Father McElroy's zeal to have a parochial school in his parish, Bishop Fitzpatrick, despite his apparent conviction that parochial schools were not financially feasible, did endorse the enterprise once it was under way.[138] Within the first year of the school's operation he was marveling that "the improvement in manners and morals observable in the children and their progress in learning is remarkable and most satisfactory."[139] He even took an active interest in finding suitable space for the schools. In 1852, for example, he proposed to Father McElroy the purchase of either the Otis or the Endicott school, both of which were apparently put up for sale by the Boston School Committee. "The building might be used as a school house during the week and on Sunday be converted into a chapel . . . The rent of seats would pay each year all the interest and a good part of the capital."[140]

Fitzpatrick's obvious enthusiasm for this enterprise, and his willingness to help finance it by making dual use of the facility, makes one wonder why he limited the efforts to St. Mary's parish, except perhaps that there he could rely on Father McElroy to put the plan into action. He noted that "Father McElroy is pleased with the proposition and will probably act on it."[141] The entries in his official diary indicate that he kept himself informed of the sisters' activities, occasionally gave assistance, and often attended functions at their schools, and he commented favorably on their "great usefulness and excellency [sic]."[142] On more than one occasion he invited the mayor, the superintendent of the public schools, and members of the School Committee to the St. Mary's commencement, and attended with them, commenting afterwards that "the performance was very good."[143] These efforts lend credence to the sense that the bishop really did favor parochial education, but that for other reasons (his conviction that schools could not be afforded, his felt need to maintain positive relations with his many Yankee connections, and the progressive lack of energy that plagued him) he did nothing to initiate or develop Catholic education through-out his diocese.

By 1853, when the sisters were beginning to recruit a significant number of Boston girls into their order, he negotiated to buy four acres in Roxbury "to establish a mother house for the Sisters of Notre Dame."[144] In 1856 he wrote to the Society for the Propagation of the Faith in Paris, begging for funds to build the mother house for them in Boston so the new recruits would not have to be sent to Cincinnati or even Belgium and perhaps never be sent back. "They apply themselves exclusively to the education of children from poor and middle class families," he noted, and "I ardently desire to multiply their colonies."[145] This was perhaps the only occasion during his episcopacy that Fitzpatrick actively sought funds for an educational enterprise not having to do with higher education, but it does further suggest that his failure to do more for parochial education was not at all based on opposition to it. By September 1856 he was supervising the building of the sisters' convent with an attached select school.[146] By 1858 a new and larger convent was built for the sisters, who were now multiplying rapidly in the diocese. By 1860 he noted favorably in his diary that the sisters had opened additional schools in South Boston and East Boston, and also that they were admitting new recruits to their convent.[147]

The Sisters of Notre Dame did not teach boys, but by 1859, as a consequence of the Eliot School controversy, St. Mary's Free School for Boys was opened in the parish by the Jesuits, apparently taught by laymen with assistance from the Jesuits. Interestingly, this was done at the very time Fitzpatrick noted in his diary that the Catholics of Boston could not afford parochial schools.

The experience of the Boston Germans gives further weight to the judg-ment that Fitzpatrick miscalculated in his view that parochial schools could not be afforded in Boston. With the Germans there was apparently never any doubt that there would be a school. Just a few months after their parish of Holy Trinity was founded in 1844, when Bishop Fenwick was still alive, they opened a school for boys and girls alike in the basement of their church. Later the school was transferred to houses on Shawmut Avenue. From 1844 to 1859, despite some severe financial problems because of overspending on a new church, the Germans managed to afford lay teachers for their school, and the children were taught half the day in English and half in German.[148] After 1859 the Sisters of Notre Dame instructed the girls and young boys, while lay teachers continued to handle the older boys. The Germans of the Boston area, though they had but one parish, also apparently established branch schools in East Boston, Roxbury, Cambridge, and Charlestown. These schools apparently prospered so well throughout Fitzpatrick's tenure that when they were asked in 1868 how many children they had in Sunday school, the Germans proudly replied that "We have no Sunday Schools, nor need of them" because all the German children attended the parochial school.[149]

Again, Fitzpatrick's diary indicates that he took an interest in this school. Although he seems to have had some problems relating to the Germans, cryptically commenting of them on one occasion that "Dutchmen don't say all they think," he did participate in their activities, and seems especially to have paid attention to their school.[150] He preached at official school exercises and distributed prizes at examination time.[151]

Finally, in addition to the Jesuit Father McElroy, one other person began to emerge before the end of the Fitzpatrick era as someone who would later be labeled a "schoolman." This was Father James Fitton, who was born in Boston in 1805 of English Catholic immigrant parents and accepted into the priesthood by Bishop Fenwick, who in 1830 sent him to work in Connecticut. Under Fenwick he had charge of all the Church's activities in that state as well as western Massachusetts, including Worcester, where he founded the antecedent to Holy Cross College in 1836.[152] In 1855 he was called back to Boston by Bishop Fitzpatrick and sent to take charge of East Boston, which had just begun to fill up with Catholics. There he founded Holy Redeemer parish in 1856, and invited the Sisters of Notre Dame to open a school, which they did. As the number of Catholics continued to increase rapidly, in the years after Fitzpatrick's death he founded three more parishes there, with schools in each.[153] "The care of children" was said to be "the great work of his life."[154] In the case of Father Fitton's parochial school crusade, too, Fitzpatrick appears to have given warm support, though it did not move him to become a public advocate for a parochial school movement.

Other isolated incidents suggest Fitzpatrick's largely private approval of parochial schools when others launched them. Thus, in 1852 he commented favorably in his diary about the opening of a large parochial school in St. Augustine's parish, Lawrence, giving credit to the pastor, who belonged to the Augustinian order; this was one of the places he visited on his trips there afterwards.[155] The Sisters of Notre Dame's schools were considered by The Pilot to be "in no conceivable respect inferior to the famous Common Schools of this city, and, in some particulars, superior to them, not withstanding our poverty, and the great sums of money which the city lavishes upon its own establishments." The girls in the Notre Dame schools, in addition to the regular subjects, were taught "plain and ornamental sewing, in which they enjoy an advantage of which girls in our common schools are deprived."[156] In 1852 the Pilot boasted that the school founded under Bishop Fenwick and run by the Sisters of Charity in the cathedral parish for the past twenty years had "first proved to the Boston public that Catholic girls lost nothing, to say the very least, by being trained in a Catholic school, instead of the famous common schools;" he even dared the snide remark that "Fortunately, no general pestilence, other than godless education, has ravaged Boston."[157]

But significantly, when this school closed after the cathedral was sold to be replaced by a new one in 1858, Fitzpatrick made no effort to reopen it. It was there when he came, and he seems to have valued it, but, typically, he did nothing to see to its perpetuation. He never initiated any leadership in any parochial school effort. The circular letters written to the parishes of the diocese during his reign contained not a single word about parochial schools.[158] When pressed, though he apparently never argued that the public schools were just fine, he fell back on the reasoning that the Catholics of his diocese could not afford parochial schools—though he had to be fully aware that Father McElroy, the Germans, and Father Fitton were able to establish flourishing parochial schools in their hardly affluent parishes.

Why the bishop took no initiative to establish parochial schools, was on record as convinced that they could not be afforded, and yet rejoiced in their presence when others took the initiative to open them, is a question open to speculation. The evidence is strong that the bishop feared offending his Yankee "friends." Also, one cannot discount the frequent comments about his lack of energy, which, as some have suggested, may have resulted from the constant inner tension of trying to please his Yankee sponsors while wanting to implement the Catholic Church's policies, which he apparently truly believed in.[159] This explanation, though less credible in the early years when he was still in his thirties and presumably robust, is more plausible during the later years, when he was sick most of the time.

Fitzpatrick's apparent judgment that to seek public support for parochial schools through tax aid would be fruitless was based on a realistic appraisal of the situation in Massachusetts. Still, the failure to protest what must have seemed an injustice probably reflects his general timidity in face of opposition from the native community. Even in the debates over a new state constitution in 1853, his mouthpiece *The Pilot* made only brief allusion to Proposition 6, which would prevent the use of state school funds for sectarian schools—and even that was merely to comment that any school that used the Bible should be considered sectarian.[160] On the other hand, *The Pilot* was very much aware of Catholic efforts going on in Maryland, Ohio, Michigan, New York, and Pennsylvania to secure state funds for parochial schools, and encouraged them.[161] In contrast to other American bishops, Fitzpatrick never made any effort either to secure state aid or to protest its refusal.

Fitzpatrick's experience in the public schools must also have contributed to his policy (or lack of it) regarding parochial schools. While he harbored a well-hidden resentment based at least in part on his experience in the public schools, the one place he had experienced the Yankee world as a youth, the experience had nonetheless been good to him. Not only had he acquired a first-rate education that enabled him to move straight into seminary training, but he had been accepted, his talents acknowledged by proper Boston. He had tasted the perquisites that awaited the assimilated Irishman. If he had done it, perhaps the children of other immigrants could too. Such thoughts must have seemed persuasive, especially in face of the herculean struggle that would have been required to construct a separate Catholic school system.

Having crossed the gulf between immigrant Irish and native Yankee in Boston and having experienced both worlds firsthand, he may well have shared the view of his most prominent convert, Orestes Brownson. Brownson, in his early years as a Catholic, which stretched throughout the Fitzpatrick era, favored public schools for the Irish Catholic immigrants for a reason not enunciated publicly by anyone else. He argued that while parochial schools would under normal circumstances be much preferred, they should *not* be preferred for the Irish. The reason was not very flattering to the Irish and did not enhance his stature in their eyes: "It is an undeniable fact," argued Brownson, "that the Irish Catholics, and I speak only of them, bring here a civilization far below that which they find here. The great body of them are but one or two removes from the state of barbarians." Further, Brownson judged that most of the Irish clergy were "only a grade in advance of the mass of our low Irish Catholics." Therefore, neither the Irish immigrants nor their leaders were capable of raising their level of civilization. In contrast, "The advanced civilization attained to by the protestant community does and will predominate in the country, and absorb in it the great body of the whole community. Those who resist it, will be outcasts." Catholic schools for the Irish would simply exacerbate the situation because "These Catholic schools, save among the French and the Germans, would be semi-barbarian . . . We cannot advance our Irish population by huddling them together and permitting them to live as they did in Ireland."

The answer, according to Brownson, was to have the Irish enter the public schools, where they would be culturally uplifted. As to the fear that the public school would destroy the faith of Catholic children, Brownson countered that "Our children will receive more advantages from being educated in the public schools than they will [at] home. They do not lose their faith or learn their iniquity there [public school], but at home, in the streets, in the haunts of intemperance, and scenes of brutality."[162]

One wonders whether Fitzpatrick, who was in communication with Brownson as his spiritual director and, to a degree, functioned as the ecclesiastical censor for Brownson's publications, might have been influenced by this view. Indeed, it could have been the other way around: perhaps Brownson had been led to adopt this position by Fitzpatrick? Fitzpatrick had, after all, experienced the very best of Yankee culture, and there are indications that he was less than enamored of Irish life in Boston. He certainly favored meetings of the Thursday Evening Club over the celebrations of St. Patrick's Day.

Finally, no doubt Fitzpatrick felt the pressure coming from the Yankee side in favor of the public schools. Bostonians were proud of their schools, and justly so: they were widely looked upon as the best in the country. They also came to be looked upon as an essential instrument in the assimilation, some would say civilizing, of the immigrant. The rhetoric of public school advocates during these years leaves little doubt that this had become a preoccupation.[163] In a word, in many Bostonians' eyes it was essential to the future of the city that the Irish immigrants send their children to public school. It was this conviction that brought pressure to bear on the immigrants, and certainly on Fitzpatrick, to comply. The Yankees wanted the Irish children in public school, not necessarily out of benevolence but as a policy of insurance for their own cherished institutions. Bishop Fitzpatrick was not about to oppose this desire.

How the Irish themselves felt about the absence of parochial schools in Boston is not clear, especially since they had no voice of their own during the Fitzpatrick years. *The Pilot* had been taken over by the bishop's men and for the most part spoke for him. Individual parishioners here and there blamed him for inaction on parochial schools, but, aside from these, there is no indication that the Irish as a group protested. One has the impression that they, even their leaders, played a relatively passive role with regard to schooling. Unlike the Germans, who seem to have, as a group, taken for granted the need for a parochial school, the Irish in this matter followed their leaders. If pastors like McElroy and Fitton provided parochial schools, the Irish willingly filled them up, but if other pastors did not provide a school, there was no widespread complaint.

Some or all of the above reasons, and perhaps others, account for the fact that the overwhelming majority of Catholic children attended the public schools in Boston throughout the Fitzpatrick era. At his death in 1866 Boston Catholics were left with substantial pockets of parochial school activity sponsored by the Jesuits, the Germans, the Sisters of Notre Dame, or individual priests like James Fitton in East Boston, but there was no semblance of a parochial school *policy or system* or effort to create one. In Boston only the parishes founded by Fathers McElroy and Fitton and the Germans had schools. Though these schools were popular in these parishes, they educated probably no more than 15 percent of the Catholic children in the city, almost all of them girls.

There was, however, hardly noticed at the time, the Jesuit Boston College, the realization of Benedict Fenwick's dream. It educated only a handful of Catholic boys in what was still not more than a classical secondary school, but it was destined to play a critical role in the education of Boston's future generations.

4

Religion over All: 1866–1907

Roman Catholicism emerged as Boston's numerically dominant religion, and Roman Catholics arguably became the city's dominant political and social force, in the last decades of the nineteenth century, from the death of Bishop Fitzpatrick and the end of the Civil War in 1866, through the first several years of the twentieth century, which coincided with the forty-year tenure of Bishop Fitzpatrick's successor. Some of this transformation might be attributed to the arrival, for the first time, of Catholic immigrants in sizeable numbers from a greater variety of European countries. By the first decade of the twentieth century in Boston there were, in addition to the predominantly Irish parishes and the single German Catholic congregation, four Italian parishes, three French, two Polish, and one each Lithuanian, Portuguese, and Armenian.

Still, it was overwhelmingly the Irish who defined Boston Roman Catholicism. The Irish had come a very long way since their first tiny parish guided unobtrusively by Bishop Cheverus at the beginning of the nineteenth century. By 1905 the Irish claimed forty parishes within the city boundaries, not to mention numerous parishes in suburbs such as Brookline and Newton. Further, the Irish had become not only both the numerically dominant ethnic/religious group in Boston, but they had also taken to heart the urging of their leaders ever since the 1820s to become citizens as quickly as possible and to participate aggressively in the political process. They had proven themselves remarkably adept at the art of politics. By the beginning of the twentieth century, though as a group they still lagged far behind Yankee Bostonians socioeconomically, they had already made an indelible mark on Boston's political life. The result must have been apparent to the Yankee guardians of the Puritan tradition: not only was the Irish vote capable of determining elections, but their demands could no longer be ignored.

Their political leaders, mostly from the Democratic Party, even though it had been identified with the Confederacy during the Civil War, began to be elected to high office.

The rising Irish politicians in Boston tended to follow two very different but not contradictory paths to power, probably neither of them a planned "conspiratorial" approach but simply reflecting the efforts of two very different types of Irishmen. The one approach, followed by a small assortment of Irish newcomers to Boston (actually enterprising individuals rather than a group), labored industriously to achieve respectability among the city's influential Yankee Democrats through education or success in business. These were more acceptable to the old-line Yankee leaders of the city's Democratic Party. The proper Yankee Democrats often turned to these more "respectable" Irishmen, whom they sponsored or at least supported, often reluctantly, into high office to represent and advance the party's values as it became obvious that the Irish, who were becoming a majority in Boston, could take over not only the party but the city itself.

It was these "respectable" Boston Irishmen who first gained political prominence, not only in the city but sometimes at the state and federal level. Though they were accepted and generally respected by the establishment, they were resented and often violently opposed by other elements of the "native" Boston population, particularly by the members of the working class, whose jobs were being threatened by the newcomers and who were most likely adherents of the more fundamentalist Christian sects. These included the so-called British Americans, more recent immigrants from Britain who resented the Irish for their adherence to Catholicism as well as their obvious success in the political arena.

Probably the earliest example of this group of "respectable" Irish politicians, and certainly an early harbinger of the inevitable Irish rise to political dominance in Boston, was Patrick Maguire. Born in Ireland in 1838, he emigrated to Canada as a boy, walked to Boston at fourteen, learned the printing trade at several city newspapers, developed real estate in various Boston locations, made connections among important Democrats, won his way onto the Democratic City Committee, and by the 1870s emerged as leader of the entire Democratic party within Boston. Though he never expanded his influence beyond the city and never ran for office, offstage he pulled the strings, and, among other prerogatives, distributed city jobs, with a more than proportionate number going to his Irish compatriots. Capitalizing on his earlier newspaper work, in 1882 Maguire founded his own newspaper, *The Republic*, which for years championed the Democratic Party as well as all things Irish and Catholic.[1]

Another of these ambitious Irishmen to rise to prominence while following a different path, by actually running for public office, was Patrick Collins. Born in Ireland in 1844 and brought to Boston by his widowed mother in 1848, he worked his way up through some education in the public schools, a lot of self-motivated learning, a series of increasingly responsible jobs, and participation in the Democratic Party, where he earned a reputation for hard work and effective oratory. He was elected in the 1860s to the Massachusetts House of Representatives, and in 1869 to the State Senate. As a legislator he consistently advocated and voted for legislation that helped secure the rights of Catholics in the state. He simultaneously attended Harvard Law School, graduating in 1871, and then opened a law practice. He worked tirelessly to advance the interests of Catholics in Massachusetts, especially the Irish. He served as chairman of the State Democratic Party and in 1882 was elected to the U.S. House of Representatives, where he served until 1889. In 1903 he became mayor of Boston but died in office in 1905.

Collins, though the first Boston Irish Catholic to attain national prominence, was not, however, the first Irish Catholic mayor of Boston. That distinction went to a contemporary who, unlike Collins, did not pursue a path to state and national office but concentrated on Boston itself. This was Hugh O'Brien, born in Ireland in 1827 and brought to Boston in 1832. After attending Fort Hill Grammar School, at age twelve he learned the printer's trade at the *Boston Courier* and at age sixteen he started his own trade newspaper. He became president of the Union Institution for Savings and Treasurer of the Brush Electric Company, was president of the Charitable Irish Society, and was a trustee of St. Vincent's Orphan Asylum. Unlike Collins, O'Brien restricted his political aspirations mostly to Boston. He served for seven terms as an alderman, four of them as chairman of the board. In 1884 he was elected the first Irish mayor of Boston and served for four one-year terms until being ousted in a violent political backlash against alleged undue Catholic influence over the city's public schools.[2]

The O'Brien experience was probably the most illustrative of the struggle in Boston over the rise of these "obnoxious" newcomers, the Irish. O'Brien worked zealously and patiently to make himself worthy of the august position of mayor, but made a serious error in the first year of his tenure when he closed the revered Boston Public Library on St. Patrick's Day. He did not make that mistake again. The fiasco that was to prove his permanent undoing was not an error of his making. In 1887 he got caught up in all-out citywide socioreligious warfare that came to be known as the Travis affair. This crisis was precipitated when Charles B. Travis, a history teacher in Boston's English High School, was asked by a student to define an indulgence. He replied that it was "a permission to commit sin that was sometimes bought with money . . . You pay so much money in advance for permission to commit certain sins."[3] In response to a protest by a Catholic pastor, the Boston School Committee, whose twenty-four elected members were now evenly divided between Protestants and Catholics, publicly censured Travis, changed his assignment from teaching history to teaching English, and banned the textbook from which the quotes had been taken.

The reaction to the School Committee's decision among the more militant evangelical Protestants, who had long feared such a Catholic "takeover" of the city's public schools, was immediate and determined. They held huge public meetings at which the decision was denounced, and passed vehement resolutions demanding that Travis be restored to his original teaching position, that the banned textbook be reinstated, and that in the future no Catholic should be elected to the School Committee or appointed as a teacher in the Boston public schools. They then formed a Committee of One Hundred to achieve these goals.[4]

The Committee of One Hundred, joined by a variety of other anti-Catholic organizations, most of them related to a nationwide movement to head off what appeared to them to be a Catholic plot to take over the nation's political and social institutions, crusaded to achieve its goals. However, the School Committee, bolstered by its Irish members, stood fast, changing none of its decisions in the Travis affair. This, in turn, led to an opposition crusade to choose an entirely new School Committee at the next elections, which they did in 1888. This time they eliminated all Catholic representation on the Committee, largely because Catholic women failed to exercise women's right to vote in school committee elections, which had been granted just a few years before.[5]

With the city's anti-Catholic organizations united against him, O'Brien lost the next mayoral election, and his days as the first Catholic mayor of Boston were over. The anti-Catholic crusade of 1888, though precipitated by the Travis affair, went far beyond purging the School Committee and denying O'Brien re-election; it led to a variety of crusades, often fostered by organizations affiliated with the nationwide American Protective Association, advocating an end to immigration, especially that from heavily Roman Catholic countries. In Boston the crusade was meant to head off the Irish and Catholic rise to power and influence in the city as well as the entire state. However, the crusade was ultimately doomed to failure, largely because the balance of power tipped increasingly in the Irish and Catholic favor.

This shift was due in part to the activities of the second group of Irish politicians. This was an amorphous assortment of Irishmen active at first in Boston politics at the local ward level, where they arose as defenders and advocates of the needs and wishes of their neighbors. Ignoring the Democratic Party's traditional Yankee leaders, as well as the larger social issues these leaders represented, these local Irishmen evolved into "ward bosses." They gained support in the communities where they lived by building friendships and especially by securing much-needed favors like civil service jobs, relief from annoying city ordinances, or even pardon for minor legal offenses. It would take some time for these local ward bosses to openly declare their independence and move out of their neighborhood base into the larger political arena, but the move was inevitable and was to come in full force by the early twentieth century.

These sons of Irish immigrants bypassed the route of educational and professional respectability so prized by Yankee Boston and entered politics directly by building loyal followings in their neighborhood. Each built his own power base on his own turf. While the individual Irish ward bosses often warred with one another and never formed a single, disciplined, citywide organization that existed in cities like New York, taken together they represented the mass of Irish voters in Boston. While the Irish ward bosses like "Smiling Jim" Donovan of the South End, Pat Kennedy in East Boston, Joseph Corbett in Charlestown, John A. Keliher of Dorchester, and Martin Lomasney of the West End were generally willing to accept the Democratic Party's Yankee citywide leadership to the end of the nineteenth century, they had not become part of the Yankee world and felt no personal connection to it.

By the 1890s some of these local ward bosses were growing increasingly restless, especially the younger men. Once they realized that they no longer needed Yankee support or approval in the political affairs of Boston, they were all too willing to part company. Finally, when the mayoralty became available in 1905 with the death in office of Patrick Collins, they scrambled for position, the two major protagonists being Martin Lomasney, boss of the West End, and John F. Fitzgerald, king of the North. The battle was waged without any significant regard to Yankee Democrats.[6] Fitzgerald gained the advantage, partly through his attractive personality and partly through the local Irish political weekly, *The Republic*, which he had shrewdly purchased in 1895 from its Irish founder, Patrick Maguire. His consequent election as mayor in 1905 marked the emergence of raw, independent Irish political power, which owed nothing of consequence to Yankee Democrats. The spoils were his.[7]

Though the spoils system was certainly not new to Boston, Fitzgerald raised it to a new level. He not only appointed his own cronies to every important position but also devised ingenious ways to increase the spoils. For example, he divided the Street Department into six separate departments, each with its own head, and created categories of jobs not covered by the civil service laws such as "brick slinger," "plank driver," and "tea warmer."[8]

The *Boston Herald* was no doubt correct when it announced that "The people have chosen such a mayor as it has never before had," and when it recalled longingly the days of a very different Irishman, Patrick Collins, "an Irishman of a different strain of blood."[9] Indeed, even the Irish Catholic press seemed embarrassed by the new political developments. *The Sacred Heart Review*, a popular Boston Catholic newspaper at the time that had been originated by a conglomerate of local pastors, at first without naming names, made distinctions identical with *The Herald's*, declaring that "If a candidate for public office lays stress on the fact that he is of Irish blood, let it be inquired if he is a decent representative of the race he boasts about," and decried the impression being created that the Catholic Church was "allied with the saloon and low politics."[10] *The Review* made every effort to distance the Church from this new breed of Irish politician, declaring that "The fact that a public official occupies every Sunday a front pew in a Catholic Church does not always prove that he is a practical Catholic," and denounced "men who pass for Catholics engaging themselves in dirty, corrupt, political practices, or condoning fraud and false dealings."[11] As Fitzgerald emerged into prominence, *The Review* explicitly labeled his effort to "trade on the Catholic name," and to "pretend that he represents Catholic interests, and speaks for the Catholic clergy" as "scandalous."[12]

Despite some internal differences and occasional aberrations among those representing Catholic and Irish interests in Boston, it was apparent that the efforts by the "reformers" and the militant fundamentalist Protestant organizations to defeat the Irish and Catholic rise to power after the Travis affair had proven only temporarily successful. Not only were the Irish skilled at the art of politics, which had enabled them to move into positions where they could influence civic policies, but they had not remained stagnant in the lowest socioeconomic status that had defined their entry into Boston. No doubt it was hard work and ambition combined with a strong sprinkling of favoritism from their fellow politically successful Irishmen that had made it possible for the Boston Irish to substantially improve their economic lot by the latter decades of the nineteenth century. For the most part that meant entry into the solid working class as well as, for an increasing number, into the lower middle class, and sometimes even higher. While in 1850 47 percent of all Irish workers in Boston had been laborers, by 1900 the Irish made up only 15 percent of the laboring-class workforce. During this half-century the Irish had also moved heavily into the skilled and civil service occupations such as masons, painters, plumbers, printers, salesmen, policemen, and teachers. Between 1850 and 1900 Irish workers went from

26.6 percent of all the masons in Boston to 47 percent; from 12.3 percent of the painters to 26.8 percent; from 18.8 percent of plumbers to 46.5 percent; from 11.6 percent of printers to 34 percent; from 7.3 percent of machinists to 24.8 percent; from 4.6 percent of the police force to a startling 42.7 percent; and from 2 percent of the teachers to 19.2 percent. Among salesmen and merchants and even professions such as medicine the Irish also made great strides.[13]

Simultaneously, there were multiple signs that the Irish were also becoming conscious that they needed to demonstrate to their fellow Bostonians that they had achieved not just a position of political power, but also one of social respectability. A campaign emerged, probably unplanned, but largely launched by Catholic publications and organizations, to convince Irish Bostonians that it was time to openly demonstrate such achievement. The truth was that it had taken the great mass of Irish immigrants to Boston a much longer time to begin to achieve middle-class respectability than it did for them to elect their leaders to high office. Thus, by the late nineteenth century, though the Irish had become a major political force, perhaps *the* major one, they were still not considered by "native" Bostonians to be "respectable" citizens. The campaign for respectability seemed to be headed not by the Irish politicians themselves, but largely by personnel, and particularly publications, associated with the Catholic Church. It became a preoccupation that lasted throughout the last forty years of the nineteenth century and beyond. One sees it in a fascinating 1867 article on "the good parish" that appeared in the official diocesan newspaper, *The Boston Pilot*. In addition to the expected exhortations to attend Mass, listen to the priest, practice charity, and the like, *The Pilot* identified the "good parish" as

> remarkable for its orderly, well-dressed people, who take pride in appearing decent, and of being proper in their homes and conversation, and no brawls or tumults are ever heard within its limits . . . The good parish is industrious, the men abroad and the women at home; the frugality that attends industry leads to the saving of many an honest penny . . . The good parish is social, intervisiting in delightful harmony, and keeping up all the pleasant relations of neighborhood. The good parish is a temperate precinct, and the baker is the only real loafer in the place.[14]

Symptomatic of this new obsession with middle-class respectability was the article's only specific advice with regard to education: "The good parish never sends its children to school unclean."[15] As early as the 1860s, *The Pilot* did offer some enlightened suggestions about the problem of youth in the emerging urban environment. In 1866 it commented on a Boston police report that

> in the evening and late at night, girls, from twelve to sixteen years of age, may be seen upon all the public thoroughfares, oftentimes behaving in the most loose and lewd manner, making assignations, and too often illicit appointments with the unscrupulous and unprincipled of the opposite sex. If now, instead of grave, solemn, and oftentimes tiresome meetings and lectures, the social arrangements for youth, could be made light and pleasant, when their exuberant feeling could find exercise in innocent hilarity; if instead of prosy and dull formalities, we would institute general and pleasant recreations, wants which are now unsatisfied in legitimate ways, would not then drive our tender lambs from the sheep-fold to the crafty and delusive and devouring wolves.[16]

Donahoe's Magazine joined the struggle to uplift the Irish to respectability. In 1883 it criticized the Irish for their avid interest in boxing, both as participants and spectators, which gave credence to the widespread belief that "wherever the Irish settle, rowdyism triumphs." The magazine exhorted the Irish that now was the time to rise above "delight in low and brutal sports" and "the semisavagery of drunkenness," a state of depravity to which they had allegedly been reduced by their long subjugation to England.[17]

Particularly zealous and continuous in its efforts to inculcate habits of middle-class virtue was *The Sacred Heart Review*, an immensely popular weekly published by a committee of local pastors, all situated in the zone of emergence, which hammered at this theme continually in weekly columns. *The Review* seldom missed an opportunity to preach the rewards of faithful hard work, though always within the context of ambition moderated by honesty, obedience, and the realization that success was not to be measured merely by economic gain.[18] It urged youth to "Remember that in the morning of life come the hard working days. Hard work never killed a man. It's fun, recreation, relaxation, holidays that kill."[19] It dispensed such worldly advice as the importance of exercising "fidelity in little things" and the value of "a good name," which "helped many a man to acquire riches." "Be assured," advised *The Review*, "that order, frugality, and economy are the necessary supports of every personal and private virtue." To the irresolute, it suggested: "What you intend to do, do thoroughly."[20]

The Review harped constantly on the ideals of life in the home, often resorting to great detail about the responsibilities of fatherhood, arguing that

"Fathers Should Govern No Less By Example than By Precept."[21] It crusaded among the men against "seeking pleasure outside of the home" and urged wives to keep their menfolk away from the tavern, the "low theatre," and the clubhouse by offering something better than "Dark and Cheerless Homes," proffering helpful hints on how the home could "Be Made Rich and Bright and Delightful by a True Woman's Industry."[22] Its pages made clear that the major concerns of its readers were no longer mere survival. It rendered advice on everything from cleaning the teeth to the proper food for breakfast to "Good Manners at Table."[23] It celebrated the wonders of Cuticura soap along-side advice on how to express one's thoughts, and instruction that excessive worry is a disease.[24] It told parents to be sure to teach their children to brush their clothes, put them away, close drawers and doors, and generally clean up after themselves.[25] But the upbringing of the young was to be done gently and with patience and, above all, love.[26] Parents should train a boy to exercise "pluck," "decisiveness," and "industry that will make him turn out afterwards neither a dunce nor a drone, but a strong sturdy worker in the world." They should bring up a girl in "maidenly modesty," practicing "thrift, tidiness and taste."[27] According to *The Review*, people liked girls who "are pleasant, don't repeat unpleasant remarks they hear, look neat and nice, look out for the happy things of life, have a good word for everybody."[28]

Such Pollyanna-ish advice obviously was meant not for a wallowing under-class but for an audience seeking direction in its path toward respectable civil-ity. A regular column by "Aunt Bride" directed itself mostly to the "working girl," obviously assumed to be office help or a store clerk, advising her not to waste money on manicures, face massages, or shampoo, but to save some and spend the rest on gym classes, to get plenty of sleep and good food, to lead a quiet life, not to flirt, not to rush for a seat on the "cars," to be polite and con-siderate, and to take her vacation at home every other year so her mother could get away for a while.[29] The adds that appeared in the Catholic newspapers also told much about the emerging middle-class respectability. "Fancy groceries," carpets and upholstery, window draperies, jewelry, gas cooking stoves, and, of course, trips to Rome and the Holy Land were regularly hawked to *The Review*'s readers by the turn of the century.[30]

The barrage of practical morality generously mixed with good etiquette and suffused with the so-called Protestant ethic says much about the self-perception of Catholic Bostonians, particularly the paper's main readers, the English-speaking Irish, during this period. Some of the rhetoric reflected concerns that had emerged much earlier, particularly the continuing exhor-tations against excessive drinking,[31] but now it increasingly concentrated on fundamental middle-class civility at home and in one's private life, and patient diligence in the world of business. Thus *The Pilot's* 1891 advice to young Catholic college graduates was to overcome the "up-hill road that lies before the young graduate" by accepting humdrum tasks like copying law documents and running errands until one's talent and education is recognized by the employer.[32]

While it was evident that the great bulk of the Catholic population was just emerging out of poverty, the publication also made much of those who seemed to be rising further, particularly by the 1890s. The Catholic press gave prominent coverage to Boston College's Young Men's Catholic Association, which catered to successful Catholic Bostonians, whether or not graduates of Boston College, "many of them successful lawyers, physicians, legislators" and the like.[33] By the 1890s *The Pilot*, in addition to remarking on "The steadily increasing popularity of Boston College," which "speaks eloquently for the general advance of the whole Catholic community in Boston and its neighborhood," also reported the activities of the Catholic Club of Harvard, as well as the fact that in 1894 a Catholic priest preached officially for the first time at Harvard.[34]

The activities of the Catholic Union of Boston, too, which had taken to fostering Catholic Reading Circles, contributed by the 1890s to the general sense of uplift. As *The Pilot* put it, "The ultimate purpose of the whole movement is the levelling up intellectually of the American Catholic people."[35] Similarly, *The Sacred Heart Review* exhorted vigorously and often on the necessity of good reading habits for youth.[36]

It is clear from all these exhortations that as a group the Irish, or at least their spokespersons, had become preoccupied with emergence into middle-class, or, more appropriately, lower-middle-class or solid working-class respectability. The reality was that large numbers of the Boston Irish, though a step above previous generations of their countrymen, were still employed as maids, gardeners, or stable hands in the homes of the "proper" Bostonian citizens. Although much was made of the fact that the Irish Catholics now had a "college," an analysis of Boston College's student backgrounds in the late nineteenth century reveals that between 1864 and 1882, only 2.4 percent came from professional families, while 79 percent of those who reported a father's occupation reported skilled, semiskilled, and low white-collar ones. Fully a third of the boys came from homes without fathers.[37]

In sum, the last decades of the nineteenth century were characterized for Roman Catholics, overwhelmingly of Irish descent, by a steady rise to political prominence in Boston, with reluctant support from the Yankee establishment that saw the inevitability of Irish political success, and by bitter opposition from more conservative fundamentalist Protestant groups that feared the consequences of a Catholic takeover of the city and its institutions. For the Irish Catholics it also meant the gradual movement into more economic security, with concerted urging from their spokespersons to take on the life habits of middle-class respectability, although many remained the maids and servants of the proper Bostonians. Indeed, the Catholic churches built in Boston's more affluent neighborhoods as well as in the wealthier suburbs during this period served mostly the servants of their Yankee employers.

John Williams, the Catholic bishop of Boston, for all practical purposes played no direct role at all in any of this—not in the rise of Irish Catholics to political prominence, not in the campaign to develop a "respectable" lifestyle, and not in the religious and education-related conflicts such as the Travis affair. Throughout his uncommonly lengthy reign (1866–1907) over the diocese, Williams seems never to have engaged in any of the political or social battles that confronted his Catholic flock in Boston, including those over education. But one can hardly understand the events that transpired in Boston during these last decades of the nineteenth century without trying to understand Williams and the role he played, and did not play, in the momentous transition of the city's Roman Catholics during these years.

In many ways the arrival of a new Boston Catholic bishop in 1866 must have promised a continuation of the Bishop Fitzpatrick years. Williams' career had paralleled Fitzpatrick's in almost every important respect—save one. Like Fitzpatrick, he had been born in Boston of Irish parentage, in 1822, just ten years after Fitzpatrick. Like Fitzpatrick, Williams emerged from the Irish immigrant slum that centered around Broad Street. His father, a blacksmith turned grocer due to ill health, died in 1830, when John was only eight.[38] Like Fitzpatrick, Williams had been early singled out by the far-sighted Bishop Fenwick as a young Irish lad of great promise, and sponsored by him. Like Fitzpatrick, though just a few years later, he had been sent by Fenwick for ecclesiastical studies first to Montreal and then to Paris. Both had returned to Boston as designated leaders, and were primed for future command. Upon his return to Boston in 1845, just four years after Fitzpatrick, Williams was assigned to the cathedral itself, where he remained for nine years, first as Fenwick's assistant and then as Fitzpatrick's. In 1857 he became pastor of St. James parish, which served the immense Irish immigrant population of the South End and was considered the most important parish in the diocese after the cathedral.[39] Before his death in 1866 Fitzpatrick had recommended Williams as his successor, which he became at the age of only forty-four.[40]

On the surface it appears that the only essential differences between the two was the ten years that separated their births, and the fact that Williams, as the junior, became Fitzpatrick's protégé. But there was at least one important difference in their life experience which, coupled with personality differences, contributed to some significant differences in their behavior as bishop. Fitzpatrick had attended the Boston public schools, graduated from Boston Latin, and maintained and fostered a lifelong relationship with the best of Boston society, whom he had first met there. Williams, in contrast, after entering Primary School No. 5 in 1826, in less than a year transferred to Bishop Fenwick's newly opened Catholic academy in the cathedral basement, where he was taught by older seminarians and newly ordained priests. He never again attended a public school. His serious, thoughtful, reliable, non-aggressive demeanor attracted the attention of his teachers, with whom he became very close. Bishop Fenwick later sent him away to the Sulpician seminary-college in Montreal and then to the Sulpician seminary in Paris, where he was ordained in 1845.[41]

Thus, from the age of five Williams had for all practical purposes retired from the public life of Boston into a Catholic seminary. By all accounts, as bishop of a diocese in the midst of explosive growth and turbulent change, Williams led a serene, patriarchal existence, religiously following a routine whose regularity harkened back to seminary days. Daily he rose at 6 a.m., took a nap after lunch, went for an afternoon walk or a carriage ride, and retired at 10 p.m.[42] Unlike Fitzpatrick, no meetings with Boston's elite at Thursday Evening Clubs or other civic affairs disturbed his orderly existence. He took an extended annual vacation, usually in the country with his friend Bernard McQuaid, the bishop of Rochester, who attested that "he knows how to take a vacation . . . No letters, no telegrams, come near him."[43]

When on the job, though, Williams worked diligently and efficiently. His journals, especially in the early years, are filled with records of transactions, mostly connected with the vast church-building programs necessitated by the rapid increase in the Catholic population. During business hours, which he held with equal though not exactly extended regularity, he functioned more or less in feudal or baronial fashion, dispensing his decisions at brief audiences held with petitioners, or in still briefer letters written with his own hand. His business letters, usually written by himself, sometimes consisted of one sentence, or markedly one word written in the margin of a letter received and returned to the sender.[44] On one occasion a person who had been granted an audience was asked, "What did he say?" The answer was, "What he always says, nothing."[45]

If he was silent in private, he was even more so in public, avoiding preaching whenever possible, though he was said to be good at it.[46] He abhorred personal publicity and did not even want the diocesan newspaper, The Pilot, to publish much about him. In his entire life he was said to have granted just one interview.[47] Thus, in the midst of great social and political change in Boston, the Williams administration took on a kind of faceless quality, even though the archbishop conducted business himself. After the Third Plenary Council of Baltimore, which was convened by the American Catholic hierarchy in 1884 and dictated elaborate provisions for diocesan administration, Williams was said to have implemented the regulations "somewhat tardily and incompletely."[48] In 1890, a quarter-century after assuming the bishopric and already in his sixty-eighth year, he secured the appointment of an auxiliary bishop to help cope with the increased volume of work, but his fundamentally individualistic mode of administration did not change.[49]

Seldom did anything interrupt his daily routine; nothing was allowed to disturb his serenity, helping to account perhaps for his eighty-five-year lifespan. Methodical and systematic, "punctuality personified," he disregarded superfluous details while concentrating on the essential. In this way it was said that "he accomplished the work of many men and yet preserved his health."[50] In his final years he could still "do a man's work."[51]

As bishop he never mixed with anyone outside the church, and within it only with a few. His reclusive, self-effacing nature led him to shun honors whenever possible. He reportedly tried to resist his promotion from bishop to archbishop in 1875, although the honor merely reflected the primacy of the Boston diocese among the several dioceses that had been split off from it over the years. When it came to the question of being made a cardinal, Williams resisted strenuously, and successfully.[52] He remained almost totally aloof from the public life of Boston, and reportedly turned down three offers of honorary degrees from Harvard.[53] In avoiding contact with the Yankees he also avoided the excruciating tensions that Fitzpatrick had experienced in trying to reconcile the interests of the church, and particularly his Irish Catholic constituents, with the pressures and expectations of mainstream Boston.

The fact that Archbishop Williams said so little, and apparently never felt the need to explain his actions, makes the task of understanding his priorities, not to mention the man himself, dependent largely on conjecture. That he rose out of the Boston Irish ghetto, for example, is a fact, but little in his adult life suggests continuing connections with Irish life or causes. After his ordination in Paris in 1845 he spent a month visiting relatives in Ireland before returning to the United States.[54] This is practically the only solid evidence of any continuing connection with family, and it was said that he never referred to his family in anything but very general terms.[55] As bishop of Boston he appears, if anything, to have preferred the company and counsel of the Yankee converts among his clergy, though not to the entire exclusion of selected Irish priests.[56]

It would perhaps be best to conclude that he was not motivated by ethnic preferences. As Italian, French, and other non-Irish Catholic groups began to multiply in the Boston diocese, he expressed a clear willingness to grant them full freedom in founding their own ethnic parishes.[57] He told a group of French Canadians that "Although all Catholics have the same faith, the same religion, and the same aspirations, language is a reasonable cause of separation for public worship."[58] Indeed, during his episcopate the number of ethnic Catholic parishes in the diocese, including mostly those outside Boston, multiplied from one to forty-two. Although the growth of ethnic diversity within the diocese did not take place without strife, Williams himself never seems to have doubted his permissive policy nor waivered in implementing it. His entire style of life seemed to some to symbolize a total break from his Irish roots. One commentator, observing that "He was reserved, silent, gravely and distantly polite, austere in his life and bearing, retiring, averse to all publicity," suggested that "One might have been tempted to conclude that the chill of New England had frozen his Irish blood, and turned a Celt into a somewhat extreme example of a well-known Yankee type."[59]

He "seldom spoke out to express Catholic views to the general public or to defend the Church when it was stridently attacked."[60] Thus, for example, there is no record that he either entered the fray over the Travis incident or publicly complained that the reaction of the militant Protestant conservatives had driven Hugh O'Brien out of the mayoralty or Roman Catholics off the School Committee. Only once did he seem to come close in public to venting anger at the periodic anti-Catholic and anti-Irish episodes that plagued his tenure. That was in a rare address in 1891 at the celebration of the twenty-fifth anniversary of his elevation to the episcopacy. As the core of his speech Williams chose to congratulate his fellow Catholics on the great restraint they had shown in the previous two years during the bitter public controversy over both Catholic influence on the public School Committee in the Travis affair and the attempted state control of parochial schools. "We are thought to be irritable; we are thought to be quick to return injury for injury," said Williams, but "when it is necessary we can be calm because we are right." Acknowledging that the virulent anti-Catholic attacks of the previous two years "came not from the better part of the community," he nevertheless leveled the most scathing part of his criticism on that "better part of the community:"

What we have against those gentlemen—those conservative gentlemen, who would not mix in such business—is that, whilst they condemned it [inwardly] and whilst they were too well bred to enter into such accusations or reviling because they knew too well their falsehood, yet they stood by and said nothing against them. Here is where I bring those gentlemen to the bar of justice. They listened to the abuse. They allowed it to be made use of. They profited by the political position of it; and yet said nothing; and when all is over they are simply ashamed of it—and we are ashamed of them.[61]

Of the handful of public statements ever uttered by Williams this comes the closest to suggesting that beneath the reserved, stately exterior, evident in the restrained and dignified tone of this speech, there smoldered a conscious resentment of the perceived indignities suffered by Catholics in Boston, and, unlike his predecessor Fitzpatrick, the courage to express it publicly, at least once.

With this one exception, Williams' dealings with the non-Catholic world were to all appearances cordial, though extremely few. That they were so few seems simply to have resulted from a combination of his retiring personality and a conscious decision to devote his finite energies single-mindedly to church affairs. He never spoke out publicly during any of the other public controversies involving Catholics during his forty years in office.

And in his devotion to church affairs in Boston and the rest of his diocese, Williams confined himself almost exclusively to those initiatives that hewed most closely to the more traditional works of the church: the building of much-needed churches and the establishment of charitable institutions to care for those in need: orphanages, hospitals, homes for working youth, and the like. In the absence of any stated principles, one would have to conclude from his actions that Williams was first and foremost a churchman. When he returned from France as a young priest, Bishop Fenwick had assigned him to duties at the cathedral, where he took charge of the vibrant Sunday school program Fenwick had initiated there. By 1847 he supervised 68 Sunday school teachers with 2,500 pupils in this parish alone, and he had taken on other such schools as far away as East Boston. In fact, he apparently became known as "the children's priest."[62] He took this work to heart and maintained a lifelong dedication to Catholic Sunday school activities.[63] Likewise in 1861, when he was pastor of St. James parish, Williams introduced into New England the first conference of the St. Vincent DePaul Society, a charitable enterprise organized on the parish level. After his appointment as bishop of the diocese he continued to promote the activities of this society in every parish and took great interest in its expansion.[64]

He also took a lifelong interest in promoting the establishment of charitable programs, especially for the young. He was instrumental, though not the originator, in starting a Home for Destitute Children in 1864.[65] In 1867 he recruited a contingent of the Sisters of the Good Shepherd to set up a house for wayward Catholic girls in Boston.[66] In 1874 he secured the services of the Brothers of Charity from Montreal to take over the House of the Angel Guardian orphanage after the death of its founder, Father George Haskins.[67] In 1882 he took the initiative in founding a home for Catholic working girls, and solicited nuns to run it.[68]

His concerns also extended beyond the purely spiritual and material care of his flock to the intellectual, though always with a Catholic intent. It was in this light that, in response to a plea from Pope Pius IX, in 1873 he established the Catholic Union of Boston, an organization dedicated to defending the Church against its numerous nineteenth-century foes on the intellectual front, in part by making it more respectable among the learned. In Boston Williams translated this into an effort at raising the general cultural level of the Catholic population, particularly its leaders. "Neglecting this duty," he argued, "we shall not be abreast with the average culture of our enlightened city!"[69] Williams initiated the Union by inviting the most prominent Catholics of the city, including Hugh O'Brien and Patrick A. Collins, both future mayors; poet and editor of *The Pilot* John Boyle O'Reilly; owner of *The Pilot* Patrick Donahoe; and significant Yankee converts like Samuel Tuckerman. In a marked departure from his general aversion to socializing and especially to venturing out of his residence in the evening, he participated regularly in the Union's activities, attending its Wednesday evening meetings every week for thirty years.[70] While his predecessor Fitzpatrick had engaged Boston's best minds at the Thursday Evening Club, Williams chose to limit his engagement to Boston's Catholic minds.

Above all, Bishop Williams labored from the beginning to provide both numerically and aesthetically adequate churches for the rapidly expanding diocese. In his first year as bishop he dedicated himself to the construction of a proper cathedral, moved perhaps by his own fond memories of the first Catholic cathedral where he had worshipped and gone to school as a child, and by the considerable delay that Bishop Fitzpatrick had encountered after abandoning that building, which had become both inadequate in size and poorly situated, in an area that had given way to commerce. Williams immediately renewed the plans, solicited pastors and wealthy Catholics for pledges, took up yearly collections in the parishes, and launched a series of fundraising fairs through the 1870s while it was being constructed. The new cathedral was dedicated in 1875, but its $1.5 million cost was not finally paid until 1895, almost thirty years after the project's inception. This project meant a great deal to Williams, and he apparently considered it his greatest achievement,[71] further proof of the firm priority he gave to his churchly obligations.

Second only to the cathedral was the archbishop's dedication to constructing a proper seminary for the education of future Boston priests. Moved perhaps by his own gratitude for the largesse of Bishop Fenwick in making a clerical education available to him, and perhaps also because his own priestly preparation, almost entirely done abroad, had necessitated a thirteen-year exile from Boston, he was determined to accomplish what his predecessors had not: to build an institution for the education of priests in Boston. He set the wheels in motion in 1872 and, after at least one false start, saw the seminary, taught by the same Sulpician order of priests that had educated him, open in 1884 on a former Brighton estate.[72]

Regarding the Boston church's material welfare, the greatest challenge during the Williams era was the building not just of a proper cathedral, but of sufficient churches to accommodate the ever-increasing number of parishioners. The surprising thing about this building boom was its tendency toward "monumentalism." In this Williams probably followed not his own proclivity toward unobtrusiveness, but the proclivity of the Irish "newcomers" to forcefully announce their presence and, above all, their "respectability." The Catholic publications like *The Pilot* and *The Republic* seemed to delight in reporting not just the addition of new churches, but their magnificence, especially in parts of the city where many of the parishioners worked as domestic servants for their more affluent Yankee employers. It was as if they wished to announce to the public that Boston Catholicism was here to stay.

However, in all of the pride and excitement expressed over the building of splendid new churches, and while funds were raised over a period of years, there was never any mention of the erection of an equally magnificent school next to a towering new church. One notes the total absence of parishes that began with a school whose auditorium was used for Sunday services, as was the practice in other American dioceses, where the school came first and then the church.

While there is no evidence that Williams promoted a crusade to build monumental churches, there is also no evidence that he seriously opposed or tried to stop it. This further demonstrates that, despite his obvious dedication to providing churches, seminaries, and charitable institutions, he was lukewarm about developing a Catholic school system. While he zealously sought religious orders of women to staff the various orphanages, hospitals, homes for working girls, and the like, there is no evidence that he ever solicited nuns to open a single parochial school. Nor is there any evidence that he applied pressure to a parish to open a parochial school.

This lack of enthusiasm was noteworthy given the controversial issues in Boston public education that arose during his reign, all the more so because several developments within the American Catholic church put heavy pressure on the American bishops to develop schools. Bishops in many of the dioceses were already distinguishing themselves by doing just that, and they served as a model for the others to follow. More fundamentally, though, the Catholic Church in the United States, spurred by dictates from Rome, was moving deliberately toward making the building of parochial schools an official policy. Thus, the Second Plenary Council of Baltimore in 1866, in which Williams participated, exhorted the American bishops to build parochial schools "wherever it can be done."[73] In 1875 the Roman Congregation of the Propaganda ruled that American Catholics could send their children to public schools only if there were no parochial schools available or if the bishop ruled that the local public schools posed no danger to the children's faith.[74]

Then, in 1884, the American bishops' Third Plenary Council of Baltimore, which had been mandated by Rome, made extensive decrees about education;[75] almost a fourth of its decrees had to do with Catholic education. Among these the Council decreed that within two years every new American Catholic parish was to have a parochial school, unless the bishop decided that unusual difficulties justified a delay. Another decree commanded Catholic parents to send their children to these parochial schools unless they were clearly able to provide for the Christian education of their children at home, or unless the local bishop decided that the local public schools would not be a danger to their faith. Although these new regulations provided room for exceptions, which would be used amply, they nevertheless provided solid grounds for fear among the opponents of the parochial school movement in the United States, Boston included.

Neither the Baltimore Council's decrees nor directives from Rome settled the question of parochial schooling for the entire United States. The issue precipitated a bitter controversy within the American Catholic Church between the "liberal" and "conservative" bishops over the necessity of parochial schools, and in particular over the desirability of the so-called Faribault plan worked out between the liberal Bishop John Ireland of St. Paul and the Faribault, Minnesota, school board whereby the town took jurisdiction over and financed the "secular" education of the children in otherwise Catholic schools while the church provided and paid for their religious instruction.

Typically, Bishop Williams did not become personally or publicly embroiled in this controversy, and he remained a very close friend of at least one of the most adamant proponents of parochial schools, the bishop of Rochester, Bernard McQuaid. While he apparently never publicly sided with Bishop Ireland, Williams clearly at least privately supported him as well as other more liberal American ecclesiastics in their efforts to work out an accommodation with the public schools. When the question about such efforts was put to him by a Vatican cardinal who had been assigned to investigate the experiments, he noted, with characteristic brevity, "think well of them" in a private written comment.[76] No hint has ever come to light, however, that Williams made any overtures to work out a similar accommodation in Boston. And, since he also never launched a serious effort to develop a parochial school system, the conclusion must be that he was satisfied to see most Boston Catholic children attend the public schools as they were.

The closest Bishop Williams seems to have come to enunciating a position on Catholic schools was his matter-of-fact endorsement of the Faribault plan. Thus, on the "school question" he internally sided with the liberals, refusing in 1892, for example, to sign a document formulated by the conservative Archbishop Corrigan of New York and sent to Rome opposing Bishop Ireland's plan. The same year he also lined up on the side of Cardinal Gibbons and Bishop Ireland in a stormy meeting of the archbishops with the Roman Cardinal Satolli over the same question.[77] He noted in his own hand that he favored the Ireland plan and would like to have it in Boston, though there is no evidence that he ever tried to initiate it.

Williams did not assume a leadership role in this dispute or in any other. He does not appear to have figured prominently as either a liberal or conservative, and in analyses of the American hierarchy on the liberal–conservative spectrum, Williams is not mentioned among the principals.[78] Most of all, although he gained a reputation as the "Nestor" of the American hierarchy, characterized by Cardinal Gibbons as a man "whose authority is very great with us," in general he did not seem to have exercised much leadership. He was said by an admiring biographer to have been more prominent at the Third Council of Baltimore than at any time of his administration,[79] although he did not make a single speech at the Council. It appears that his reputation among fellow bishops rested mostly on his ability to give sage advice rather than initiate policy. One less admiring student of the period concluded that "the passive element within the American hierarchy could be typified in the person of the Most Reverend John Joseph Williams, archbishop of Boston."[80] At best, he seems to have succeeded in straddling the major controversies embroiling the Catholic hierarchy during this period, remaining cooperative with both sides. When he became a close advisor to the conservative Michael Corrigan, bishop of New York, he was nonetheless thought of as a "moderate liberal" member of the hierarchical faction headed by Cardinal Gibbons of Baltimore.

Despite the bishop's lack of interest in a parochial school system for Boston and failure to try to implement Bishop Ireland's Faribault plan in Boston, during his tenure a substantial number of parochial schools did develop in the diocese. By the end of his service, of fifty parishes in Boston, there were twenty-five Catholic parochial schools with an enrollment of approximately 16,000 children. Nineteen of these schools had been founded during Williams' episcopate.[81]

The reason for this unexpectedly large growth of parochial schooling despite the absence of a parochial school mandate in Boston was not Williams' actions, but the continuation and growth of the phenomenon begun during the Fitzpatrick episcopate, namely the "schoolmen." These were individual pastors who took it upon themselves to have schools in their own parishes, some of whom then encouraged other parishes to do likewise. The schoolmen's continued existence was likely made possible by Williams' generally hands-off policies, but there is no evidence that they were the result of his urging. There is no record that he opposed their efforts either.

The singular dedication to parochial schools on the part of the "schoolmen" had begun during the Fitzpatrick era in the inner-city St. Mary's parish, which was manned by the Jesuits, and whose pastor, John McElroy, had secured the services of the Sisters of Notre Dame to conduct a school. Once ensconced in Boston, these sisters had expanded their educational work to open more schools in other parishes at the invitation of the local pastors. They also established a more exclusive private school for girls, and they substantially increased their own numbers both by bringing in more sisters from elsewhere and by recruiting some of their schoolgirl graduates into their convents and schools.

Then in 1873, during the Williams episcopate, the Sisters of St. Joseph were brought into Boston by Father Thomas Magennis to start a school in a new parish in the rapidly developing Roxbury/Jamaica Plain section of the city. The Sisters of St. Joseph rapidly expanded their numbers, staffing still more schools in the area and elsewhere in Boston and its environs. During the Williams era the Sisters of Notre Dame and the Sisters of St. Joseph staffed all the parochial schools in the English-speaking parishes of Boston. The foremost promoter of the schools was the pastor of St. Mary's in Cambridgeport, Father Thomas Scully, who not only developed a vital parochial school program in his own parish but forcefully crusaded for the same in all Boston parishes, making some bitter clerical enemies in the process. Williams entered the ensuing controversy on Scully's side, but characteristically did not force the opposing pastors to open schools.[82] The archbishop's "hands off" behavior regarding the parochial school issue in this instance seems to have typified the stance he took with regard to most matters having to do with the parishes and their pastors. Williams, while he did not oppose the development of parochial schools, did not advocate it either and did not exert a systematic effort. Not a single piece of correspondence exists in which he solicited a religious order to conduct a parochial school in the diocese. His correspondence abundantly reveals his active promotion of numerous other Catholic activities, including frequent negotiations to obtain sisters or brothers to conduct various benevolent institutions. But the procuring of religious teachers for the parochial schools was conducted exclusively by the pastors of parishes who wanted them.

In 1897 Williams did get around to appointing a Diocesan Supervisor of Schools, but this was a position that had been mandated ten years earlier by the Third Plenary Council of Baltimore. This position would gradually, if belatedly, shape the parochial schools of Boston into something resembling a school system. He also, in conformity with the Council's decrees, belatedly established a diocesan school board, made up of parish priests. While conforming to these Baltimore Council decrees, and despite his proclivity for Catholic separateness, he never became an active advocate of parochial schools. Why? He could not be numbered among the large number of clerics, including his predecessor Fitzpatrick, who had been educated, apparently without harm, in the public schools. His own educational as well as personal life had been led in separation from the non-Catholic world, and why he did not desire this for his Catholic followers remains unclear. In his failure to understand how schooling was gradually replacing the family in the formation of children, and how the common school movement in many respects fed on the realization that the family in rapidly urbanizing and industrializing America was no longer up to the task, Williams was not alone, though perhaps the misapprehension persisted in him much longer than in most others.[83]

Whatever the explanation, the fact remained that the large majority of Catholic children continued to attend the city's public schools. In this, nothing had changed all that much since the beginning of organized Catholicism under Bishop Cheverus in the first quarter of the nineteenth century—except, of course, the looming threat that the rise of Catholic political power now posed that the Boston Catholics would take over the public schools themselves. This threat probably provoked even more dread among concerned Protestants in Boston than the Third Council of Baltimore's decrees in 1884 regarding the need for parochial schools. What many Bostonians apparently considered the most serious imminent threat was that the Boston Catholics, rather than developing a comprehensive parochial school system, were about to take over the cherished public schools themselves. After all, by the 1880s Catholics were moving increasingly into public school teaching positions, occupying almost a quarter of them by the end of the Williams era, with the proportion increasing each year.

More threatening still, with the exception of several years after the Travis affair, Catholics held half the seats on the School Committee, which was entrusted with the duty of perpetuating the values that Boston had held dear ever since its Puritan origins. It was becoming increasingly apparent that the Committee might easily pass into Catholic hands, just as the mayoralty itself had.

It was apparent to some that the uneasy balance of power was only maintained because Archbishop Williams preferred it that way. He seems to have been embarrassed by the emergence of the Irish into the public and particularly the political life of Boston, and might have preferred that it had never happened.[84] Though he was powerless to prevent the rise of Irish political power, his own reticence as their spiritual head kept the Church itself from achieving a corresponding status. As the official history of the diocese put the matter, "To some impatient Catholics at that time it seemed that the archbishop was too self-effaced, too passive, too silent, too timid, and that the Church was quite too long and too unnecessarily hiding in the Catacombs."[85]

Still, few questioned his competence. He was, indeed, a retiring administrator, though able, as witnessed by the numerous parishes he brought into being as well as the charitable activities and organizations he initiated. But the results of his reclusiveness and his patriarchal lifestyle support the conclusion that he was a man whom time had passed by. He had grown up in a more bucolic, more pastoral Boston, and in a Catholic Church more familiar to him than the city itself. But this was a Boston and a Catholic Church that had disappeared well before he took charge of the diocese. This was a situation that Williams would have preferred not to see emerge. It did not fit with the cherished memories of his youth, of a simpler time when he had attended Mass and school at the only Catholic establishment in Boston, when the faces of the priests and parishioners were familiar to him, when the bishop knew everyone by name. No doubt this was the perception that became frozen in his memory during his thirteen years of study away from Boston. The Boston Catholic church he returned to in 1845 had already undergone a radical transformation, and the Church he inherited upon becoming bishop in 1866 bore but faint resemblance to the Church of his childhood. Even the beloved cathedral, where he had worshipped and gone to school as a child, was gone, with only paper plans to replace it.

None of this had been Williams' doing: the Catholics had simply kept coming and multiplying in Boston and Massachusetts. He had reacted to the deluge by recruiting priests and seeing to the building of churches as best he could. But all the while it seems that he might have preferred that it had not happened, that the single Catholic congregation of his youth would have been enough. And he continued to administer the diocese as his patron Bishop Fenwick had done—indeed, as the bishop of his early childhood, John Cheverus, had done.

If there was a single greatest failure of the Williams administration, it was probably this: he failed to make the transition to modernity either in his outlook or his behavior. He was incapable of or chose not to adjust to the fact that Boston was now a major city and no longer the small town of his youth, and that the Catholic Church of Boston and its constituents had emerged from hardly noticeable minority status to become the region's dominant religious group, on the verge of political dominance as well.[86] All this in one man's lifetime! This was a transition difficult for any human to comprehend or embrace, and all the more difficult for a man of Williams' profoundly conservative propensity.[87]

His apparent inability to make this transition had a profound and possibly deleterious effect on his stewardship in a variety of ways. One was the antiquarian style in which he continued to administer the diocese, as if he were conducting the affairs of a feudal manor. The result, given the sheer magnitude of business that now had to be conducted, was inevitable. The administrative vacuum that resulted from Williams' failure to tend personally to such a vast development was filled by others at the local level. What emerged was a multiplicity of local fiefdoms run by powerful parish priests functioning in relative independence of the archbishop and of one another. The local pastors functioned very much like their counterparts who were emerging at the same time in politics, the local ward bosses.[88] This diffusion of power to the local level makes it impossible to discern diocesan-wide policy on a variety of issues, including the school question.

Williams' stance on the school question may also have been determined by his failure to grasp the profound social changes taking place in his lifetime. One critic has argued persuasively that Williams' lack of enthusiasm for the parochial school movement was rooted in his antiquated belief that the Catholic family could supply for its children what the public school could not.[89] It is strange that he actively promoted Sunday schools, routinely solicited religious orders to run charitable and social welfare institutions such as orphanages and homes for working girls without families, and even advocated strictly Catholic organizations for cultural uplift—indeed, in every respect except schools he strove to create a sort of Catholic island of activity within the city and diocese.

This was the legacy that Archbishop Williams left to his successor at his death in 1907: a Boston Catholic Church that, clearly unintended by the archbishop himself, was well on its way to dominance in the city, and that only awaited the emergence of a leader with the determination to make that dominance a reality. For better or worse, it was about to be visited with just such a leader.

5

Catholic Schools Triumphant?
1907–1944

The development of Catholic education in the Boston area during the nineteenth century had not been impressive. The first Catholic bishop of Boston, John Cheverus, had intended to provide schools for the children of early nineteenth-century Irish Catholic immigrants, but the resources were not available. The second bishop, Benedict Fenwick, exerted herculean efforts to provide a Catholic alternative to the public schools but succeeded mostly in laying the groundwork for Catholic higher education that would come to fruition long after his demise. The next two bishops, John Fitzpatrick and John Williams, whose combined tenure spanned sixty years, from 1846 to 1907, did not energetically promote Catholic schooling, though some individual parish priests who came to be known as the "schoolmen" did produce a fairly respectable number of parochial schools.

Through all this time the Irish immigrants themselves, who made up the vast majority of Boston Catholics, did not demonstrate great zeal for Catholic education either. And the Yankee guardians of Boston tradition, who controlled the public schools, reluctantly made necessary accommodations to what they considered the legitimate demands of the Catholic newcomers, as well as to what they considered necessary to keep Catholics sending their children to the public schools. All of these factors resulted in a Catholic school effort in Boston that paled in comparison to that in other major American urban dioceses.

As late as 1908, exactly a century after the founding of a Catholic diocese in the "Athens of America," and more than two decades after the Third Council of Baltimore had decreed that every American Catholic parish must have a school with a seat for every child, only 35.9 percent of the diocese's parishes with resident priests had schools. In Boston itself, where Catholics made up over 40 percent of the population, only 15 percent of all the school-children attended Catholic schools. Even in many parishes that had schools, most of the children did not attend them: overall only about one Catholic child in five attended Catholic school.[1] In Boston and its suburbs within a ten-mile radius, for every Catholic child who attended parochial school, two others attended only catechism class in 1907, and many others did not even do that or attended only long enough to prepare for First Communion or Confirmation. Boston was known throughout the United States as a notable exception to the generally accepted, though still unrealized ideal, of every Catholic child in a Catholic school.

But the next man to occupy the Roman Catholic bishop's throne in Boston after the death of Archbishop John Williams arrived loudly proclaiming his determination to change all that. William Henry O'Connell, like Fitzpatrick and Williams, was also the child of Irish immigrants, this time born in Lowell (1859) instead of Boston itself. O'Connell, like Fitzpatrick, attended the public schools through high school, claiming to have experienced both severe anti-Catholic and anti-Irish prejudice and, especially in high school, the encouragement of inspirational teachers.[2] After attending St. Charles Seminary in Maryland and then Boston College, he went to Rome for his higher ecclesiastical studies and was ordained in 1884. Then O'Connell, upon returning to Boston, began his surprisingly rapid rise to churchly power. Through a combination of ability, luck, and cunning ambition he rose from obscure ranks as a curate in Boston's West End to prominence, first as a gifted orator and then as rector of the American College in Rome (1896), at that time probably the single most influential position an American could hold at the papal seat. Through friendships made in high places at Rome O'Connell secured appointment to the vacant position as bishop of Portland, Maine, in 1901, special papal envoy to Japan in 1904, and then coadjutor with right of succession in Boston in 1906, assuming full command upon Archbishop Williams' death in 1907. He had been recommended for neither bishopric by the consultors of either diocese but used his connections in Rome behind the scenes.[3]

O'Connell's unusual rise to power revealed the fundamental cleavage between himself and his two immediate predecessors. Whereas they had timidly accepted the status quo and allowed external events to shape their policies, he chose to seize the moment and make events bend to his own wishes and desires. In an ominously ill-disguised affirmation of this radical difference, O'Connell took advantage of the first public opportunity to distinguish himself from his predecessor. In a speech given before Williams in the cathedral in formal celebration of his appointment as coadjutor, O'Connell referred to himself as "no weak copy of a great original" and suggested that people "accept me for what I am."[4]

What he was, among other things, was a man determined to take Boston Catholicism out of the catacombs, which he did both by word and deed. O'Connell made no secret of how he perceived the position of Catholics in Boston. He took the occasion of the centennial celebration of the Boston diocese in 1908 to deliver his Boston manifesto. His "In the Beginning" speech was a statement both triumphant and peacemaking.[5] The Puritans treated us miserably, argued O'Connell, but now we are in control. We will not exercise vengeance, but instead will forge a new harmony both with the descendants of the Puritans and with the newcomers now arriving.

O'Connell spoke of the "dreadful gulf" that historically separated Puritan and Catholic in Boston. "To begin even to understand the cause of things which happened during the past century that gulf must be explained," he affirmed. Further, "until a bridge has been thrown across that chasm, still very deep, the people of New England will never live in perfect concord. The first step in the remedy is the admission of its existence." O'Connell then went on to analyze the gulf and its sources. His analysis reveals a certain ambivalence regarding the New England Puritans, whom he admired as "sturdy men" with "sturdy ideals" who "stand as an exemplification of what a high ideal, even imperfectly conceived, but tenaciously held, can give man the power to accomplish against seemingly insuperable odds." But he also perceived them as people with "temperaments not easily adaptable" and whose religion constituted a "reversion to the Old Law rather than an acceptance of the New Testament." "There was little of love but much of terror in their laws." Their most grievous offense was that they "frankly hated the Catholic."[6]

Thus, the Puritans' basic intolerance, coupled with their hatred of Catholicism, according to O'Connell, had set the stage for perilous confrontation once Catholics arrived in Massachusetts:

> The Englishman and the Puritan stood for the first time face to face with the Catholic and the Irishman. The inevitable followed. The contrast offered by these diverse types of men could not have been greater; the antithesis could not have been stronger. Never in the history of the whole country was there such a problem given to solve by two factors so utterly opposite in all their bearings.

The "dreadful gulf," argued O'Connell, "though narrowed," was still there. What had changed was that "the Puritan has passed; the Catholic remains. The city where a century ago he came unwanted he has made his own. The child of the immigrant is called to fill the place which the Puritan has left. He must learn to fill it worthily and well." Whereas "the charity of the Puritan was for his own only; the charity of the Catholic must be for all."[7]

O'Connell's "In the Beginning" speech was in many respects a tour de force. First, it trenchantly delineated the essential Boston social history of the past century as well as the state of affairs in 1908. But its greater significance lay in the fact that for the first time an official Catholic leader stated publicly what every thinking Bostonian must have known—that the Irish Catholics had now become top dog. The archbishop's words must have stirred proud sentiments in many hearts that had sat quietly in the catacombs for half a century. No doubt his comments were intended to do just that. O'Connell's speech was intended to do more than merely affirm Catholic hegemony in Boston. It attempted to give that hegemony direction, conciliatory, peacemaking direction, founded no doubt on his perception of Christian charity, but surely also both on his apprehensions about the new breed of Irish Catholic politician beginning to take over in Boston, and on his considerable admiration for the Puritan culture and his desire to become a part of it himself.[8]

Thus, O'Connell attempted both to assert the dominance of Catholic Boston and to guide it into acceptable respectability, with himself in the vanguard. Unlike the retiring Williams, he plunged into public life, participating with Protestants in such wildly diverse organizations as the not exactly prestigious Massachusetts Milk Consumers Union (1910) and the revered board of the Boston Public Library (1932–1936). He became a member of the Boston Chamber of Commerce (1910) and belonged to the Boston Wednesday Evening Club, where he associated with some of Boston's first citizens, among them the reformer James Jackson Storrow, with whom he apparently developed a friendship. In these and many other activities he resembled Bishop Fitzpatrick, except that unlike Fitzpatrick, he never practiced quiet acquiescence. Indeed, he seemed to seize every opportunity to flaunt the presence of Catholicism, as in the triumphal parade on his return from Rome after receiving the cardinal's hat in 1911 or with the U.S. Catholic Missionary Congress hosted by the Boston diocese in 1913, said to be the largest Catholic gathering ever held in the United States.[9]

Throughout his Boston career O'Connell tried to pursue this dual, sometimes seemingly contradictory theme of celebrating the triumph and greatness of Catholicism in Boston while acknowledging the enduring importance of the Puritan culture by attempting to achieve acceptable standing for himself and his followers in it. Thus, he could speak publicly not only about "The Nobility of the Celt" but about "The Real Influence of the Puritan," whose "best qualities were the Christian virtues common to all true and sincere Christians." He concurrently critiqued them as a people whose "fanaticism and intolerance" resulted from separation from Rome and led to that "dour stubbornness" that recognized "only hard work and harsh duty as the highest virtues." Yet even in condemning them O'Connell could not repress his admiration ("the Puritan, whatever his failings, was a man who stood straight up for his principles. It was that uprightness and sturdiness that gave strength to him and to his community"), so much so that O'Connell deigned to hold up this Puritan as a model of simplicity, sturdiness, and loyalty for Catholics to emulate.

The Puritan devotion to culture, too, O'Connell clearly admired. "Nowhere in all America," he claimed, in a statement worthy of the most seasoned Boston Brahmin, "is the cultivation of mind or pursuit of the intellectual life held in higher honor than in this Athens of America."[10] He could be both belligerent and deferential. At the Mass celebration of his elevation to cardinal in 1911, he declared with regard to his Irish Catholics that "never again shall we shrink from the intolerance of mere ignorance, which could place us in a position inferior to anything but the best in this city and this community."[11]

Yet he was aware that Catholics still maintained a tenuous position in the city. Though they were moving into almost absolute political control, their financial position remained weak. Catholic membership in the Boston Chamber of Commerce was negligible, much less their participation in the great banking and financial institutions. Economically and culturally they remained outsiders. Further, in O'Connell's eyes even the political dominance was tainted by the likes of John F. Fitzgerald and James Michael Curley, whose questionable political consciences cast Irish and Catholic Boston in an unfavorable light. It was the cardinal's self-appointed task, then, both to celebrate the triumph of Catholicism and to make it a triumph worth the name.[12]

In his position on education O'Connell chose to reach back beyond his two immediate predecessors, Williams and Fitzpatrick, to the man he felt had established not only the true Catholic position on the school question but also the authentic response to the place of Catholics in Boston society. This was Bishop Benedict Fenwick, who had ruled the diocese from 1825 to 1846. Fenwick had tried valiantly, though with very modest success, to establish a Catholic educational tradition in Boston in open defiance of the Yankee pressure to accept the public schools. It was he who established the Ursuline nuns in their exclusive girls' boarding school in Charlestown, who built Holy Cross College, and who laid the first plans for Boston College. In every Boston church built under his direction schoolrooms were included either in the basement or in the back, even though, because of financial and other difficulties, schools did not actually materialize in all.

In a 1914 speech at the dedication of a new school in St. Mary's parish, Cambridge, a longstanding center of Catholic educational activity, O'Connell made his admiration for Fenwick open and explicit. Calling him "a really great man to whose name altogether too little glory has been given. . . . by great odds, the ablest and noblest chief this Diocese has ever had."[13] O'Connell saw him as a man of "courageous manliness" who broke the Catholics of Boston out of "conditions of strange timidity" and "apologetic reserve." "He knew full well that unless his flock took on its measure of self respect by standing openly and fearlessly for its fundamental principles it could never expect to be either respected or understood by the Puritan enemies who surrounded it." "He gave himself heart and soul to the founding and maintaining of Catholic schools, academies, and colleges." His "valiant" efforts O'Connell considered truly miraculous, "considering the means at his disposal and the hostile spirit of the time." Unfortunately, according to O'Connell,

> when Bishop Fenwick died the idea of the necessity of the parish school and of Christian education went to sleep and lay dormant for many years, until it literally required a strong word from Rome and the solemn warning of a plenary council to stir from their apathy and their indifference, what might appropriately be called armed neutrality, those who might well have continued what had been so well and so nobly begun.[14]

Based on the forthright statements in O'Connell's address, he both disdained Fitzpatrick and Williams and admired Fenwick, with whom he shared much both in temperament and conviction, particularly conviction in favor of a bold public stance for Catholics in Boston, including open defiance of the public school. O'Connell openly advocated the cause of Catholic schooling from the very beginning of his episcopacy, and his celebration of Bishop Fenwick as the model who should have been followed throughout the nineteenth century appears to have reflected his true feelings.

On numerous occasions, both public and private, he reaffirmed his view that religious, particularly Catholic, schooling was the proper response to the question of education. "Happy the parents who, when the day comes for sending their child out from the tender and watchful care of the home, may take the lamb of the flock to a religious school," he declared in a 1913 pastoral letter. "How is it possible that any Catholic parent can hesitate for a moment to send his child to a Catholic school when such opportunity is open to him! . . . The short hour in the Sunday school is altogether insufficient to give the child that grasp of the doctrines and principles of our holy religion . . ."[15] "There is, as you know, just one point of view and that is, Catholic children should attend Catholic schools," he told an inquiring Catholic in 1930.[16] And he assured the Catholic teachers of the archdiocese that the Catholic school movement "really must occupy the first place in our hearts and minds."[17]

Hardly had O'Connell assumed command in Boston when he invited the Catholic Educational Association to hold its sixth annual meeting there, which it did in 1908. The move both underlined O'Connell's determination to flaunt Catholicism openly in Boston by holding mass meetings and demonstrations and confirmed publicly his commitment to Catholic education itself.[18]

O'Connell's position on the school question was not surprising, not just in view of his declared independence of Puritan domination, but especially in view of his generally conservative philosophy. He was first of all an avowed Romanist. As a young seminarian he had determined somehow to find a way to study in Rome, and then he later won appointment to the directorship of the American College in Rome. His connections there had made all the difference in his career. O'Connell later lost influence at the Vatican because his closest connections, such as Pius X, either died off or were replaced in curial reshufflings, and apparently also because of a scandal within his own chancery involving the marriage of a nephew whom he had sponsored into the priesthood and appointed as his influential personal secretary. Even so, he never shed his conviction that Rome was in every respect the center of Catholicism.[19]

Most of all, he believed in Rome as the church's center because he totally endorsed the church's hierarchical nature. He believed that God willed the word to come from Rome and then be passed down through the bishops to the priests and thence to the faithful. "There is coordination and subordination all along the line of the whole diocese, with all its varied activities, to the Bishop, and of the Bishop to the Holy See." This, argued O'Connell, "constitutes the real strength of the Church's position."[20] "We are not units," he contended, "each working his own way, but an organic body in which the members are directed from the head."[21] And, after all, the "head" had spoken on the school question, through its approval of the Third Council of Baltimore's decrees in favor of parochial schools and through its settling of the internal controversy over the school question in the American church in 1892. It was to speak again during O'Connell's tenure through Pius XI's encyclical in 1929 on the Christian education of youth. If Rome had settled the question, then O'Connell, given his brand of ecclesiastical theology, was ready to act instead of question.

But even aside from his readiness to obey authority, it appears that O'Connell's deep convictions about the nature of man and society would have led him to advocate parochial schools anyway. His advocacy of them was often heavily imbued with reflections on man's immense potential for self-destruction. In O'Connell's view, seething chaos lay always just beneath the surface and could be held in check only through the authoritative influence of religion. He saw human nature as "an elemental force with awful possibilities for evil unless it is held in check and balanced by the mighty power of religion."[22] It was this view that probably motivated O'Connell's respect for the Puritans, despite their ill treatment of Catholics. That is, they had recognized man's flawed nature for what it was, and acted accordingly. Unfortunately, in O'Connell's view, their descendants of the early twentieth century had all but abandoned this basic truth of human existence. O'Connell was fond of pointing out what he considered the emasculation of Protestantism and the fact that only Catholicism was now exercising that powerful conservative force in society.

At the same time, he decried the loss of this potentially useful ally in the battle against the secular humanism that seemed to be poisoning men's minds. O'Connell's condemnation of modernism was no mere conformist reiteration of Pius X's decree.[23] The cardinal saw the inroads of this incorrect view of human nature in the prevalent philosophies of education, which he was ever quick to condemn. "Some of the widely advertised and boasted educational systems of the day," he contended, destroyed "docility" and "discipline." "Teachers deliberately encourage little ones to say and do whatever fancy or chance puts into their small heads."[24] "Formerly children were brought up to be obedient. Now children are being brought up to be quite self-conscious and self-sufficient. This is entirely foreign to the system of Christian education."[25] In O'Connell's view children needed more training in "will power" and "simplicity of life;" they needed less "self-confidence" and more "confidence in God." In a word, "human nature cannot be uplifted by its own bootstraps."[26]

For O'Connell this was the nub of the matter: human nature cannot do it on its own. This conviction came out in perfect clarity in the cardinal's condemnation of the Italian educator Maria Montessori. In 1913, as Montessori was being lionized in America and other parts of the world for her educational innovation, O'Connell dismissed her as having contributed to the exaggerated use of the senses in education and having responded to individual needs, but even more so as having committed the most fundamental of errors: "In her eyes the child is sufficient unto itself. His environment is the only enemy. Give him liberty and freedom and he will educate himself."[27] Montessori, in a word, failed to understand the depravity of human nature, mistakenly concluding that only the environment impedes progress. In contradistinction to this false philosophy of education, based as it was on a false theology, O'Connell posited his own, which he believed to be the Church's as well. Children needed training and discipline, not freedom: "If the holy years of childhood are to be left without moral restraint or guidance, if youth and young manhood are to be cast out upon life without rule or compass, what inevitably will be the end of civilization and society?"[28]

Montessori was not the only educator at fault. O'Connell saw the public schools as having at worst deliberately embraced the secular humanist philosophy, and at best capitulated to it by default, since religion, the only adequate conservative force against the powers of darkness lurking in every childish heart, had been excluded from the public school classroom. "The absence of a religious motive in the system of education generally prevailing in our country," he argued, "has resulted in the undermining of that respect for authority which is a necessary condition for the observance of law."[29] Thus, he condemned the trend in public school thinking toward the secular humanist philosophy, criticized the schools for abandoning religion, and supported the widespread efforts born in the early twentieth century to find an acceptable way to return religion to public education. "Many of the denominations," he argued, "are coming to see that the public schools, even while doing the best they can do under the circumstances, are by their very nature unequal to the task of educating properly. They cannot teach religion without violating the rights of one pupil or another." He concluded, "It is an encouraging sign that the people of this country are now awakening to the vital need of moral training in education."[30]

In this context his advocacy of parochial schools went beyond mere ecclesiastical obedience; in every respect it squared with his deepest convictions about human life. The parochial school, he assumed, both recognized the child's true nature and offered the only true remedy, religion.

O'Connell took a keen interest in parochial school affairs, involving himself in everything from the training of teachers to the construction of school buildings. His involvement demonstrated his commitment to Catholic schooling as well as his view that Catholic education, at whatever level, was a part of the Church's total effort and must therefore come under central control. He once told Catholic educators that "you are but the helpers of the hierarchy in the feeding of the flock of Christ. Teaching is not a thing apart, a profession isolated from the general work of the Church."[31]

To see that the Boston Catholic educational effort remained responsive to episcopal control, O'Connell submitted it to the same process of centralization as he did every other Catholic activity in the archdiocese. Under his predecessor, Archbishop Williams, the Boston diocese had been administered as a kind of loose federation, with Williams as a sort of patriarch who intervened only in unusual situations. Each pastor functioned as the ecclesiastical equivalent of the local ward boss. Catholic educational, charitable, and other activities mostly originated from individual local initiative and proliferated in uncoordinated disarray. In such a permissive atmosphere not much administrative structure was needed, and not much was afforded. For the most part Williams had administered the archdiocese personally, working out of the cathedral rectory rather than an office complex, and conducting his own correspondence by hand.

But O'Connell's penchant for Roman discipline changed all that—immediately. In the first year his administration produced more records than Williams did in his entire forty-year tenure. O'Connell moved the "chancery" or administrative function away from the cathedral, first to Granby Street in Back Bay, and later to the grounds of St. John's Seminary in Brighton. He upgraded the functions of his official secretary and chief administrative assistant, the chancellor. He filled positions mandated by the Third Council of Baltimore but left unfilled by Williams, such as a book censor, a matrimonial court, a moderator for theological conferences, and the like. He immediately created a Diocesan Charitable Bureau to coordinate, systematize, and regulate all charitable activities, and appointed a director for it. He even organized the multitudinous Catholic organizations that had developed in the archdiocese into the Federation of Catholic Societies in 1908, a huge organization that had 40,000 members by 1911. O'Connell gave it a great deal of attention and depended on it for displays of mass Catholicism in Boston. He also promoted the creation and organization of many other societies in the attempt to unify and coordinate all possible activities, everything from a Holy Name Society in every parish to a League of Catholic Women, to a Guild of Catholic physicians, and so forth.

To gain control over the communications media, he bought the faltering *Boston Pilot*, which had been under lay ownership since the 1830s, and he tried intermittently either to take over or suppress *The Sacred Heart Review*, a popular Catholic weekly published, with collaboration from many colleagues, by a powerful local pastor, the Rev. John O'Brien. After a bitter decade of struggle, in 1918 O'Connell finally succeeded in killing *The Review*.[32] O'Brien called O'Connell "ungracious and incriminating" and accused him of "a disposition to fabricate grievances,"[33] but his complaints produced no results.

In 1911 O'Connell ousted the Sulpician order from the diocesan seminary and ensconced his own clergy, thereby gaining direct control of priestly training as well as delivering a bit of vengeance on an order that had apparently not treated him well as a junior seminarian. He took much autonomy away from local parishes by requiring regular financial and administrative reports, reserving to himself approval of all construction, and regulating the activities of priests in minute detail, such as forbidding absence from the parish without his approval and restricting speaking engagements and the like to those explicitly approved by him. He reduced the power of old-line pastors by breaking up what had sometimes grown to be immense fiefdoms into more numerous smaller parishes, appointing priests of his own choosing to the latter. In the first four years alone he created thirty-two new parishes, often by subdividing larger ones.[34]

This same penchant for centralization, organization, and control he applied to the administration of Catholic schools. Before O'Connell's advent to power, the schools had only a modicum of organization. In 1889, in conformity with directives of the Third Council of Baltimore, Archbishop Williams did get around to appointing a twelve-member school board from among the pastors, and in 1897 he appointed the Rev. Louis Walsh as supervisor of schools, though without a staff.

Some of the sisters who taught in the schools had already initiated a degree of organization, at least within the schools of their own religious order. The two communities that together conducted most of the parochial schools in Boston, the Sisters of Notre Dame and the Sisters of St. Joseph, each had its own plan of studies in force, and each had at least the semblance of a program by which the members of their orders were trained and updated for their teaching duties.[35]

In at least some parts of Boston a certain unity had held the schools together. This was particularly noticeable in East Boston, where the Rev. James Fitton had functioned as a champion of parochial schools since the 1850s. From his own original parish he had initiated the founding of parishes in East Boston, with a school in each, all taught by the Sisters of Notre Dame. In a sense these schools had long functioned as a kind of mini-system, but for the diocese itself not much central organization had ever been set up. Under Williams the diocesan school board had been largely inactive and therefore ineffective from the beginning. Father Walsh, the superintendent appointed by Williams, though he had no office or clerical staff, took his position seriously and annually visited each of the schools, spoke to the sisters both at the schools and in their summer retreats, wrote annual reports, and took one important step toward the creation of a modern school system in 1902 by initiating an annual meeting of the supervisors of all the parochial schools as well as a second meeting for the parish priests in charge of these schools.[36] Out of this arrangement had developed an agreement in 1902 on a common exam given as an option to students in the final year of elementary school and later extended to all students as a requirement for graduation.

O'Connell seized all of these beginnings and put the teeth of his own considerable authority into them. In 1908, apparently disturbed by a lack of enthusiasm in some parish priests who were expected to look after their parish's school if there was one, O'Connell told the superintendent "to send me at once a list of those who were absent" from the meeting recently held for them to discuss school affairs.[37] But more important indications of his determination to organize the schools into an efficient system were at hand. After a two-year experiment with co-superintendents, the Rev. John Graham and the Rev. George A. Lyons, O'Connell gave the ball to Lyons until 1913. Lyons worked diligently visiting classrooms and writing reports rife with what would have to be described as excessive subservience to O'Connell.[38]

This may have led to a change in 1913 when the Rev. Augustine Hickey was given the job, which he handled until 1926. Hickey worked in close cooperation with O'Connell and apparently enjoyed the latter's complete confidence. It was he, under O'Connell, who shaped the Boston Catholic schools into what could reasonably be called a Catholic school system, at least at the elementary school level. Hickey, for the first time among the superintendents, set up an office separate from his own residence, a modest one at the cathedral, but at least with some provision for secretarial help.[39]

Educationally, with O'Connell's approval (as with everything he did), Hickey took steps to bring the various religious communities working in the schools into a cooperative working relationship. To this end in 1914 he created a body of twelve community supervisors, one member from each community having at least two hundred pupils in the archdiocesan schools, each member appointed by their respective religious orders.[40] This group of sisters from diverse religious orders he immediately set to work devising a common curriculum for all the schools. By 1915 they had developed and put into effect an outline of requirements in religion, English, history, geography, arithmetic, and physiology for all eight grades. The cardinal, who had a strong interest in the subject, appointed a special supervisor to coordinate the music program in all schools of the diocese.[41] By 1923 the sister supervisors had revised the outline of requirements into a thoroughly detailed course of study for each of these subjects, and in addition courses in patriotism and civics, physical training, and hygiene. Not only did the course of study contain a complete outline for each course, but it even specified the amount of time to be spent on each. The introduction of a common course of study made possible the use of common examinations, and these were instituted on a mandatory basis for grades three through eight in 1919.[42]

By the time the Rev. Richard J. Quinlan became superintendent in 1926, the Boston parochial schools were welded into a system complete with superintendent, a board of community supervisors from the major religious communities teaching in the schools, a common course of study, and uniform exams. It was left to Quinlan merely to consolidate in minor ways, such as his decision, with the cardinal's approval, to make the Italian pronunciation of Latin mandatory in all schools of the diocese.[43] In all of this consolidation the superintendents maintained close liaison with O'Connell, seeking his approval for each significant, and often insignificant, development.

In no issue was this more apparent than in the development of an adequate teacher training program for the parochial schools, in which the cardinal took an active and interested part. Here again teacher training did not begin with the O'Connell administration: each religious community had always had its preferred means of preparing recruits for the classroom, usually consisting of instruction by more experienced members of the community and then on-the-job supervision by veterans. As formal teacher training gained headway during the nineteenth century in the secular world with the creation of normal schools and their gradual development and extension, Catholic teaching communities often responded with a somewhat more organized form of preparation than they had employed in the past. Thus, by the 1890s the Sisters of Notre Dame, who at that time conducted the most parochial schools in Boston, were inviting guest lecturers to their various houses to speak on pedagogical topics.[44] The first supervisor, Father Walsh, also spoke to the various communities on educational questions. By 1908 the Sisters of St. Joseph, who by that time were the second-largest teaching order in the archdiocese and the fastest-growing, held a summer institute for their own teachers.[45]

The Sisters of St. Joseph's institute attracted O'Connell's attention and prompted him to express an interest in having one for all the religious teachers of the archdiocese.[46] This led to the first diocesan-wide teacher institute, held for six days in the summer of 1910, and attended by some 450 sisters. O'Connell promoted the idea, selected the speakers, and addressed the gathering.[47] The institute was repeated annually thereafter, supervised by the diocesan superintendent of schools but ultimately controlled by the cardinal, to whom all important decisions, such as the selection of speakers and topics, had to be submitted for approval.[48] Though perhaps authoritarian in the extreme and at times petty, the practice did at least underline O'Connell's keen interest in building up his perception of educational quality for the Catholic schools.[49]

The annual institute, begun in 1910, fulfilled an important function beyond the specific lectures delivered over a six-day period. For the first time it brought the sisters of different religious communities together in one place and exposed them to a common set of ideas; probably more significantly, it brought them in contact with one another. This may have been part of O'Connell's intent, for surely it furthered the unifying thrust of his administration.

The annual summer institute was only the first of several developments, all initiated and/or carefully supervised by O'Connell, designed to further upgrade, modernize, and unify the education of teachers for the parochial schools. In 1917 the practice of having a "visiting day" was initiated: each school closed on a given day to enable the teachers to visit another parochial school and observe the practices there. The intent was to counteract the "narrowing" effects of having schools run separately by each religious order without communication between them.[50] In 1919, again under the cardinal's auspices, extension courses were offered during the fall at the cathedral, under the aegis of Boston College. In the first year alone five hundred sisters attended this course, which consisted of thirty pedagogical lectures given on Saturdays.[51] In 1920 St. John's seminary began offering a course in principles of education to better prepare the future priests to work more cooperatively with the schools. Then in 1924 Boston College began a summer school for parochial school teachers, attended by 321 sisters and 20 brothers by 1927. And in 1926 the college opened its graduate school of education, enrolling 157 sisters and 5 brothers in degree programs the very first year.[52]

At the same time, apparently reluctant to give up their traditional practices, individual religious orders also continued to pursue their own teacher education programs. The Sisters of Notre Dame, for example, provided anything from sending a few sisters to their Trinity College in Washington to sending others for a summer program at their Notre Dame Academy in Boston.[53]

The involvement of Boston College in the archdiocesan teacher education program, which had begun with the extensive use of its Jesuit faculty as lecturers in the diocesan summer institute in 1910, was to O'Connell the most natural of events, for he thought of every educational activity, program, and institution in the archdiocese as merely one aspect of the Church's single mission. Institutions of higher learning were no exception. Thus, O'Connell thought of Boston College as an integral part of his educational system and expected it to comply, which it did. O'Connell, considering himself its most illustrious alumnus, maintained a special relationship with the college, not only approving but materially aiding its move from the South End to spacious and prestigious Chestnut Hill in 1913, and in future years encouraging its development, organizing parish support for its major fund-raising drive in 1921, and even donating substantial amounts of his own money.[54]

He also exercised his episcopal authority over the college, everything from investigating the quality and orthodoxy of its religious and theological programs, to approving the outside speaking engagements of its Jesuit faculty, to dictating the conditions and direction of its curricular expansion. Thus, at one point, at O'Connell's command, the supervisor of diocesan schools submitted a report on all religious activities at Boston College. The report assured the cardinal that all the faculty were Catholic, that only thirteen non-Catholic students attended, that all students were required to take two credits of religion each semester as well as to pursue a course in scholastic philosophy, that all made an obligatory annual retreat, and the like.[55]

All of these involvements illustrate not only the degree of O'Connell's authoritarian control over the diocese, in marked contrast to his predecessor, but his concern for Catholic education in Boston. Records of the O'Connell years are replete with correspondence, negotiations, directives, and the like having to do with educational affairs. He did everything from encourage the founding of Emmanuel College (1917) and Regis College (1927) for women, to purchasing land for an exclusive school to be run by the highly regarded Madames of the Sacred Heart in Newton. At one point he refused permission to the Sisters of Notre Dame to build a new gym and dormitory for their academy in Roxbury, accusing them of "rank imprudence" in financial matters and a "proclivity to create enormous debts."[56]

But generally the direction was toward the encouragement of expansion. The number of Catholic colleges went from one to three during his administration. Enrollment at Boston College went from 143 to 3,837, and each of the two women's colleges went from nothing to about 500. The number of private academies and prep schools increased from ten to twenty-four, and their enrollments grew by 500 percent to 5,510. Parish high schools as extensions of the parochial elementary schools grew from twenty-two to sixty-seven, a number that also included parishes within the diocese but outside of Boston. The cardinal professed that

> The Catholic high school is essential to the work of Catholic education. The distinctive Catholic training of the individual must be continued during the entire period of intellectual and moral growth and development. May God bless abundantly every effort and every sacrifice in the advancement of the Catholic high school movement.[57]

But even as O'Connell directed his energies to the development of a vital Catholic school enterprise that would compete successfully with the public schools at every level, he was ever-cognizant of the dangers that loomed against his efforts and, specifically, that not just endangered the existence of a Catholic educational program but also threatened to overly control its very nature. This is what drove him to engage in the educational politics that embroiled Massachusetts at the time. His support of Catholic education led him into most of his forays into the political arena, which as a matter of policy he normally shunned, at least publicly. But when Catholic educational interests seemed at stake he was ready to take action, though aside from articles in his weekly newspaper, most of his efforts took place behind the scenes. Not all of his political activities in the educational arena, though, were aimed merely at preserving the interests of parochial schools as such. In fact, he took positions on a broader variety of educational issues, and these often seemed formed from a combination of a certain paranoia that led him to suspect an anti-Catholic intent behind otherwise innocent legislation and the genuine conservatism that motivated his politics as it did his religion.

Thus, his position on the so-called anti-sectarian issue, for example, which embroiled Massachusetts citizens in controversy for almost two decades after 1900 and culminated in an amendment to the state constitution, can probably be attributed more to paranoia than anything else. First legislation and then a constitutional change had been proposed to outlaw the use of public funds for any sort of denominational educational activity. O'Connell took this as a direct effort to cut the Catholic Church off from the possibility of funds, even though, by his own account, a small proportion of all the monies given for such purposes in the past had gone to Catholic institutions.[58] Many Catholic politicians supported the proposition because they wished to cut off institutions like Harvard from the funds they had long gotten, believing that Catholic interests would be hurt much less than Protestant ones. But O'Connell seems to have genuinely believed that "the state had acted wisely in giving financial support to private efforts that furthered the general welfare, especially when the total operation actually saved the state money." This position fit into his general opposition to "big government" and his belief that government itself should let the private sector do as much as possible, aiding where appropriate.[59]

O'Connell remained convinced of an anti-Catholic plot and stood staunchly opposed to the amendment right down to the day of defeat. He took passage of the amendment in 1917 with extreme bitterness and publicly vowed to correct the injustice once Catholics gained absolute control of the state. After first petulantly dismissing the defeat as meaningless, since Catholics were only receiving a pittance anyway, he then, in the same statement, resorted to undisguised threat:

A new generation of Catholic statesmen already well to the fore, who value truly the interests of their faith, will in a few years, sweep indignantly aside the time-servers who have constantly attempted and often succeed in harassing Catholic forces to their cheap individual interests. In that day, now dawning, this amendment will be swept away from the law books as the blue laws have been wiped out of existence.[60]

His opposition to the continuous proposals in the early twentieth century to upgrade the powers of the state department of education and to create a federal department of education, as well as to initiate federal funding of education, was motivated as often by his conservative political philosophy as it was by desire to defend Catholic educational interests. His political philosophy was stated as clearly as possible in a 1919 letter to Congressman J.N. Baer, responding to a bill Baer had introduced into the House of Representatives, a copy of which the congressman sent O'Connell for his opinion. O'Connell characteristically minced no words:

> Your bill, and several others recently introduced, would seem to indicate that we are well along the road to the centralization of legislation concerning every phase of human life which will prepare the way for an autocracy far more iron than any ever devised by the rulers of Germany. What we eat, what we drink, where and how we shall do both; when, where and how we shall study; how we shall think, and whether we shall think or not, or whether we shall even be allowed to think—all these seem to be well advanced in becoming entirely controlled by centralized bureaucracy. I am a firm believer in the phrase that the "best governed people are the least governed people, the strongest Government is the Government which encourages the maximum of private initiative and action."[61]

Strange words, perhaps, from a man who had already concentrated all power over the Archdiocese of Boston into his own hands. But if one accepts this fundamental illogicality, the truth was that O'Connell genuinely opposed centralization of political power, and expressed that opposition on numerous occasions, perhaps most notably in his speech at the 1919 meeting of the National Catholic Educational Association in St. Louis on "The Reasonable Limits of State Activity." His well-known opposition to the Child Labor Amendment was based not on a desire to see children work, but on fear of vesting too much power over people's lives in the federal government instead of in the state and, more importantly, in the family. In education he argued that "the medical inspection of schools, the physical examination and treatment of school children, the supplying of food for the indigent pupil, and other similar provisions which have been added to the educational program of the State, all are signs of the spirit of machine centralization and control."[62] Efforts to create a federal department of education he labeled as the "wish to Prussianize American institutions," and he vehemently argued that "Federal Control of Education Usurps State and Parental Rights"[63].

In contrast to other ecclesiastics like Cardinal Mundelein of Chicago, who opposed federal involvement in education as detrimental to parochial schools, O'Connell was more likely to oppose it as the unwanted centralization of political power. In none of his public or private pronouncements on the issue of federal control of education during the 1920s did O'Connell voice any concern that parochial schools might be harmed. He was not, however, averse to explicitly defending the interests of parochial schools against hostile legislation. Thus, in 1913 and again in 1919, when a state legislative commission recommended the taking of approval of non-public schools out of the hands of local school committees and placing it in the state department of education, O'Connell opposed the move both as too much centralization of power and as detrimental to Catholic school interests. The issue here was the foreign-language schools. State law mandated the teaching of the major subjects in English but left the enforcement of this mandate to local school committees, and the local committees had over the years ignored the fact that certain French-speaking and other foreign-language parochial schools in Massachusetts were not in conformity with the law. The state department wished now to vest that authority in itself and see that the law was enforced.

O'Connell, who seems to have genuinely favored the cultural diversity of Boston Catholicism, and who prided himself in his mastery of the Italian language, went to the defense of the foreign-language ethnic schools, basing his opposition publicly on fear of state centralization but privately sympathizing with the ethnics, insisting that they be assured that the regulation obliging them to teach in English "does not come from His Eminence, but from the state authorities." Actually, O'Connell's concern, as his correspondence reveals, extended beyond protection of the bilingual schools: he also feared that any move to strengthen the state department of education's control over these schools might easily be extended to parochial schools in general.

A similar issue developed in 1919 over the question of sex education.[64] The cardinal had first taken notice of this development in 1913 when the Chicago public schools adopted a "sex hygiene" program. O'Connell called it a "pernicious fad." "What the schools want is morality based not upon hygiene but upon religion." So worked up did he get over this that he urged in The Pilot, "Let Catholics never cease their efforts and their sacrifices until there is a parochial school in every town and village, with a desk for every Catholic boy and girl."[65] The sex hygiene issue did not develop in Massachusetts until 1919, and again the issue had two aspects: the mandatory introduction statewide of health education, which included sex education, and the vesting of authority to coordinate and administer the program in the state department of education. O'Connell opposed the measure on both grounds; working as always behind the scenes through a legislative committee with important connections to friendly politicians, he succeeded on both counts. The final legislation gutted the program of all semblance of sex education, changing its name from "health education" to "physical training," and left its implementation to the local authorities. The legislative committee consisted of the supervisor of schools, Father Hickey, several other trusted clerics, representatives of the League of Catholic Women, several prominent Catholic lay people, and Mr. Henry V. Cunningham, who served as legal counsel.[66] Thus, though motivated by several different factors, O'Connell's record in the political arena indicates that prominent among those motives was adamant opposition to any public action he deemed detrimental to the cause of Catholic education, in addition to his fundamental opposition to the liberalizing, more child-centered tendencies in early twentieth-century public education.

But despite his strenuous efforts to defeat legislation that might, in his opinion, harm Catholic education, his loud pronouncements about the importance of Catholic education, and the fact that the number of Catholic schools greatly increased during his tenure, the actual expansion did not match the cardinal's rhetoric. The historical record reveals discrepancies between his pronouncements and the actual results.

For instance, he often referred to the growth of the Catholic schools and his own role in that development. In 1915, taking stock of his first eight years, he claimed that "the most striking work has been the fostering of the Catholic school." "Just as soon as a parish was found able to undertake the work of establishing its own parochial school," he stated, "so soon was it done."[67] And the cardinal's correspondence with individual parishes does include numerous instances of his prodding pastors to build a school, often with reference to financial priorities. In 1915, when the Rev. Daniel Riordan of Sacred Heart parish in Newton requested permission to install side altars in his church to celebrate its twenty-fifth anniversary, O'Connell replied that these "should be not at all elaborate" and that "you should keep in mind the need of planning for a parochial school."[68] In 1926, shortly after appointing a new pastor for St. Stephen's parish in Framingham, he wanted "to know whether or not it is time to begin preparations for a school."[69] A year later, when no school seemed to be materializing, his secretary wrote again, saying that O'Connell "notes that as yet there is no parochial school in St. Stephen's parish and he wishes you to send him information regarding the prospect of opening a school within a year." In 1927, referring to the "extremely large balance on hand" at St. Catherine's in Charlestown, which already had a parochial school, O'Connell wanted "to know whether or not you have considered the erecting of a high school."[70] In 1927, O'Connell even requested of the superintendent a list of parishes that had no schools, together with an indication of those "in which parochial schools might be established in the immediate future."[71]

Judging by O'Connell's rhetoric and the numerous examples of his prodding subordinates to build schools, and his exhorting parishioners to send their children to them, one would expect that Boston had finally become a primary example of the Catholic Church's parochial school ideal. Indeed, during the O'Connell years Catholic education did grow quite remarkably in comparison to what he had inherited in 1908. And judging by the core of the educational enterprise, the elementary schools, the growth in comparison to the past was substantial. In the diocese as a whole, which included much more than the city of Boston, the number of parochial elementary schools increased from 75 to 158 and the enrollment from 49,352 to 80,143.

Yet, despite this growth and the cardinal's conviction that Catholics should attend Catholic schools, the net results were less than spectacular: the reality did not match the rhetoric. In the city of Boston, more than three of every ten parishes still did not have schools when O'Connell died in 1944; in the ten-mile suburban fringe only a little more than half the parishes had schools. In the entire diocese only 48.6 percent of the 325 parishes had schools. The comparative figures for 1907 were 45.3 percent in the city, 36.7 percent in the ten-mile suburban ring, and 35.9 percent in the diocese, so under O'Connell the parochial school system had grown substantially relative to what he inherited. However, compared to the situation in other dioceses, where practically every parish had a school, and relative to the archbishop's rhetoric, the expansion was less than dramatic.

The actual results of O'Connell's efforts can be seen even more clearly if we examine enrollment growth, particularly in the slightly more than two decades of O'Connell's administration prior to 1930, into which were concentrated most of his administration's energy.[72] Between 1907 and 1930 the Catholic elementary school population in Boston and its ten-mile suburban ring almost doubled, from 33,018 to 63,304, a 91.7 percent increase (to be exact, a 72.85 percent increase in the city and a 101 percent increase in the suburbs). But during this same period the total Catholic population increased by 46 percent overall (17.5 percent in the city and 85.35 percent in the suburbs). In the suburbs, where ostensibly the greatest expansion took place, in 1907 one Catholic in twelve was in a Catholic school, and by 1930 the ratio had been reduced to one in 10.6. In the city the ratio improved from one in 15.9 in 1907 to one in 10.8 in 1930. Perhaps more telling, in 1907 the proportion of elementary school pupils attending parochial schools was 16.3 percent overall (15.7 percent in the city and 17 percent in the suburbs). By 1930 the proportion had risen to 19.2 percent overall (18.3 percent in the city and 20 percent in the suburbs). This modest growth of 2.9 points was mitigated by the fact that the Catholic proportion of the total population had increased from 32.9 percent to 36.1 percent overall (a decrease in the city from 42.7 percent of the total population to 40.2 percent, and an increase in the suburbs from 28.1 percent to 33.2 percent). Thus, the overall increase in the percentage of children attending Catholic schools was accounted for in large part simply by the increase in the Catholic proportion of the total population.

The statistics, therefore, do not support such statements as *The Pilot*'s in 1915 that "Just as soon as a parish was found able to undertake the work of establishing its own school, so soon was it done"[73] or its confident exhortation in 1913, "Let Catholics never cease their efforts and their sacrifices until there is a parochial school in every town and village, with a desk for every Catholic boy and girl."[74] O'Connell's pronouncement before the Catholic Educational Association Convention convened in Boston in 1909 that "The Diocese stands in the vanguard of Christian education" was not true then, nor was it to become true during his lifetime.[75] Nor were his remarks to the archdiocesan clergy assembled for the fourth synod in the diocese's history that same year any closer to the reality: "We may well congratulate ourselves," he boasted, "on the flourishing condition of our schools. Nowhere, I would venture to say, is better and more efficient work being done for the cause of Catholic training than here."[76]

O'Connell sincerely believed in Catholic schools: the considerable growth during his administration relative to the past documents this conviction. Yet, the ambivalent outcome demands a closer look. Were there circumstances beyond the cardinal's control that prevented realization of his dream of a desk in a Catholic school for every Catholic child? Or was his own determination itself halfhearted and ambivalent? The two questions are difficult to separate from one another. Certainly there were circumstances beyond the hierarchy's control that limited the success of a Catholic educational enterprise. Certainly also the cardinal stopped short of the kind of absolute fiat that might have produced a total Catholic educational system, and that many have thought he had the absolute power to issue. Thus, although the synod he called in 1909 pronounced, in line with the Third Council of Baltimore, that every parish must have a school and that all parents are bound to send their children, its decrees left ample room for noncompliance by exempting parishes where a school was "impossible" and also excusing parents who sufficiently attended to the Christian education of their children at home. In both cases, of parishes and parents, the bishop reserved to himself the right to enforce these provisions.

When looked at in the hard light of reality, the cardinal's achievements would have to be judged far less than spectacular, and far less than his pronouncements might lead one to believe, despite the substantial growth of the Catholic educational enterprise during his era at all levels from elementary school through college, and including a variety of non-school educational activities. The gulf between rhetoric and reality is most pronounced when we look at the core of any community's educational enterprise: elementary schools. Many parishes opened no school at all, some even after being prodded by the cardinal. O'Connell's mandate to build a school in every parish was not carried out universally. On occasion he pressured local pastors to build a school, but the pressure was not uniformly applied. It was so sporadic, in fact, that one is hard pressed to understand what was taking place. This powerful prelate had spoken out clearly and forcefully in favor of parochial schools and against lavish expenditures for elaborate churches—yet much of what happened did not square with those pronouncements.

For instance, the Dorchester area during this period was growing rapidly with the southward movement of the city's Irish population, and O'Connell founded parishes to meet this growth. St. Paul's parish was founded here in 1907, and by the 1920s it had a church worth $264,000, which a noted architect, Ralph Adams Cram, allegedly termed "undoubtedly one of the really fine Catholic churches in the United States."[77] The parish also sported a $46,000 rectory by that time. It had more than 7,000 parishioners by 1930 but never built a school, nor is there any record in the parish file that O'Connell ever brought pressure to do so. St. Angela's in Mattapan was also founded during O'Connell's first flurry of parish building in 1907. Yet, as late as 1930, with 5,000 parishioners it still had no school, though its priests lived in a $60,000 rectory, and again O'Connell apparently brought no pressure upon the pastor to build a school.[78] St. Ambrose parish, founded in Dorchester in 1914, by 1930 had over 4,000 parishioners but no school, although it did have a $212,000 church and a $73,000 rectory. When the pastor had submitted plans for this expensive rectory in 1928, arguing with perhaps dubious reasoning that "the people are anxious to have a new rectory here," O'Connell answered that "a less extensive house would be more serviceable." The pastor then had his architect shave approximately one foot off each side of the house, reducing the cost by $3,000, resubmitted the plans, and got them approved. O'Connell initially objected to an expensive rectory but capitulated after a token adjustment, again without any reference to possibly using the money to open a school.[79]

It was not until 1927, twenty years after assuming control of the diocese, that the cardinal got around to asking his superintendent of schools for a list of parishes without schools, together with an indication of those that might be ready to open one. The superintendent submitted a list of twelve parishes ripe for a school. But, except for St. Stephen's parish in Framingham, O'Connell did not pressure any of these to build a school; indeed, as late as ten years later only seven of the twelve had done so.[80]

Also, during the O'Connell years, no enforceable sanction was levied against Catholics who avoided the Catholic schools.[81] There is no record that he ever adopted the policy used in some dioceses of excommunicating or denying the sacraments of the church to parents who refused to send their children to Catholic school. There was just one instance in 1929, more than twenty years after he assumed command, when he told the sisters and brothers gathered at the twentieth annual Teachers' Institute, "I want it to be known that absolution is not to be given to a woman who sends her children to secular school for no reason except that she wants them to be brought up in a secular way." This remark, which seemed to include mothers but not fathers, seems to have stemmed from O'Connell's disdain for Boston's Catholic social climbers, whom he saw as trying to get into society through their children, but how he hoped to distinguish those mothers who sent their children to other than Catholic schools for "merely social reasons" from those who did it for other reasons remained a mystery.[82] There is no such directive in pastoral letters and other more authoritative pronouncements, so it may have been uttered in a moment of frustrated anger because the cardinal on numerous occasions expressed concern about Catholic social climbers.

Judging from their expenditures on church structures and housing for the clergy, many parishes that could easily have afforded schools neither built them nor were ordered or even pressured by the cardinal to do so. Parishes with a more marginal financial status were never asked to do what was done in certain other dioceses committed to building parochial schools. Already in the nineteenth century a practice had entrenched itself in some dioceses that placed a high priority on Catholic schooling of starting a parish by building first a school and using its auditorium as a church, sometimes for years while the parish collected money for a permanent church.[83] This was not the case in Boston, however: in a new parish where funds were scarce, the practice was to build first the basement and roof it over as a church while funds were collected over a period of years for the "upper" church. Usually only after the entire structure was completed and adequate housing provided for the clergy did thoughts turn to a school, and often not even then. O'Connell did not really alter this procedure, except to insist more than his predecessors on sounder financial planning at each step of the way. He repeatedly refused permission to expand the debt too far or take out too large a mortgage, but is not on record as ever having suggested the alternative of a combined church and school.

Only one or two instances of the church–school concept appear in the Boston diocese during these years, and then only as the result of a local decision. The pastor of the new St. Charles Borromeo parish in Waltham in 1909, "somewhat to the dismay of his people," chose to build a school first, "convinced that nothing else would do so much to consolidate a new parish."[84] O'Connell appears never to have entertained the idea; in fact, his thinking reveals a clear distinction between church and school, and an apparent view that the church had to be a distinctive place on a different and higher plane than a school. Thus, at the dedication of one new parish school he stated, "While I am always happy to bless a church, from whose altars radiate the countless blessings of God to humanity, it gives me almost as much satisfaction to bless a school, which is almost on a par with a church in many ways."[85]

The ambiguity regarding O'Connell's educational policy deepens when one looks at the development of non-parochial Catholic schooling during his administration: it appears that the cardinal paid more attention to it than to the parochial schools. He maintained close contact with Boston College and supported and encouraged its growth and development. He endorsed the establishing of the two women's colleges, Emmanuel and Regis. He also supported the development of exclusive private Catholic academies, in prestigious locations, even purchasing the property to enable the highly respected Madames of the Sacred Heart to open an academy in Newton.[86] The Catholic country day school, too, came into its own during the O'Connell era. He encouraged the founding, for example, in 1927, of the Walnut Park Country Day School in Newton "for Catholic boys from wealthy Catholic families," and the diocese itself ran St. Sebastian's Country Day School for boys in Newton.[87] O'Connell seems to have thought first of Catholic higher institutions and more exclusive schools, and only then of the parish schools. When addressing the Catholic Educational Association in 1909, he characteristically referred first to "our flourishing college, now at the birth of a new and glorious era, our numerous preparatory schools advancing steadily, our many academies for young women," and only then to "our ever growing number of splendidly equipped parish schools."[88]

Yet, given his penchant for "higher" education, he failed to keep pace with what was probably the most significant development in American education, both public and non-public, during the first half of the twentieth century: the development of the high school. When O'Connell took office in 1907 the notion that a high school education ought to belong to everyone was still relatively new and not at all universally accepted, but before his administration was ten years old educators, and most of the public too, no longer questioned the idea. The expansion of the American high school during these years was phenomenal. This era saw the development of the large public high school, usually a comprehensive one to meet the educational needs of a diverse student population that a previous generation, in the 1890s, was never expected to see the inside of. To keep pace with this development Catholic educators followed one or both of two alternatives. One was the "Central Catholic" high school, either run directly by the diocese or shared by a number of parishes in a particular part of the city. The other was to promote the expansion and transformation of the numerous existing small Catholic academies, conducted by individual religious orders, into large private Catholic high schools; usually the elementary grades were dropped and only the four-year high school course was kept. In both instances the result was a large Catholic high school that served a population beyond the parish boundaries.[89]

However, during the O'Connell years neither of these two developments took place in Boston, except for the development of Boston College High School as a separate institution after the college department relocated from the South End to Chestnut Hill in 1913. For the rest, the diocese continued not only to maintain but to expand the idea of the small, often exclusive private academy for girls, modeled on the old European convent school. Beyond that, instead of building multi-parish "central" high schools as the counterpart to the large public high school, the diocese stuck with the informal development, which had begun in the latter part of nineteenth century, of the small local parish high school. These were simply extensions of the parish elementary school, sometimes including only two grades, sometimes expanding into the full four years, but in most cases serving just a handful of the local parish children. Thus, by 1944, the 61 such schools in the entire archdiocese educated only 10,567 youth, an average of only 173 per school. When the Rev. Edward Hurley of St. Matthew's parish in Dorchester proposed a regional (central) Catholic high school for that heavily Catholic area in 1929, he was told that "the matter of a regional high school will be taken care of at a later date"—but it never was.[90]

So we are left with an intriguing question: Why did the O'Connell administration fail to implement its self-imposed mandate to create a total Catholic educational system in Boston? There are probably a variety of causes, a prominent one being the ethnic makeup of Boston Catholics.

By far the dominant Catholic ethnic group, the Irish, in the beginning had expressed little interest in parochial schools—in fact, not much interest in education generally. By the twentieth century the Irish had certainly become interested in education, but they lacked an established tradition of supporting *Catholic* education, as opposed to simply sending their children to the local public schools. This may have accounted to some degree for their failure to follow the cardinal's push for parochial schools.

Among Boston Catholics, there was not a large foreign-language contingent. In other dioceses the foreign-language groups, most of whom embraced the American church's willingness to allow them to create their own separate parishes where their native language was honored and used, not only in their churches but in their own parochial schools.[91] This created a strong incentive among the foreign-language groups to build parochial schools. In fact, the Catholic foreign-language groups in Boston did substantially outdo the Irish in developing parochial schools, but these groups were not as large as in many other American dioceses and were far outnumbered by the Irish. The German Catholics had only one parish in Boston; the single French parish in the city, as well as the six that existed in the suburbs by the end of the O'Connell era, all had schools. The German and French Catholics had committed themselves 100 percent to parochial schools, but they made up, combined, just eight of all the parishes in the city and its ten-mile radius.[92]

Not as many Eastern European Catholics moved to Boston as they did to some Midwestern cities during the huge second migration to America between the 1880s and 1920s. In 1907 there was only one Polish parish in Boston proper, and three more newly formed Polish parishes in Cambridge, Chelsea, and Lynn. By the end of the O'Connell era the Poles had only two parishes in the city and three more in the ten-mile ring. But all the Polish parishes, except a small and struggling one in Hyde Park, had schools.

The Italians, who became a noticeable presence in Boston by the early twentieth century, did not distinguish themselves generally in American cities for their devotion to parochial schooling. Since most of the Italian parishes in the Boston diocese were taken over by religious orders that had resources of their own to draw from, the Italian parishes did much better generally, including the building of schools, than in many other cities. But even then, by 1930, only four of the ten Italian parishes in Boston and its ten-mile radius had schools. They were hardly contributing to the overall percentage of Catholic parishes with schools in the area, nor were they providing leadership or a challenge in the field of Catholic education for others to emulate.

Other ethnic groups that might have added to the Catholic school movement and perhaps provided more incentive for the Irish were not found in abundance in the Boston area. Only one of the two Lithuanian parishes had a school; the other, in South Boston, had been plagued by internal dissension for years, and this may have accounted for its departure from the usual Lithuanian Catholic practice.

When one combines the German, French, Polish, Lithuanian, and Italian parishes in Boston and its ten-mile radius, 66.6 percent of their parishes had schools. Over 70 percent of the Polish and Lithuanian parishes combined had schools, substantially above the diocesan average. Had these groups made up a larger proportion of the Catholic population, they might have made a greater difference. Others, like the small groups of Portuguese, Armenian, and Syrian Catholics, made no practical difference in the overall school movement. Yet, even counting the lack of interest of the Italians and the inability of other foreign-language communities to launch schools because of their dispersion or small size, the national parishes of Boston and its suburbs still had a better parochial school record than the Irish, with over 65 percent having schools by the end of the O'Connell era. But, even combined, they did not pose a challenge to the overwhelmingly more numerous Irish. Because of the preponderance of Irish Catholics in Boston, the kind of intra-Catholic rivalry to build the most and the best Catholic schools that existed in some other Catholic centers never developed in Boston.

The second factor that probably contributed to the statistically modest development of Catholic education in Boston during the O'Connell era may have been the desire of some upwardly mobile Catholics for acceptance into the city's old-line mainstream. They may have seen participation in the long-established Boston public schools, so revered by the city's establishment, as an entrée into that establishment. O'Connell saw this phenomenon as a direct threat to his parochial school campaign. O'Connell's *The Pilot* complained in 1918 that "There have been some cases where what is called the 'better class' of Catholics have frowned upon Catholic education. They wished their children to gain social prestige and so have sent them to schools where the name of God is never heard. The bad example set by such parents affects not only their own children, but others of a vacillating or dubious faith." Despite *The Pilot*'s allegation that "At the price of the character of their children they have purchased a fading social status," many continued to do so.

Ten years later the cardinal still wondered how "a so-called Catholic mother with wealth and such opportunities, can take her children away from a Catholic school." The phenomenon of Catholics with money rejecting the Catholic school annoyed him acutely, so much so that he decided to refuse absolution to those "who, for mere social reasons, deprive their children of their highest birthright." The move apparently had little effect, for a year later he was still asking, "Now, what do you find among the so-called better class? You find as they come into a little more wealth that the spirit of the world controls them." Thus, at least according to their bishop, a certain segment of the Boston Catholic population subtracted from the Church's educational effort because they had become "social climbers." But their numbers could hardly have made a huge difference in the net result.

A third factor was likely more influential as a drag on the development of a large-scale parochial school system in Boston: the apparently longstanding policy regarding the rights of local pastors of parishes. The parish pastor, once the proceeds of collections from parishioners had been allocated to the upkeep of the church and other necessary "running" expenses, was allowed to keep the excess for his own use. Some pastors might choose to pocket the excess dollars rather than allocate them to a fund to establish a parochial school. It would be difficult to accurately assess the degree to which this practice might have detracted from the parochial school effort, but it could have been substantial.

A fourth factor that might have deflected enthusiasm among pastors from the parochial school effort was that many of the Boston Catholic parents and priests had gone to the city's public schools and had come out unscathed, with their faith intact.[93] They, or their faith, may have been ridiculed, but they had survived, and their children could too. The public schools had also profoundly changed in ways that made them a far less likely threat to the faith of Catholic children. In fact, it often became increasingly difficult to distinguish between the public schools and the Catholic parochial schools. What had happened to the Boston public schools is a fascinating story in itself and highly relevant to an understanding of why the city's Catholic schools did not develop more fully during the O'Connell era.

6

Public School/Catholic School: 1914–World War II

Cardinal O'Connell resolutely believed that Catholic schooling was the only adequate answer to the education of Catholic youth, but he did not come close to fully implementing this conviction. Did not actually have as much power that he appeared to have? Were his convictions about Catholic education not as absolute as his bold pronouncements made them sound? Probably both of these possibilities were true, but even more fundamentally, the events that developed on the Boston sociopolitical scene largely took schooling out of O'Connell's hands.

The relationship between Catholicism and the larger society and particularly with the public schools had changed radically by the beginning of the twentieth century. Through much of the nineteenth century Catholics in Boston, as elsewhere, had every reason to shun the public schools, which were often avowedly anti-Catholic. By the O'Connell era, however, the vast majority of Boston Irish Catholics had attended the public schools and apparently their Catholic faith had survived. Accusations that the public schools deliberately undermined the faith of Boston's Catholic children could no longer be made. Especially as Catholic personnel became more prominent in the public schools, it was difficult to distinguish between public and parochial schools. As the Dillingham Commission had reported, almost a quarter of the public school teachers in Boston were Roman Catholics by the time Cardinal O'Connell had assumed the episcopal chair. The proportion was increasing every year, apparently reflecting the fact that the Irish seemed to be attracted to civil service occupations like teaching, which offered job security and respectability as opposed to the insecurity and often disrespect afforded factory and/

or domestic workers. Supervisory positions in the public schools carried even greater respectability, and grew noticeably in terms of numbers and importance among Boston's Roman Catholics during the O'Connell era, though quite independently of his influence.

The change was caused by the area's shifting political and social fortunes. The second half of the nineteenth century had seen the gradual but inevitable rise of Catholic political power in Boston, brought about both by an ever-increasing numerical strength at the polls and by the Irish penchant for and facility in the world of politics. The first Catholic had been elected to the city council in 1857, the first to the Boston School Committee in 1859, and the first to the Board of Aldermen in 1870. But after these minor yet, to Boston establishment eyes, alarming inroads, the progress (or regress, depending on one's point of view) had been ineluctable. By 1884 Irishman Hugh O'Brien had been elected the first Catholic mayor of Boston, and Catholics had gained control of all the important bodies in city government, including the school committee. True, in 1888 their handling of an alleged anti-Catholic incident in a Boston public school, the Travis affair, had triggered a violent backlash that galvanized a large enough segment of the "native" population to drive O'Brien and most high-level Catholics out of office and temporarily reduced their representation on the school committee to a token. Yet, the Catholics could not be held off forever; the balance of power inevitably lay on the side of the Irish. For a decade and more after 1888 Irish Catholic power had been held in check, or, as some thought of it, within the bounds of respectability, by the fact that influential, forward-looking Yankees wielded influence far exceeding their numbers within the Democratic Party, which was the dominant force in city politics and the party to which most of the Irish belonged. The Yankee Democrats had sponsored for public office either Yankees acceptable to the Irish or Irish acceptable to the Yankees. Most notable among the latter had been Patrick Collins. Collins was the kind of man who could and did serve as a hero to the Irish, having been born in Ireland and having made it in the world through a combination of hard work and talent. He could also be firmly endorsed by fellow Yankee Democrats not only because of his proper political views, but because he had pursued a personal course leading to respectability. In face of the inevitable Irish numerical hegemony in the city, forward-looking Yankees preferred to hitch their wagons to stars like Collins rather than fight the hopeless battle to maintain Yankee superiority as such.

But this strategy was doomed to failure because it did not recognize the reality of the political situation in Boston, namely that the Irish already possessed the majority power. They would accept respectable minority status only so long as the Yankees could hold together the coalition, which began to come apart with the death in office in 1905 of Mayor Collins. The struggle for power within the Democratic Party after Collins's death was strictly an Irish affair, as the Yankee Democrats who had held together the coalition were shunted aside. John F. Fitzgerald, with his base in the Irish wards, had emerged victorious first within the party and then in the mayoral elections of 1905.

Fitzgerald's election signaled the demise of effective Yankee–Irish collaboration in Boston politics, for he represented a new generation of Irish politicians who had been waiting in the wings—or, more properly, in the wards and precincts, where they amassed loyal followings of constituents on whom they had bestowed jobs and other favors. These, like Fitzgerald himself, were mostly second-generation Irish Bostonians who had made politics their profession at an early age and who had a strong base in the Irish community. They had never associated much with Yankees, nor did they see any reason to do so. They were, in fact, disdainful of Yankee Boston.

Thus, almost exactly coinciding with Cardinal O'Connell's assumption of ecclesiastical authority in Boston came the emergence of Irish political domination. First Fitzgerald and then James Michael Curley, who bested him for leadership in 1913, dominated Boston politics, supported by lesser but like-minded lights in the city council and most of the important governmental positions.

As for the fate of the public schools in this political transformation, Fitzgerald's newspaper, *The Republic*, had made the public school situation very clear in 1904 when it declared: "Boston is a Catholic city and has been for a considerable period . . . Were the Catholics of Boston to organize and strive to control the schools of Boston, it could be done easily."[1] This inevitability was held off for a time through the skillful maneuvering of coalition-minded Yankees like James Jackson Storrow and the other influential Yankees who had formed the Public School Association (PSA). They got the Irish to agree to an arrangement whereby the Boston School Committee would be for the first time legally limited to five elected members, by mutual agreement two Catholics, two Protestants, and one Jew, all nominated by the PSA. Why the Irish, who already had so much political power, agreed to this is a mystery, but it appears that they were still more in awe of the schools as a cultural institution than they were of the more mundane aspects of city government that they now controlled—or possibly because they were not that interested in education. In any case, for a little more than the first decade of the twentieth century they accepted the strong and respectable, but minority, status allotted them by the PSA. That organization continued to wield strong influence over the public schools for several more years, during which the PSA was even able to nominate the two Catholic Irishmen to run for membership on this influential body.

The Irishmen whom the PSA nominated for the School Committee were invariably respectable, but also invariably of lesser standing than their Yankee counterparts. Thus, while Yankees like Storrow and Joseph Lee, prominent men who claimed ancient New England lineage, wealth, and prominence in the city, served as if by right on the School Committee controlled by the PSA, the committee saw that Irishmen like Thomas J. Kenny, a South Boston lawyer, and William S. Kenny, an East Boston businessmen, were also elected to serve. Both were certainly respectable, but not prominent city-wide and not troublemakers either. John Fitzgerald, who apparently disdained this arrangement, argued that the PSA deliberately put up less prominent Irishmen so they would not be as influential on the committee as Storrow and his colleagues.[2] It became clear early on that the Irish, influenced by their leaders like Fitzgerald, were not about to stand off and let these "proper" Bostonians continue to run the show.

As early as 1910 the foundations of this "cooperative" arrangement began to break down when Storrow, the architect of the School Committee arrangement that would keep Irish members in the minority, foolishly over-reached his position by challenging Fitzgerald for election to the mayoralty itself. Predictably, Fitzgerald made Storrow's record in the schools an issue in the campaign, and thus with one blow returned the schools into the political arena from which the reformers had tried to remove them. Storrow was defeated, and Fitzgerald again became mayor. The alliance between the established prominent Yankee Democrats and the upstart Irishmen was breaking down.

Then, when fellow Irishman James Michael Curley beat out Fitzgerald for the mayoralty in 1913, the alliance eroded still further. Curley delighted in making School Committee elections fair game for politics. The Catholic *Boston Pilot*, too, angry especially over the PSA's control of the coalition committee and therefore its ability to control appointments to the high-level school personnel positions, renewed its campaign against the PSA, claiming it was "of the same ilk with that arrogant band of dictators known as the 'Good Government Association'." In 1917 *The Pilot* even claimed that one candidate pushed by the PSA "is known to represent a certain class of capitalists who are trying to gain control of education so that the children of the immigrant and the wage earner generally may be kept out of the professions and be forced to learn trades and thus maneuvered into a state of insurmountable dependence. It is for this reason that he is such a warm advocate of 'vocational training and allied fads'."[3]

Though this interpretation of events in Boston may have seemed odd coming from the cardinal's militantly conservative and anti-Communist newspaper, it represented common opinion among Catholics in the city. It also helps explain why by 1915 the idea of a coalition School Committee made up of a fixed proportion of Protestants, Catholics, and a Jew had completely broken down. Catholic voters had ignored the agreement to limit their representation on the School Committee and had broken the PSA's hold on the nominations for and election to the committee. The coalition had splintered and political realities had taken over. After that year the Irish went their own way, and, throughout the O'Connell era and beyond, always maintained a controlling majority on the committee. It was a decisive advantage they were not to relinquish, enabling them to determine public school policy almost at will.

Further, the Irish Catholics who emerged on the School Committee after 1915 tended to be much more forceful and prominent, and also much more publicly Catholic and Irish. Men like Edward M. Sullivan, a prominent trial lawyer and assistant district attorney for Suffolk County, for example, outspokenly defended his mother country as well as his church against all comers, and argued forcefully for "a return of the schools of Boston to the fundamentals of public school education."[4] His namesake on the committee, Michael H. Sullivan, judge of the Dorchester District Court and a professor at Suffolk University Law School, was also prominent as president of the Charitable Irish Society.[5] He was not a man who could be controlled by the Boston elite.

So dominant had the Catholic control of the School Committee become by the teens that *The Boston Transcript*, a bastion of Brahmin superiority, which had habitually published detailed news of the committee, including the complete text of its monthly meetings, now seldom ran even the biggest news items. It was almost as if *The Transcript* had written off the public schools as lost forever. Indeed, as far as the interests of its subscribers were concerned, they probably were, and for several decades *The Transcript* simply abandoned the fruitless effort to influence Boston public school policy.

As just one example, *The Transcript* did not even mention a stormy meeting of the committee more than a decade later, in June 1939, that probably marked the nadir (if there was a single one) of Yankee influence on the committee. Yankee Joseph Lee, now a minority of one on the committee, had complained that when the students of Roxbury Memorial High School asked for speakers on both sides of "the Spanish question," they were threatened with denial of graduation by the principal, an Irish Catholic, whose threat was upheld by every member of the School Committee but Lee; the committee labeled such a request as subversive. Lee accused Chairman Henry J. Smith of religious intolerance and discrimination, assuming that the majority opinion had been dictated by the social teaching of the Catholic Church. This precipitated stormy proceedings, including the demand for retraction, a vote of confidence in Smith, and also Lee's accusations that the Catholic Church runs the schools and, though not teaching its specifically religious tenets, imposes its positions on social questions, calling all opposing positions communistic and subversive. But Lee's plea "to make sure that a boy can go through school without having to revamp his ideas and his family's ideas in regard to social, political or international questions, in accord with policies taken by the Church," was smugly, even abusively dismissed as groundless and having nothing to do with religion.[6]

Thus, from roughly the mid-1910s, the Irish Catholics controlled not only the mayoralty but the School Committee. The committee had come a long way, indeed, since it was set up to guard the cherished Puritan tradition; now it ensured that Irish and Catholic interests would be satisfied. No longer did the Irish Catholics have to depend on the PSA for a token favor here and there, like the inclusion of a little Irish history as an option in the high schools, some Gaelic in night school, and the naming of schools after prominent Catholics like the former Catholic bishops of Boston. The real prizes, particularly the most influential personnel positions, were now theirs.

In fact, it was failure to secure appointment of what appeared to be a highly eligible Catholic for the six-year term of Superintendent of Schools in 1906 and again in 1912 that finally dissolved the attempt at coalition School Committee politics. In 1912 *The Pilot* announced that Catholic candidates were rejected simply "because they were Catholics." Conceding that "We have been rather careless in regard to this matter of schools," *The Pilot* outlined its perception of the problem and the solution:

> We are not outsiders. We do not ask that a man be chosen simply because he is a Catholic. But we do demand that our Catholic men who have given their best efforts to our schools not be discriminated against, when there is a question of promotion, simply because they are Catholics. That, in the present instance, is the real reason for the rejection of Boston teachers and the appointment of an outsider. Surely it is time that the Catholics of Boston broke up this monopoly and show that they are no longer to be deceived by the cry of "keep the schools out of politics," which means "keep Catholics out of the schools."[7]

Six years later, when the next appointment of a superintendent rolled around, *The Pilot* did not even comment. It did not have to, for by 1915 the Boston School Committee had come firmly and permanently into the hands of a Catholic majority, so firmly that the appointment of a Catholic superintendent seemed a foregone conclusion—and it was. In fact, all three principal candidates were not only Boston school insiders but publicly active Catholics. One of them, Frank Thompson, a lifelong Catholic who had already held several supervisory positions in the Boston public schools, was named superintendent. After Thompson died just a year later, the committee selected Jeremiah Burke, a devout Catholic who had already held significant supervisory positions in the Boston schools and who had sought the superintendent's position openly for over ten years. It was a position that Catholic candidates would maintain for the duration of O'Connell's tenure and, in fact, for decades to come. Burke dominated Boston public school policy through the 1920s, serving ten years as superintendent until his death in office in 1931, at the beginning of another six-year term.

Burke, who had excellent educational credentials, was not a political spoilsman for Catholic interests but did maintain close ties with the Catholic Church. For example, Cardinal O'Connell felt free to call on him to use his influence to help kill the Towner Sterling Bill for federal involvement in education, as well as for other favors that might help Catholic educational interests. Burke was in frequent contact with the cardinal or the cardinal's assistants and placed more emphasis on religion, particularly Catholicism, in the public schools. However, he appears to have done so in good faith and not as a reprisal against the decades of alleged religious prejudice that many Boston Catholics still apparently chafed under.

In particular, Burke worked to implement policies he considered essential to education, especially those related to religious belief and contrary to what he considered the pernicious influence of more modern movements such as progressivism. In its place, Burke advocated character education. But, he observed, "in later years a shadow obscured the horizon of our idealism . . . While in the quest of strange gods we discovered a pernicious philosophy which would elevate success above virtue and knowledge above wisdom . . . Such words as 'duty,' 'conscience', 'sin' became obsolete, even in the vocabularies of school men." But now, reasoned Burke, after the cataclysm of the First World War, the world was turning again to "its ancient idealism and faith." We are recognizing once again, said Burke, that "no civilization can prosper which ignores great moral and spiritual realities." The schools stood ready to do their part in this great renewal, "for the development of spiritual habits; of unselfish conduct, of unfaltering loyalty to conviction; of moral robustness and vigor; of righteousness of living; and of the ability to distinguish between right and wrong."[8]

Burke acknowledged that religion itself could not be taught in the public schools, but the character education program he developed and implemented went as far as it could in that direction, including the insertion of religious heroes wherever possible as models of upright character. Specifically Catholic heroes came in for their share of adulation. Thus, in the single complete "specimen" outline published for the program, for grade six, one reads that "the spirit of morality must dominate the entire life of the school." The list of appropriate reference books included *The Catholic Encyclopedia* and *Murray's Catholic Heroes.* The curriculum suggested John Boyle O'Reilly and Father Damien as examples of self-reliance. Others recommended as exemplars of various virtues were St. Elizabeth of Hungary, Joan of Arc, Sir Thomas More, Pere Marquette, Thomas à Kempis, St. Francis of Assisi, St. Columba, St. Isaac Jogues, the founder of the St. Vincent de Paul Society, St. Teresa, and St. Patrick. Indeed, the "story of Ireland's devotion to nationality" was suggested as a prime example of loyalty to an ideal. And, in an obvious slight, the kindness of the "French missionaries to the Indians" as well as the success of New York as the result of allowing religious freedom was contrasted with "the effect on the Puritans of their refusal to allow others to become members of their church." A reading of the document leaves little doubt as to who was in command of the Boston public schools.[9]

It was in the character education program introduced by Burke that the public schools of Boston came closest to the Catholic schools. Not only did Catholics control the public schools, but they taught essentially the same morality in both. Indeed, a comparison of the specific virtues inculcated in the character education programs of both the public and the parochial schools reveals little difference except in nomenclature: self-control, duty, and obedience in both; self-reliance in one, self-respect in the other; reliability in one, honor in the other; good workmanship in one, love of one's work in the other; kindness in one, unselfishness in the other; loyalty in one, fidelity in the other. While the public school program put a little more stress on the bodily virtues like health and clean play, the Catholic one added a few more specifically Christian virtues like forgiveness and humility. But the core of both programs was nearly identical.[10]

Certainly the Catholic-inspired and -directed character education program in the public schools added one more justification for Catholic parents who wished to send their children to public school. Not only did the Catholics run the schools; they had succeeded, to a degree at least, in "Catholicizing" the curriculum. The character education program was also explicitly meant to counter what were considered the deleterious effects on children brought on by the "progressive" education movement, which was popular in certain quarters at the time but abhorred by O'Connell and his ilk. Thus, the Catholic-inspired character education program essentially did away with progressivism in the Boston public schools, and in the process came extremely close to introducing religion itself.

In fact, character education, not progressivism, became the most significant and widely heralded public school development in Boston during the 1920s, and was formally adopted in 1924. Character education had been introduced formally into the Boston public schools in 1921 and mirrored the program already operating in the Catholic schools. Communication about character education seems to have passed freely beginning in the early 1920s between Cardinal O'Connell; Father Augustine Hickey, the superintendent of Boston Catholic schools; and Arthur Gould, the assistant superintendent of Boston public schools and a devout Catholic. This was just one of numerous examples of public school–Catholic school cooperation that emerged once the public schools had come under Catholic control.

The issue of Catholic teachers in the public schools had long been a sticky one. Much more than the supervisory positions, this was not just a matter of Catholic power over school policy, but a matter of jobs, especially for aspiring young women. Teaching had become in the nineteenth century a position to which the daughters of many immigrants aspired. While it did not pay that much, it offered solid respectability, and it certainly beat other alternatives like domestic service or the factory. Thus, by the late nineteenth century an ever-growing number of Irish Catholic young ladies had been seeking entrance into the Boston schools as teachers; the Boston Normal School, the training school for teachers, was said to be at least half Catholic by the turn of the century.[11] The proportion of Catholic teachers in the public schools was ever on the increase, though it is difficult to determine the exact proportion since they were not required to state their religious affiliation. Over the years various estimates were flung back and forth, often no doubt distorted by the heat of controversy. Despite alleged attempts to limit the number of Catholic teachers earlier, the proportion had already become high at the beginning of the twentieth century. By 1908 the Dillingham Commission of the U.S. Congress found that 23.8 percent of Boston teachers were either the children of Irish immigrants or Irish immigrants themselves. If one added the uncounted third-generation Irish, plus Catholics of other ethnic origins, the actual percentage of Catholic teachers in the schools must have been substantially higher.[12].

Despite the predominance of women in the profession, by the 1920s fully 30 percent of the male graduates of Boston College joined the staff of the Boston public school system. By 1930 the list of teachers, both male and female, in the Boston public schools read like a roster from the Ancient Order of Hibernians. Taking only the very most obvious Irish names, there were 78 Sullivans, 50 Murphys, 37 O'Briens, 25 Kelleys, and 24 Lynches; one teacher in ten was a Barry, Brennan, Fitzgerald, Kelley, Kelly, Lynch, McCarthy, Murphy, O'Brien,

Riley, Ryan, Shea, Sheehan, Sullivan, Sweeney, or Walsh, not to mention the numerous Careys, Carneys, Dolans, Dooleys, Finns, and Fitzpatricks.[13]

In short, the Catholic presence, overwhelmingly Irish, in the Boston public schools had become dominant by the 1910s. By the 1920s Catholics were in almost total control, from the school committee, to the superintendency, to the assistant superintendency, right down to the teachers' college, the headmasterships, and the positions in the classrooms themselves.

Given all this, it is not surprising that many Catholics saw little difference between the parochial schools and the public schools; in many respects both were now Catholic school systems. This may explain why Cardinal O'Connell's promotion of parochial schools fell short of a crusade, and why the large majority of Catholics felt comfortable frequenting the public schools. Catholics controlled both school systems and established many interrelationships between them at every level. For example, the principal of one parochial school, who had gone to public normal school before entering the convent, had two sisters teaching in the Boston public schools and "really depended very much on them to carry to her any new things that were going on in the schools in Boston."[14] Relationships like this one, not uncommon among Boston Irish Catholics, expanded the communication between the two school systems to the intimate, family level.

Teacher training became a shared responsibility of the two systems. Prominent Catholics in the public school system were called upon regularly to lecture at the summer institute for parochial school teachers, and they offered courses for them at the local Catholic colleges: Boston, Emmanuel, and Regis Colleges. During the 1920s alone three present or future superintendents of the public schools were listed on the faculties of Boston's Catholic colleges, plus three assistant superintendents, three deans and professors from the teachers' college, two headmasters, and nine teachers. Yearly the superintendent of Catholic schools sought permission from the cardinal to appoint these people to teach the sisters in-service courses, frequently assuring him that people like assistant superintendent Mary Mellyn or future superintendent Arthur Gould were not only "recognized authorities" but "exemplary Catholics."[15]

The communication went both ways. Jesuit-run Boston College in particular exercised a continuing influence over public education. Its graduates had been entering the public schools as teachers in such numbers that by 1913 the college had organized a Teachers Club intended "to keep together in friendly co-operation the graduates of the College engaged in the Public School service." Then, to meet the demand for graduate-level teacher education, the Boston College School of Education came into existence in 1919, almost coincident with the Catholic ascendancy in the public schools. Conveniently, "with the opening of the School of Education an arrangement was effected between the School Committee of Boston and Boston College whereby courses leading to the degree of Master of Arts are offered to residents of the City of Boston who are graduates of colleges approved by the Board of Superintendents."[16] What this neat arrangement did was allow college graduates to substitute work at Boston College for the formerly required teacher training courses at the Boston Teachers College.

Even neater was the fact that the two principal participants in this cooperative venture were the Rev. James Mellyn, a Jesuit priest and director of all teacher education activities at Boston College, and his sister Mary, assistant superintendent in charge of teacher development for the public schools. James provided the coursework for the students; Mary supervised their practice teaching. This homey situation probably constituted the capstone of public–Catholic school cooperation at the grassroots level. James taught the principles of Catholic education to both public and Catholic school teachers from his school of education at Boston College. Mary not only supervised teachers from her position in the school system but regularly taught courses at Boston College and even received an honorary degree there in 1925. The relationship could hardly have been closer: the training of teachers for both systems was literally "all in the family."

Catholic school advocates, including Cardinal O'Connell, continued to emphasize the uniqueness of the parochial school. While the public schools had undertaken the teaching of morality, they had to keep it divorced from explicit religious teaching. In this the two systems differed, and Catholic school spokesmen made the most of that difference.[17] Thus, though now largely under Catholic hegemony and no longer explicitly offending Catholic beliefs and practices, the public schools fell short of the explicit inculcation and support of specific Catholic interests and beliefs. In Catholic schools, the garb of the sister teachers themselves spoke of religious orientation, as did the crucifixes and the holy pictures that adorned the classroom walls, the occasional visits by the parish priest, the closing of school on important holy days, and the marching of the children to the nearby church on others. The prayers before class and the four common prayer periods each day were constant religious reminders. The plan of studies adopted in 1923 allotted 150 minutes each week to the formal teaching of religion in the parochial schools, insisting that "Religion is the great motive power of life in the classroom of the Catholic School. Every lesson taught must include a presentation of the truths and standards of Christ in such a manner as to touch the life of the child."[18]

In addition to those 150 weekly minutes, religion colored other areas of the curriculum. In the teaching of American history, for example, the 1923 course of studies admonished teachers to "Direct the pupils' attention to the great share Catholics have had in the discovery and civilization of America, in its commercial and political prosperity." It was especially concerned that "the children should be taught the Catholic side of American History, especially the stories of the self-sacrificing missionaries who were among the first explorers; also biographies of those great Catholics whose names brighten the pages of the past, or Catholics who have played a prominent part in shaping the nation." The syllabus detailed these heroes, from the Carrolls of Maryland to the cardinals of the American church.

The English syllabus recommended the frequent use of religious topics for the children's written compositions, suggesting such themes as "What My Conscience Tells Me," "My Patron Saint," "How I Pray at Mass," and "Keeping Lent Well." In the choice of reading material teachers were told to "use freely selections from Father Abram [sic] Ryan, Father Blunt, Father Tabb, Father Garesche, and Denis McCarthy" in the first grade.

Even geography was to be used for "the inculcation of the fundamental truths, particularly of man's dependence on God Who in His Providence has created the earth as a wonderful home for man." And physiology and hygiene, in addition to teaching the specifics of cleanliness and warning third graders about the dangers of cigarettes, was to develop an appreciation of the human body as a "temple of the Holy Ghost."

All of these prescriptions were duly carried out in textbooks especially written for the Catholic schools. Not a single one of the textbooks reported most in use in the parochial schools of 1915 was on the approved list for the Boston public schools; they were too explicitly impregnated with religion.[19]

No doubt in addition to religion the parochial school communicated to some youngsters a more comfortable sense of belonging than did the public school. In the "bi-lingual" schools, as Catholic authorities called them, even though by the 1920s state law required and enforced teaching in English as the medium of instruction, French, Polish, or even Italian could still be taught, as well as the mother history and literature. And in the Irish Catholic schools, which constituted by far the majority, the teaching of Irish history was mandatory, at the instigation of the cardinal himself.

The distinctively religious and ethnic atmosphere was not the only thing that distinguished the parochial school from the public in the minds of at least some Catholics. Despite the renewed emphasis on character training and discipline in the public schools, their reputation had suffered greatly in the minds of many as a result of the progressive movement. The notion that the public schools had "gone soft" was very much in the air, and not just from Catholic critics. Whether their argument was based on truth or not, the Catholic schoolmen made much of the idea that Catholic schools stood for discipline while the public schools at least tolerated, if they did not out and out endorse, anarchy.

The parochial schools projected an image of firm discipline tempered by loving care from the dedicated sisters. In the educational philosophies of the religious communities who taught most of the Boston parochial school-children, one sees just such an intent. Emphasis was placed on "enforcing good habits of order, cleanliness, industry, and economy."[20] "Good order and discipline" were mandated in general and spelled out in considerable detail, with the children made to "form into columns and march to places." All class movements were to be "executed quietly, quickly and with military precision." Teachers were told to "tolerate as little noise in the school as possible;" in general "everything had to be very exact."[21] These were hardly progressive approaches to the education of children—far from it—and no doubt this firm attention to discipline attracted the more conservative Boston Catholic parents.

Despite the rigor, the sisters also stressed the humane treatment of their pupils. The Sisters of Notre Dame were advised to "rule by kindness rather than severity. For some of your pupils their school days may be the only happy period of their lives; therefore, make them all sunshine." The sisters were told never to use corporal punishment; not to punish faults done from ignorance or by accident; and, if punishment were necessary, afterwards to forgive and forget. "In class we should be mild, yet firm," the sisters were taught; "simple, but dignified; amiable, though grave."[22]

The Sisters of St. Joseph's teachers' manual expressed this same humane concern, for the most part spelled out in practical form. The sisters were told not to use corporal punishment and never to punish without reason, but also simply to avoid problems of this nature by keeping the children busy in a constructive way; to try to keep children quiet without something useful to do was "cruelty." "Kind words and a cheerful, helpful manner, are most potent influences in governing children," the sisters were reminded. Teachers were told not to punish children by making them stay in during recess, because the youths needed the recreation. They were also advised to finish all their work during the assigned hours, for "to keep the pupils longer is barbarous." Concern for the children's sensitivities was paramount, too. "No good teacher scolds;" rather, "Encouragement inspires confidence, and children more than others need it." Teachers were told "not to wound the sensibilities of the duller pupils by making comparisons of one child with another."[23] The emphasis on discipline always tempered by humaneness, though it was no doubt not always carried out in practice given the overcrowded classrooms and overloaded schedules, must have added to the conviction among some Catholics that the parochial school was the proper place for their children.

By at least the 1920s, the public and parochial schools of Boston had taken giant steps toward one another in theory and practice under the leadership of the Catholics who presided over both systems. The public schools taught the same morality as the Catholic ones, and, in the generous use of Catholic saints and heroes as moral exemplars, they came dangerously close to breaching the wall of separation between religion and the public school. The public schools no longer championed Yankee superiority; the presence of so many Irish teachers and administrators assured at the minimum a fair attention to Celtic interests. And the notion that discipline and humane caring was the exclusive preserve of the parochial school was not shared by all Catholics.

Though Cardinal O'Connell and his circle continued to preach the need for Catholic children to attend parochial schools, parents knew that with the public schools now controlled by Catholics, their children's Catholic faith would no longer be derided or undermined. The choice of a public versus a parochial school could no longer be viewed as a choice between good and evil, God and Satan, Christ and Anti-Christ—and not even the Church tried to pretend that it was. This helps explain why the hierarchy did not try to enforce parochial school attendance as a moral obligation, why so many Catholic parents chose public schools, and why the Cardinal's dream of a total Catholic school triumph did not materialize.

Other factors might help explain the less-than-enthusiastic development of parochial schools during the O'Connell era. Even before Catholics had gained so much control over the City's public schools, most Boston Catholics had attended the public schools and apparently had maintained their Catholic faith. This served as a detriment to parochial school development because the inertia of the past deeply affected the present. Catholic leaders recognized this: as early as the 1890s, during one of the intermittent attempts to beef up the parochial school effort, *The Sacred Heart Review* had noted that "The present generation have nearly all been educated in the public schools and we have become so accustomed to consider them better than any other, that now that Catholic schools are being established in many parishes, there is found a strange reluctance on the part of many to send their children to them."[24] O'Connell referred to "the former tepidity of interest" as one of the obstacles he had to overcome in building up the Catholic system.

Actually, the inertia and the "tepidity of interest" were not confined to the children's parents: many of the Boston priests had been educated in the public schools, again without apparent harm. O'Connell was one of these. Some, like the cardinal, had experienced anti-Catholic and anti-Irish prejudice there, but some, again like the cardinal, had met with understanding and supportive teachers. For this reason many of the clergy probably did not experience the parochial school movement as an urgent necessity.

Another factor that may have dampened the enthusiasm of some Boston pastors for building parochial schools was the tradition of allowing pastors to keep any monies left over after payment of parish expenses, in addition to their regular salaries and special collections such as that at Easter designated for their personal use. For example, the cardinal, who had made himself rector of St. Cecilia's parish in the Back Bay even though he did not reside there, in addition to the usual salary and special collections, also accepted checks for the "surplus," sometimes amounting to thousands of dollars in a single year. Some pastors accumulated considerable wealth in this way. The cardinal not only participated in this system but made no attempt to change it, though he donated the excess dollars accumulated in the parish officially assigned to him to other charitable causes. The practice, however, must have influenced some pastors to forego the added expense of a parochial school in favor of their own pockets.

Economics certainly influenced the parochial school movement in other ways. Earlier explanations of why Boston did not have an extensive parochial school system tended to stress the poverty of its Catholic population, but the reality was more complicated. For one thing, the Boston tradition did not include the solution to poverty adopted elsewhere of building combination church–schools. In fact, in Boston the trend had been just the reverse, in favor of monumental churches that severely taxed the financial resources of the Catholic population. One finds in nineteenth-century Boston Catholic rhetoric frequent and proud reference to churches built "on a scale of magnificence hitherto unparalleled in this region." Catholics tended to measure the status of their churches by the height of the steeple, with special honor going to those adorning churches already sitting on high ground.

O'Connell did attempt to put a stop to the monumentalism. "We have work besides piling stone upon stone," he declared in 1909. He adopted a policy against "enormous, costly churches, modeled upon the cathedrals or basilicas of Europe, and involving mountainous debts," and favored instead "simple, inexpensive, but graceful churches, unpretentious but devotional."[25] He tried to maintain a tight control over the amount of debt allowed in each parish, though his efforts to stamp out monumentalism did not entirely succeed, possibly in part due to the poor example of his own extravagant personal tastes. He never turned to the more radical economic solution of mandating or even encouraging the church–school concept. Thus, poverty, neither in the nineteenth century nor during the O'Connell era, adequately explains the relative dearth of parochial schools.

Other ethnic groups that might have added to the Catholic school movement and perhaps provided more incentive for the Irish were not found in
abundance in the Boston area. The French, for example, mostly of Canadian
origin, were vehemently dedicated to parochial schools of their own where
not just Catholicism but French culture could be propagated. In face of the
threat to ban languages other than English from the schools of Massachusetts
during the 1910s, the French took considerable initiative in opposition. But
the French had only one struggling parish in Boston itself, founded in 1880
and already declining in numbers by the O'Connell era. Its parishioners were
so scattered over the city that they could not send their children the long
distances to a French-speaking parochial school.[26] The Eastern European
Catholics, too, might have served as a better model for the parochial school
movement had they come to the Boston area in the numbers they did to some
Midwestern cities during the huge second migration to America between the
1880s and 1920s.

But they did not. In 1907 there was only one Polish and one Lithuanian
parish in Boston proper. By 1944 the Poles had only two parishes in the city
and three more in the ten-mile ring, while the Lithuanians had only one in the
city and another outside. True to their reputation elsewhere, all the Polish parishes except a small and struggling one in Hyde Park had schools. The Poles
in Boston as elsewhere tried to maintain a tight cohesiveness, even founding
their own orphanage and sponsoring several newspapers from time to time.
Only one of the two Lithuanian parishes had a school. The other, in South
Boston, had been plagued by internal dissension for years, and this may have
accounted for the parish's departure from the usual Lithuanian Catholic practice. Even so, more than 70 percent of the Polish and Lithuanian parishes combined had schools, substantially above the diocesan average. Had these groups
made up a larger proportion of the Catholic population, as they did in other
American cities, they might have made a greater difference. Others, like the
small groups of Portuguese, Armenian, and Syrian Catholics, made no practical difference in the overall school movement.

Even counting the admitted lack of interest of the Italians and the inability of other foreign-language communities to launch a school because
of their dispersion or extremely small size, the national parishes of Boston
and its immediate suburbs still had a better parochial school record by the
end of the O'Connell era than the Irish-dominated territorial parishes.
Of the national parishes, more than 65 percent had schools in 1944; the
figure for the territorial ones was 60 percent. Thus, in the last analysis,
those ethnic groups large enough to provide the exemplary leadership for
Catholic schooling in Boston lacked the dedication, and those ethnic groups

dedicated to the idea of Catholic schooling lacked the size to serve as a model for the rest. The kind of intra-Catholic rivalry to build the most and the best Catholic schools that existed in some other Catholic centers never developed in Boston.

The educational achievements of Boston Catholicism during the O'Connell era were considerable: the number of parochial schools more than doubled and their enrollments grew by over 60 percent. Catholic secondary school enrollment, which had never been very large, increased by over 600 percent during the same period, while Catholic colleges went from fewer than 200 students to more than 4,000. Organizationally, too, the O'Connell regime brought the Catholic schools of Boston to maturity. During this period, both in official doctrine as expressed by the cardinal and in actual practice, the Boston archdiocese came somewhat more in line with the American Catholic pattern. Although the majority of Catholic children continued to attend the public schools, the public system was now firmly in the hands of Catholic, mostly Irish, personnel, from the teachers to the school principals, to the superintendent, and to the Boston School Committee itself.

Epilogue

By the 1920s the Boston public schools were solidly in the hands of the city's Catholics, mostly Irish. The majority of the members on the Boston School Committee were Catholic. The school superintendent was Catholic. The principals of all the prominent public schools, including Boston Latin School, were Catholic. A substantial and ever-growing percentage of the city's public school teachers were Catholic. The large majority of all of these were of Irish descent. The natural result was that the morality taught in the public schools was, if not officially, at least in fact consonant with Roman Catholic teaching. This prominence of Irish Catholics in the public schools would continue for several decades.

At the same time, other significant changes were beginning to take place on the Boston educational scene. One was the fact that the highly education-oriented Jewish population was leaving Boston for the more education-rich suburbs such as Brookline, thus removing from the Boston public schools a significant educational asset. A second new ingredient was the challenge to Boston's public schools from new sources, in particular the significant influx of blacks migrating from the South, which produced years of stress and conflict. And then, by the 1960s, came large numbers of immigrants from Asian countries as well as Latin America and the Caribbean.

A third ingredient was the fact that Cardinal O'Connell's efforts since his arrival in Boston in 1907 to develop a more vital parochial school system were beginning to pay off handsomely, despite their slow start. Thus, although the city's parochial schools educated only about 23,000 students in 1920, more than a decade after his arrival in Boston, by 1960, thanks especially to the hard work of the Sisters of Notre Dame and the Sisters of St. Joseph, they had more than 52,000. The public schools were no longer a monopoly.

Notes

CHAPTER 1

1. See Oscar Handlin, *Boston's Immigrants: A Study in Acculturation 1790–1865* (New York: Athenaeum, 1941), 17ff.; Howard Mumford Jones, *The Many Voices of Boston, A Historical Anthology, 1630–1975*, ed. Howard Mumford Jones and Bessie Zaban Jones (Boston: Little, Brown, 1975), 157ff.; Roger Lane, *Policing the City, 1822–1885* (New York: Athenaeum, 1971), 3ff.

2. Stanley K. Schultz, *The Culture Factory, Boston Public Schools, 1789–1860* (New York: Oxford University Press, 1973), 211.

3. James Russell Lowell, *My Study Windows* (Boston: Houghton Mifflin, 1895), 95–96.

4. Edmund Quincy, *The Life of Josiah Quincy of Massachusetts* (Boston: Ticknor and Fields, 1867), 396.

5. Robert H. Lord, John E. Sexton, and Edward T. Harrington, *History of the Archdiocese of Boston in the Various Stages of Its Development, in Three volumes, 1604–1943*, vol. 1 (Boston: Pilot Publishing Company, 1945), 133, from Mass. Council Records, 8:71, August 22, 1724. Hereafter this source is referred to as "Lord," the principal author of the three-volume work.

6. Governor Belcher to Sheriff of Suffolk, March 17, 1731; quoted in Lord I, 158–9.

7. Lord I makes numerous references to various Dudleian Lectures; see 218, 235, 244, 258, 344, 497, 772–4.

8. John Adams, "On the Canon and the Feudal Law," *Boston Gazette*, August 12, 19, September 30, 1765 (Works, III, 449–54), in Lord I, 236–7.

9. See Lord I, 236, 251, 259; John Adams, *Diary*, September 11, 1774 (Works, II, 380) in Lord I, 270.

10. Lord I, 270–1; 276–7; 285–7; 321ff.

11. See Lord I, 561.

12. Lord I, 156, from G. Donovan, "Pre-Revolutionary Irish in Massachusetts" (Ph.D thesis, St. Louis University, 1931); George Francis Donovan, *The Pre-Revolutionary Irish in Massachusetts, 1620–1775* (Menasha, WI: George Banta Publishing Company, 1932).

13. Lord I, 606.

14. Lord I, 604.

15. Lord II, 126; the *Jesuit*, January 16, 1830; Bishop Benedict Fenwick Memoranda, Boston Archdiocesan Archives (BAA), December 31, 1825. The *Jesuit* was the first Catholic newspaper published in Boston, by Bishop Benedict Fenwick. See Chapter 2.

16. Lord II, 35.

17. Lord II, 188–9.

18. Lord II, 190; I, 620–2.

19. Father Thayer to Bishop John Carroll, January 6, 1790, in Lord I, 425.

20. Lord I, 512.

21. From Fr. Matignon to Bishop John Carroll, May 1, 1798, Baltimore Diocesan Archives., 5G9. In Lord I, 545.

22. Lord I, 559.

23. Lord I, 580–3.

24. Lord I, 604, Matignon to Carroll, January 23, 1802, Baltimore Dioc. Arch.

25. Rev. Mathew O'Brien to Archbishop Carroll, September 16, 1813, Baltimore Dioc. Arch. Quoted in Lord I, 643.

26. Bishop Cheverus to Carroll, March 18, 1814, Baltimore Dioc. Arch., in Lord I, 643.

27. Cheverus to Father Brute, October 9, 1816, University of Notre Dame Arch., in Lord I, 697. Not every Catholic was destitute; John Magner, a pillar of the church, died in 1816 at the age of 81, leaving $24,000 from a blacksmith business and real estate (Lord I, 675).

28. Lord II, 202, and see *Columbian Sentinel*, June 21, 1823, and *Boston Patriot and Daily Mercantile Advertiser*, June 23, 1823.

29. Ray Allen Billington, *The Protestant Crusade* (New York: Macmillan, 1938), 44; see Lord I, 771.

30. See Lord II, 184–5; 649.

31. Quoted in Lord II, from *Boston Recorder*, May 5, 1818, January 1, 1820, April 19, 1821; *Christian Watchman*, January 1 and 22, 1820, November 23, 1822.

32. Lord I, 427–42.

33. Ibid., 500.

34. Ibid., 555.

35. Ibid., 698, 705–6.

36. Ibid., 493.

37. See Walter Muir Whitehill, *A Memorial to Bishop Cheverus with a Catalogue of the Books Given by Him to the Boston Athenaeum* (Boston: Boston Athenaeum, 1951); and Lord I, 558, 581–2.

38. Cheverus to Cardinal Litta, Arch. Prop Fide, Am. Cent., III, 416, 417, June 18, 1817, quoted in Lord I, 696–7.

39. Lord I, 767–8.

40. Lord I, 769–70; Lord II, 182. Failure to discern that friendship toward Catholics in Boston came mainly from Unitarians, and to an extent from Episcopalians, during the entire period prior to the Potato Famine immigration of the late 1840s was probably the source of Oscar Handlin's mistaken conclusion that Boston experienced little anti-Catholicism until mid-century. See Oscar Handlin, *Boston's Immigrants: A Study in Acculturation 1790–1865*. Rev. and enl. ed. (Cambridge, MA: Belknap Press of Harvard University Press, 1991).

41. Lord I, 768–71.

42. Ibid., 770. The documentation for this statement is a bit shaky.

43. See Schultz, *Culture Factory*, 5.

44. Ibid., 5–7.

45. *The New England primer improved, For the more easy attaining the true reading of English. To which is added the assembly of divines' catechism.* Glasgow, MDCCLXXXI. [1781]. *Eighteenth Century Collections Online.* Gale. CUNY- College of Staten Island. April 13, 2017, pp. 11–12.

46. Schultz, *Culture Factory*, 11.

47. Ibid., 8–14.

48. Ibid., 14–15.

49. Schultz, *Culture Factory*, 16–17, lists *The Child's Companion, Beauties of the Bible, American Preceptor*, by Caleb Bingham; *An American Selection*, the third part of Noah Webster's *Grammatical Institute.*

50. Schultz, *Culture Factory*, 20–21.

51. Acts and Laws of Massachusetts, June 25, 1879, Chapter 19, in Raymond B. Culver, *Horace Mann and Religion in the Massachusetts Public Schools* (New Haven: Yale University Press, 1929), 22.

52. *The System of Public Education Adopted by the Town of Boston, 15 October, 1789*, bound in *American Antiquarian Society Pamphlets*, 10, in Widener Library, Harvard University.

53. Carroll to Father Thayer, May 9, 1793 Baltimore Diocesan Archives. 9AI2, in Lord I, 498–9.

54. Lord I, 499.

55. Matignon to Carroll, November 25, 1806, BAA photostat, Lord I, 599, letter originally in French.

56. Lord I, 599. No explanation is given of what happened to the building purchased by Thayer.

57. Book of Accounts, p. 19, BAA, quoted in Lord I, 597.

58. Lord I, 597.

59. Ibid., 597.

60. Ibid., 647.

61. Ibid., 647–9.

62. Ibid., 674–5.

63. Cheverus to Father Brute, March 23, 1816, Notre Dame Arch., in Lord I, 680.

64. Cheverus to Archbishop Marechal, June 25, 1818, Baltimore Dioc. Arch., photostat in BAA. Also in Lord, I, 681.

65. Lord I, 723. Note that at the time girls in the Boston public schools also attended for only a half day, it being assumed they were too delicate to endure an entire day's schooling.

66. Lord I, 724–5.

67. See Schultz, *Culture Factory*, 32ff.

68. Stephen C. Blyth to Harrison Gray Otis, Otis Papers, Mass. Historical Society, April 3, 1806, in Lord I, 599.

69. Schultz, *Culture Factory*, 33.

70. Lord I, 781–812.

71. Ibid., 806.

72. In Lord I, 800–801, from original in Arch. Nationale, Paris.

73. In Lord I, 803, from Grand Almonier to Bishop Cheverus, July 12, 1823, in Arch. Nationale, Paris.

74. Lord I, 729, quoting William Ware, a disciple of the Rev. Joseph Tuckerman, in *New York American*, May 15, 1823.

75. Cheverus to Papal Nuncio, December 29, 1823, Arch. Secret, Vat., Sec. di Stato, Rub. 248, no. 30858, quoted in Lord I, 807.

CHAPTER 2

1. See Schultz, *Culture Factory*, for an account of the historical development of public schools in Boston.

2. See Schultz, *Culture Factory*, 90, and entire Chapter 4, "Schoolhouses and Scholars."

3. Oscar Handlin, in *Boston's Immigrants*, makes this mistake, emphasizing the potato famine of the 1840s as the beginning of serious religio-ethnic conflict in Boston.

4. Lord II, 125.

5. Bishop Benedict Fenwick to the Society for the Propagation of the Faith, August 25, 1835, in Fenwick Memoranda, 1835.BAA. The 1835 estimate could have been exaggerated because it was contained in a letter seeking financial aid. However, the bishop was not given to exaggeration, and the figures are consonant both with the recorded growth in baptisms and later independent estimates. The "Fenwick Memoranda" are the diaries kept by Bishop Fenwick throughout his tenure in Boston, and are preserved in the BAA in their entirety. They are frequently cited as sources in the present work, and are identified simply as "Fen mem" or simply as "memoranda."

6. Lemmuel Shattuck, *Report of the Committee of the City Council appointed to Obtain the Census of Boston for the Year 1845* (Boston: J. H. Eastburn, 1846), 125.

7. Ibid., 125.

8. Ibid.

9. See Peter R. Knights, *The Plain People of Boston, 1830–1860: A Study in City Growth* (New York: Oxford University Press, 1971), 23.

10. Lord II, 355–60.

11. Fen mem, May 31, 1835; July 24, 1836; Fenwick's report to Primate of Austria, 1836 in Fen mem.

12. Fen mem January 22, November 10, 19, 26, 1837; July 2, 1841; June 14, 1842; January 22, 23, 1843; April 8, May 10, 1844; Very Rev. Brasseur de Bourbourg, Vicar General of Boston, to Society for the Propagation of the Faith, in Archives of the Archdiocese of Boston, February 24, 1847.

13. Fen mem, May 20, 1846.

14. Shattuck, *Report*, 110.

15. Ibid., 118.

16. Ibid., 129.

17. Ibid., 157.

18. Ibid., 155–6.

19. See, for example, Lord II, 140, 252.

20. Fenwick to Primate of Austria, 1836, copy in Fen mem.

21. Lord II, 144, 295–6; Fen mem September 17, 1840; July 2, 6, 1841; May 10, 1844.

22. Lord II, 134.

23. See, for example, Fen mem August 19, 1825; September 10, 1828.

24. Boston *Pilot*, March 17, 1838. *The Pilot* was a newspaper initiated by Bishop Fenwick and would become the long-term official organ of the diocese.

25. Lord II, 110–23.

26. Ibid., 127–8.

27. Ibid., 56–8.

28. Bishop Fenwick to Society for Propagation of Faith, Fen mem, August 29, 1837. See also frequent references to the economic depression.

29. See Fen mem, February 6, 1829, November 16, 1841, November 24, 1844; Lord II, 345.

30. Lawrence diary, June 13, 1837, Lawrence papers, Massachusetts Historical Society. Lawrence also added that the Irish were disliked because they were "good at a fight."

31. *Pilot*, October 26, 1839 [editorial].

32. Lord II, 258–9.

33. The tensions, conflicts, and open violence, from the celebrated burning of the Charlestown convent and school to the riots in the street and other instances of hostility, are thoroughly treated in Lord II, chapters VII, "The Revival of Opposition;" VIII, "The Burning of the Charlestown Convent;" and IX, "Native Americanism." The material presented here is heavily dependent on this material.

34. See Billington, *Protestant Crusade*; Fen mem, Lord, etc.

35. Fen mem, December 29, 1834.

36. *Pilot*, February 13, 1841, quoting Dr. H. B. C. Greene in the Massachusetts House of Representatives.

37. Lord II, 243.

38. Resolution of the Independent Boston Fusiliers, February 9, 1838, in Adj. Generals Archives, Massachusetts State House, transcript in BAA.

39. *Pilot*, February 16, 1839; also February 2 and 9.

40. Fenwick to Society for Propagation of the Faith, Fen mem, August 25, 1835.

41. Fen mem, December 25, 1834.

42. Fen mem, December 29, 1834.

43. Fen mem, June 14, 1837.

44. *Pilot*, March 30, 1839.

45. See Jonathon Messerli, *Horace Mann: A Biography* (New York: Alfred A. Knopf, 1972), 237; Mann Journal, June 11, 1837, Massachusetts Historical Society.

46. *The Pilot* complained of this frequently in the late 1830s.

47. *Pilot*, April 6, 1839.

48. *Jesuit*, January 18, 1834, 21. The newspaper begun by the new bishop, Benedict Fenwick, was named the *Jesuit*, and only later named *The Pilot*.

49. *Pilot*, January 26, 1839 [editorial].

50. *Pilot*, February 16, 1839 [editorial].

51. *Pilot*, May 25, 1839 [editorial].

52. Quoted in *Pilot*, June 22, 1839 [editorial].

53. Ibid.

54. *Jesuit*, July 13, 1833, 1.

55. *Jesuit*, January 18, 1834, 21; see January 25, 1834, 39.

56. *Pilot*, January 26, 1839 [editorial].

57. *Pilot*, November 16, October 29, November 30, 1839; February 19, 1842.

58. *Pilot*, April 1, 1843 [editorial], 102; see also April 8, 112; April 29, 136; May 13, 150.

59. Handlin, *Boston's Immigrants*, 190–1.

60. Fen mem, November 15, 1844.

61. *Pilot*, August 21, 1844, 278.

62. Ibid.

63. *Pilot*, January 18, 1845, 22.

64. *Pilot*, September 7, 1844, 285; also, *U.S. Catholic Intelligence*, April 27, 1832, 246.

65. *Pilot*, Jan. 11, 1845, 14.

66. *Pilot*, August 24, 1844, 278.

67. *Pilot*, January 4, 1845, 3.

68. Green was the only known Catholic among the group, and he was a convert. *Pilot*, February 8, 1845, 47.

69. *Pilot*, February 1, 1845, 38; also December 6, 1845, 389.

70. *Pilot*, January 4, 1845, 6.

71. *Pilot*, January 18, 1845, 22.

72. *Pilot*, February 8, 1845, 47.

73. *Pilot*, October 25, 1845, 342.

74. *Pilot*, June 14, 1845, 190; November 22, 1845, 374; and many others.

75. *Pilot*, January 17, 1846, 6.

76. *Pilot*, August 21, 1844, 278.

77. Ibid.

78. Ibid.

79. *Pilot*, September 14, 1844, 294.

80. *Pilot*, September 24, 28, October 2, November 30, 1844.

81. See, for example, *Jesuit*, September 26, 1829, 2; January 16, 1830, 157–9; January 22, 1831, 165–6; *U.S. Catholic Intelligence*, March 16, 1832, 197; May 18, 1832, 270; *Jesuit*, January 19, 1833, 10; October 12, 1833, 162; January 11, 1834, 12; June 14, 1834, 190; *Pilot*, June 23, 1838; October 5, 1839; October 19, 1839.

82. *Pilot*, March 16, 1832, 197.

83. *Pilot*, June 23, 1838.

84. *Pilot*, September 12, 1840, 271.

85. *Pilot*, July 6, 1844, 214.

86. *Pilot*, May 24, June 6, 13, July 18, August 1, 29, 1840; January 23, July 3, November 6, 20, December 4, 1841; January 1, 8, 15, 22, February 12, April 16, 1842.

87. *Pilot*, July 9, 1842, 232.

88. See Lord II, 3ff.

89. Ibid., 35.

90. Ibid., 30–31.

91. Ibid., 36–37.

92. Fen mem, June 14, 1829.

93. Fen mem, 1836.

94. Fen mem, November 20, 1842.

95. *Pilot*, June 7, 1845.

96. *Pilot*, February 25, 1843, 62

97. Fen mem, February 13, 1826; Lord II, 36–37.

98. Fen mem, May 17–18, 1826.

99. Lord II, 36–37.

100. Fen mem, May 18, 1826.

101. See for examples Fen mem September 30, 1827; April 15, 1829; January 9, 1833; June 10, 1834; January 24, February 28, 1836; July 30, 1840; July 5, 1841; August 5, 1846.

102. Lord II, 36; *Jesuit*, January 19, 1833, 10; Fenwick to Society for the Propagation of the Faith, February 3, 1833, copy in Fen mem.

103. Fen mem, July 3, 1826.

104. See, for example, Fen mem April 14, May 21, 1828.

105. Fen mem is full of details about such matters.

106. See, for example, Fen mem, August 19, 1825; September 29, October 3, 1828; April 27, 1829; July 18, 1829; January 25, 1830; November 30, December 20, 1831; December 16, April 25, July 22, 1832; January 3, February 11, April 12, July 2, December 31, 1834; April 5, 24, 1835; July 25, 1841; January 24, 29, December 6, 1842; January 11, 17, 1843; January 7, 8, 1844; October 2, 28, 1845.

107. *Jesuit*, April 27, 1833, 67.

108. Fenwick to Fr. Dzierozynski, August 27, 1842, Fordham archives; Fen mem, December 13, 1836; September 24, 1838; October 9, 1839; October 6, 1840.

109. Fenwick to Bishop Rosati, April 24, 1832, *Illinois Catholic Historical Review*, vol. X, no. 2, 149–50.

110. Fen mem, January 22, 23, 24, 25, 26, 1838.

111. *Jesuit*, October 16, 1830, 52. See also Fen mem, October 13, 1829. He had been delegated to do this by the American bishops, who intended to use the books in other dioceses as well.

112. Fen mem, September 30, 1827.

113. *U.S. Catholic Intelligencer*, March 16, 1832, 197.

114. *Jesuit*, January 15, 1831, 156.

115. Fen mem, December 30, 1832; see also *Jesuit*, March 9, 1833, 37; Lord II, 186, 650; Rules of St. Aloysius Sunday School, pp. 25–31 (BAA).

116. Fen mem, September 30, 1827.

117. See Fen mem letter to Rome April 24, 1831; *Jesuit*, January 19, 1833, 10.

118. Fen mem, October 7, 1827.

119. Fen mem, May 13, 1832.

120. Fen mem, July 14, 1833.

121. Constitution and By-Laws of the Young Catholics Friend Society, Boston: Patrick Donahoe, 1839 (BAA).

122. Lord II, 345–46.

123. *Pilot*, February 27, 1836.

124. *Pilot*, September 3, October 1, 1836.

125. Fen to Frs. Wiley and O'Bierne, August 12, 1836, Fen mem.

126. *Pilot*, July 9, 1842, 232.

127. Fen mem, January 24, 1836; July 5, 1841.

128. Fen mem.

129. Fen mem, November 14, 1841.

130. Fen mem, February 28, 1836.

131. Fen mem, July 30, 1840; August 2, 1842; August 5, 1846; *Pilot*, August 6, 1842, 264. *The Pilot* regularly published accounts of these excursions.

132. Fen mem, October 15, 1843.

133. Shattuck, *Report*, 124.

134. *Pilot*, February 27, 1836.

135. Printed in *Pilot*, December 1, 1838, 358.

136. See Schultz, *Culture Factory*, 22–30.

137. Fen mem, October 1, 1827.

138. *Jesuit*, January, 22, 1831.

139. Fen mem, October 1, 1827.

140. Ibid; also, Lord II, 310–1.

141. Fen mem, October 1, 1827.

142. Ibid. *Jesuit*, January 22, 1831, 165–6.

143. Fen mem, January 15, 1832.

144. Fen mem, March 11, April 30, May 3, 5, 6, 1832; *U.S. Catholic Intelligencer*, May 18, 1832.

145. *U.S. Catholic Intelligencer*, May 18, 1832, 270. For about a year, in 1832, the *Jesuit* changed its name to the *U.S. Catholic Intelligencer*, but it was the same paper.

146. See frequent articles in *Jesuit* (e.g., October 12, 1833, 162) and frequent references in Fen mem (e.g., July 15, 1838).

147. See, for example, *Pilot*, September 14, 1839.

148. Fen mem, September 8, October 2, 1845; Lord II, 329–31.

149. *Jesuit*, June 14, 1834, 190; Fen mem, June 10, 1834.

150. *Jesuit*, June 14, 1834, 190.

151. Fen mem, July 13, 1842.

152. *Jesuit*, January 19, 1833, 10.

153. Fen mem, September 19, 1832.

154. Ibid.

155. Fen mem, January 9, 1833.

156. *Jesuit*, January 11, 1834, 12; June 14, 1834, 190; Fen mem, January 24, 1839.

157. Fenwick to Society for Propagation of the Faith, August 25, 1835. Copy in BAA.

158. Fen mem, October 16, 1832.

159. Fen mem, July 10, 1834.

160. *Pilot*, September 12, 1840, 271; September 19, 1840.

161. Fen mem, January 18, 1842.

162. Fenwick, *History of Boston Diocese*, 66 (BAA).

163. Fenwick to Society for the Propagation of the Faith, 1843.

164. *Historical Records and Studies*, Vol. VII: The United States Catholic Historical Society, 1914; Paul H. Linehan, "Holy Trinity Parish, Boston," *Historical Records and Studies*, vol. VII (New York: The United States Catholic Historical Society, 1914), 134.

165. See *U.S. Catholic Intelligencer*, June 1, 1832, advertisement on 288; *Pilot*, May 6, 1843, 143.

166. Bishop John England, to Society for Propagation of the Faith, October 27, 1825. Copy in BAA.

167. Lord II, 3–12.

168. Fen mem, March 17, 1828; Fenwick to George Fenwick, March 17, 1831, Fordham University Archives. See also Fen mem, March 17, 1831.

169. Fen mem, March 17, 1843.

170. Fen mem, July 9, 1834; November 15, 1844. See also Fen mem July 9, 1834; November 15, 1844.

171. Fen mem, September 18, 1827.

172. See Fen mem, May 18, 1831; December 16, 1832; July 2, 1834.

173. Lord II, 40; Guilday, *History of the Councils of Baltimore* (publisher unknown), 122.

174. See Fenwick report to Rome, April 24, 1831 (copy in BAA); Lord II, 142, 266.

175. Fenwick to Frs. Wiley and O'Burne, August 12, 1836 (BAA).

176. Fen mem, February 7, 1836.

177. Fenwick to Charlestown Church, 1830 (BAA).

178. *Pilot*, February 26, 1842, 81; March 12, 1842, 93; February 26, 1842, 81; March 12, 1842, 93. Fenwick had settled numerous disputes over the years. See Fen mem, May 6, 1833; April 5, 1835; September 3, 1835; July 12, 1836; January 22, 1837; November 10, 19, 26, 1837; see also Lord II, 298–9, 308–9.

179. Quoted in *Daily Mail*, April 20, 1842. See Ibid., May 11, 1842.

180. See Fen mem, September 13, 1835.

181. Ibid.

182. Quoted in *Daily Mail*, April 27, 1842.

183. Ibid.

184. Fenwick to St. Mary's Catholics, February 11, 1842 (BAA).

185. *Pilot*, January 26, 1839 [editorial].

186. *Pilot*, June 1, 1844, 173.

187. *Pilot*, July 26, 1845, 239.

188. *Pilot*, August 15, 1846, 4.

189. See quotes in *Pilot*, August 2, 1846.

190. *Pilot*, August 29, 1846, 7.

191. *Pilot*, September 19, 1846, 1.

192. Fenwick to Fr. Dzierozynski, December 24, 1825, Fordham Archives (copy in BAA).

193. Fenwick to Bishop Rosati, St. Louis, June 10, 1836, *Illinois Catholic Historical Review*, vol. X, no. 2, 158–9. See also Fenwick to Bishop Eccleston, August 11, 1836, Baltimore Diocesan Archives.

194. Fenwick to Society for the Propagation of the Faith, August 29, 1837 (copy in BAA).

195. Fen mem, March 29, 1826.

196. Fen mem, June 21, 1826.

197. Fen mem, April 2, 1832; August 31, September 11, 1835; Fenwick to Bishop Rosati, April 24, 1832, and to George Fenwick, August 1, 1833; Lord II, 320ff.

198. Fenwick to Society for the Propagation of the Faith, December 1836 (copy in BAA).

199. Fenwick to Dzierozynski, April 11, 1826, Fordham Archives.

200. Fenwick to Prefect of the Sacred Congregation for the Propagation of the Faith, April 24, 1831 (copy in BAA).

201. Fenwick to George Fenwick, April 31, 1831 (copy in BAA).

202. Fen mem, September 29, 1838; October 9, 1839; October 6, 1840; Fenwick to George Fenwick, November 29, 1838 and October 3, 1842, Fordham Archives; Fenwick to Dzierozynski, August 27, 1842.

203. Fenwick to George Fenwick, December 8, 1842 (copy in BAA).

204. *Pilot*, June 23, 1838; October 19, 1839; May 2, 1840; Lord II, 320ff; Fenwick to George Fenwick, October 3, 1843; Fenwick to Dzierozynski, January 11, 1843 (copies in BAA).

205. Dzierozynski to Fenwick, Jan, 1843; also to Father General of the Jesuits, February 1843; Fenwick to Dzierozynski, February 4, 1843.

206. Fenwick to Dzierozynski, February 4, 1843; Dzierozynski to Father General of Jesuits, February 1843.

207. Fen mem, June 18, 21, 1843, and Bishop John Fitzpatrick memoranda, July 28, 1852 (BAA).

208. Fen mem, November 1843; see also Fen mem for 1844–5.

209. Fenwick to Society for Propagation of the Faith in Paris, February 26, 1845. W. F. Clarke, Georgetown to Rev. Samuel Barber, May 11, 1845, Fordham Archives,

indicating that Fr. Verhagen of St. Louis, official Jesuit Visitor, had proposed this and Fenwick had agreed.

210. See Joseph Wightman, *Annals of the Boston Primary School Committee: From Its First Establishment in 1818 to its Dissolution in 1855* (Boston: G. C. Rand & Avery, city printers, 1860), 153, describing the building of a two-story public primary school for $2,528. This did not include the ongoing payment of teachers' salaries, which was a concern to Fenwick.

211. Fen mem June 18, 1843.

212. Fenwick to Congregation for Propagation of the Faith, February 26, 1845.

213. See Culver, *Horace Mann*, and Messerli, *Horace Mann*, who document these debates.

214. See Fenwick to Society for the Propagation of the Faith, August 25, 1835.

215. Fenwick to Brimmer, January 28, 1843 (copy in BAA).

216. Fenwick to Boston School Committee, care of Mr. Edward Wigglesworth, February 23, 1843. See also Fen mem, February 23, 1843. Unfortunately, the letter has not survived either in BAA or in the BSC archives, only Fenwick's reference to it in his diary.

217. Boston School Committee (BSC) minutes, February 7, 1843, 50, Boston Public Library (BPL).

218. BSC minutes, March 7, 1843, 66–67. Unfortunately neither the report nor the BSC discussion on it has survived. The context suggests that the subcommittee wished to reject Bishop Fenwick's petition but that the BSC as a whole did not accept that position. This is not certain, however.

219. BSC minutes, April 4, 1843, BPL; "Revised Statutes of the State of Massachusetts." BSC minutes, 1835, chap. 23, section 723.

220. BSC minutes, April 4, 1843, BPL.

221. BSC minutes, April 5, 1843.

222. Brimmer to Fenwick, April 8, 1843, together with a copy of the resolution.

223. 1828 and 1843 editions, Massachusetts Historical Society (MHS).

224. 1850 edition, p. 194

225. From City Directory; *Transcript* obituaries; Richard Hildreth, *Our First Men: A Calendar of Wealth, Fashion and Gentility, containing a list of those persons taxed in the city of Boston credibly reported to be worth one hundred thousand dollars* (Boston, 1846).

226. Fenwick to Society for the Propagation of the Faith, February 26, 1845, Notre Dame University Archives. Actually, throughout his tenure in Boston, Fenwick, although he truly admired the Bostonian love for learning and the intellectual achievement, was always put off by the fact that it was produced by Protestants and colored by Protestantism.

227. Ibid.

228. BSC minutes, 1843, 59–60, in BPL.

229. See Memoirs of Rev. John Pierce, Brookline, 1846, MHS; also Lord II, 381–5.

230. *Pilot*, August 29, 1846, 7.

231. The Catholic educational experience in the textile mill town of Lowell during this period differed greatly from that in Boston. The differences are instructive,

and indeed the Lowell situation deserves separate study in its own right. The first Catholic school was established in Lowell in 1824 or 1825, just about the time that Irish immigrants were beginning to move into the mills. It was attached to the single Catholic church. But financial resources did not suffice for the growing number of Irish children. At this point the textile company, which dominated the town, stepped in. In 1828 Kirk Boot, the company's agent, offered Bishop Fenwick a building lot for a more permanent school, and in 1830 the town school committee allocated $50 to the school. By 1835 the school committee adopted the school and another existing in a second Catholic parish, with the understanding that only Catholic teachers would be appointed, and that the curriculum and the textbooks, though controlled by the committee, would contain nothing derogatory to Catholics. Fenwick went along with all this, and *The Pilot* praised the "liberality" of the Lowell citizenry. The arrangement continued until 1852, several years after Fenwick's death, though it ceased working well in 1843. Apparently the troubles stemmed not from any change of heart in the school committee but from a cantankerous Catholic pastor who in 1843 demanded the dismissal of seven of the nine Catholic teachers. Many Catholics opposed him, and the school committee refused his demand. After that, relations began breaking down, and teacher vacancies in the Irish schools were routinely filled with Protestants until in 1852 the arrangement ceased entirely.

The ease with which Lowell accommodated the Irish Catholic educational needs, contrasted with its opposite in Boston, was almost certainly related to the fact that Lowell was so completely a company town. The textile manufacturers were more concerned with maintaining a satisfied workforce than they were with transmitting the New England heritage. If the Irish wanted Irish Catholic teachers, why not? In fact, the textile manufacturers often donated land for Catholic churches, and even sometimes contributed to the building of the churches themselves. Interestingly, while Bishop Fenwick accepted this arrangement, he does not appear to have made an issue out of it or to have tried to get it adopted in Boston. See Lord II, 313ff; Fen mem, October 26, 1828, July 13, 1830, January 4, 1836, January 24, 1842, July 25, 26, 1841, December 13, 1842; Fenwick to Philip Scanlon, March 26, 1831, U.S. Catholic Historical Society Records and Studies, XI, 1900, p. 403; Fenwick to Society for Propagation of the Faith, August 29, 1837; *U.S. Catholic Intelligencer*, May 25, 1832, 278–9, June 1, 1832, 287; *Pilot*, March 10, 1838, 55; October 22, 1842, 352; July 6, 1844, 214.

CHAPTER 3

1. For an excellent summary of the potato famine and the exodus that followed, see Thomas H. O'Connor, *Fitzpatrick's Boston* (Boston: Northeastern University Press, 1984), chap. 4, "The Immigrant Flood," which draws heavily on Marcus Lee Hansen and Arthur M. Schlesinger, *The Atlantic Migration, 1607–1860: A History of the Continuing Settlement of the United States* (Cambridge, MA: Harvard University Press, 1940). See also George Potter, *To the Golden Door: The Story of the Irish in Ireland and America* (Boston: Little, Brown, 1960); Cecil Woodham-Smith, *The Great Hunger: Ireland, 1845–1849* (New York: Harper & Row, 1962); and Thomas Gallagher, *Paddy's Lament: Ireland, 1846–1847 Prelude to Hatred* (New York: Harcourt Brace Jovanovich, 1982).

2. Edward Everett Hale, *Letters on Irish Emmigration* (Boston: Phillips, Sampson, 1852), 5.

3. Oscar Handlin, *Boston's Immigrants: A Study in Acculturation, 1790–1865* (New York: Athenaeum, 1941; enlarged ed., 1991), 242ff.

4. Richard J. Grozier, "The Life and Times of John Bernard Fitzpatrick, Third Roman Catholic Bishop of Boston" (unpublished Ph.D. thesis, Boston College, 1966), 207–8.

5. Handlin, *Boston's Immigrants*, 246.

6. Grozier, "Life and Times," 208, referring to the 1850 State census of Massachusetts, p. 34.

7. Handlin, *Boston's Immigrants*, 255.

8. See Ibid., 55–66.

9. Labor statistics are derived from Ibid., chap. III, "The Economic Adjustment," and the tables that document it.

10. Ibid., 85, derived from the *Third Annual Report of the Bureau of Statistics of Labor*, 1872, 517–20.

11. See Shattuck, *Report*.

12. Fitzpatrick memoranda, June 13, 1847 (BAA).

13. Boston Committee on Internal Health, *Report of the Committee on Internal Health on the Asiatic Cholera*, 1849 (City Document 66, pp. 9–15).

14. See Handlin, *Boston's Immigrants*, 101–17; Lord II, 452–4.

15. Handlin, *Boston's Immigrants*, 256–7. Grozier's analysis of crime rates shows definitively that between 1850 and 1865 the Irish represented an average of 18.4 percent of the serious offenders in state prisons while representing 14.2 percent of the population in the state ("Life and Times," 7–63). It was only for petty crime that the Irish incarceration rates were far above the average. See *Abstract of the Returns of the Keepers of the Jails and the Overseers of the Houses of Correction of Massachusetts*, 1851–1863, Massachusetts State Library.

16. *Pilot*, July 31, 1847, 6.

17. Quoted in Schultz, *Culture Factory*, 248. See *Reports of the Annual Visiting Committee of the Grammar and Writing Schools of Boston for 1847* (Boston, 1847).

18. *Boston School Report*, 1847, 54–55.

19. *Pilot*, October 23, 1852, 5.

20. O'Connor, *Fitzpatrick's Boston*, 79.

21. Edward Everett to Dr. Henry Holland, March 25, 1847 (Everett Papers, MHS).

22. McCaffrey, p. 194, from *Boston City Documents*, 1852, No. 11, p. 3.

23. See O'Connor, *Fitzpatrick's Boston*, 89–90, referring to Edward Everett, his nephew Edward Everett Hale, and others.

24. Handlin, *Boston's Immigrants*, 70–71.

25. Edward Everett to N.W. Senior, March 2, 1851 (Everett Papers, MHS).

26. *Pilot*, January 19, 1850, 5.

27. Handlin, *Boston's Immigrants*, 75–82.

28. Ibid., 82.

29. Ibid., 74.

30. Ibid., 86.

31. *Pilot*, August 14, 1847, 6; September 4, 1847, 6.

32. Handlin, *Boston's Immigrants*, 82.

33. Edward W. Everett to N.W. Senior, April 29, 1851, MHS. There was certainly no Bostonian more prominent in his time than Edward W. Everett. Having attended Boston Latin, graduated from Harvard College, and then earned a PhD at the University of Gottingen, he served consecutively as pastor of the Brattle St. Unitarian church, professor of Greek literature at Harvard, editor of the *North American Review*, U.S. Representative to Congress, Governor of Massachusetts, U.S. Minister to England, President of Harvard, Secretary of State, and U.S. Senator!

34. Horace Mann, *Ninth Annual Report*, 1845. See Schultz, *Culture Factory*, 230.

35. "Immigration: Its Evils and Their Remedies," *New Englander*, XIII (May 1855), 275.

36. BSC minutes, October 7, 1851.

37. Ibid.

38. *American Annals of Education*, III (November 1843), 495.

39. BSC minutes, Nov. 28, 1854.

40. Edward Everett, "Boston Public Schools," *Eclectic Magazine*, LX (September 1863), 68–70, quoted in Schultz, *Culture Factory*, 260.

41. BSC Report, 1850, 29–30.

42. BSC Report, 1841 (Boston, 1841), 55–56.

43. *American Annals of Education*, III (September 1833), 412–3; in Schultz, *Culture Factory*, 229–30.

44. *Report of the Annual Visiting Committee of the Grammar and Writing Schools of Boston for 1846* (Boston, 1846), 34.

45. Whightman, *Annals of the Boston Primary School Committee*, 218.

46. BSC minutes, February 2, 1848.

47. "Report on Truancy," Boston City Documents, 1846, Doc. no. 18, pp. 2–3; address by Josiah Quincy, Jr., in *Common School Journal*, X (June 15, 1848), 178.

48. BSC minutes, December 29, 1847. See also March 7, 1849.

49. BSC minutes, Aug, 11, 1848.

50. Schultz, *Culture Factory*, 296–301.

51. BSC Report, 1853, 25.

52. BSC minutes, September 22, 1847. Schultz, *Culture Factory*, 276.

53. Whightman, *Annals of the Boston Primary School Committee*, 232, 251.

54. Schultz, *Culture Factory*, 283, quoting Edward Twisleton, *Evidence as to the Religious Working of the Common Schools of the State of Massachusetts, with a Preface* (London, 1855), 9.

55. Wilkie. One weakness of this otherwise enterprising and revealing study is the fact that Wilkie, having to rely on census data, is forced to assume that school enrollment reported to the census takers means the same for everybody. This takes no account of actual attendance rates. For example, one child might have attended school for one week during the year, another for twelve months, but both are counted the same in the census data. It is likely that actual attendance rates for lower-class children were much lower than for higher-class ones.

56. Schultz, *Culture Factory*, 79.

57. Based on Schultz, *Culture Factory*, 282.

58. BSC Report, 1849, 27–28; BSC Report, 1850, 32, 36–37.

59. BSC Report, 1850, 32, 36–37.

60. See O'Connor, *Fitzpatrick's Boston*, 59–60.

61. See Lord II, 389ff. Family tradition has it that Fitzpatrick's maternal grandfather fought in the American Revolution and that his mother was born in this country but returned as a child to Ireland, where she later married Bernard Fitzpatrick and immigrated with him to Boston in 1805.

62. See Lord II, 202–3.

63. See Grozier, "Life and Times," 12, from *Catalogue of the Boston Latin School* (ed. Henry F. Jenks, Boston, 1886), 170–1; O'Connor, *Fitzpatrick's Boston*, 8.

64. The exact sequence of events is not entirely clear. Fitzpatrick completed Boston Latin in 1829. He seems to have been linked to Fenwick since 1825. See O'Connor, *Fitzpatrick's Boston*, 11; Lord II, 292–3.

65. See Lord II, 293.

66. Lord II, 293–4.

67. See Grozier, "Life and Times," 18–23; Lord II, 397–403.

68. Cited in Lord II, 396, quoting Father George Haskins, *A Panegyric on the Rt. Rev. John B Fitzpatrick, D.D., in Memoriam of Rt. Rev. John B. Fitzpatrick* (Boston, 1866), 33. Haskins, a native Yankee Bostonian, had attended the meeting.

69. Edward Everett to Duchess of Argyle, February 3, 1852 (Everett Papers, MHS).

70. Memoranda, October 30, 1846; November 5, 1846. These are often noted in his diary—for example, an evening party at Richard Henry Dana's on December 30, 1847. See Edward Warren, *The Life of John Collins Warren, M.D.: Compiled Chiefly from His Autobiography and Journals* (Boston: Ticknor and Fields, 1860).

71. Henry Cabot Lodge, *Early Memories* (New York: C. Scribner's sons, 1913), 56.

72. See Grozier, "Life and Times," 506–8, referring to Fitzpatrick to Sumner, January 10, 1863 (Sumner Papers, Harvard University Archives).

73. Grozier, "Life and Times," 35. Lord II, 406; memoranda, Feb. 13, 1856.

74. This copy is among the holdings in the library of St. John's Seminary, Brighton, Mass.

75. Memoranda, July 14, 1859.

76. Grozier, 504–28. He left for Europe May 30, 1862, and traveled through Italy and France before taking up residence with the U.S. Legation in Belgium. O'Connor, *Fitzpatrick's Boston*.

77. Amos A. Lawrence diary, June 20, 1861 (Lawrence Papers, MHS); Lord II, 756.

78. Grozier, "Life and Times," 25.

79. Grozier, "Life and Times," 33, quoting Bishop Bayley of Newark in Hildegarde M. Yeager, *Life of James Roosevelt Bayley, First Bishop of Newark and Eighth Archbishop of Baltimore, 1814–1877* (Washington: Catholic University of America Press, 1947), 42.

80. Memoranda, June 7, 15, 16, 1847.

81. Memoranda, June 26, 1847.

82. See Lord II, 625–7, on the continuing struggle to gain entrance of priests to the House of Industry and Deer Island.

83. Grozier makes this argument in "Life and Times."

84. John Fitzpatrick to Eleanor Fitzpatrick, January 12, 1838 (Boland Collection, BAA), quoted in Grozier, "Life and Times," 15, who had access to photocopies of the Fitzpatrick letters in the possession of Msgr. Harrington that are no longer extant. The originals were in the possession of the Boland Sisters.

85. Fitzpatrick to John B. Purcell, Archbishop of Cincinnati, August 20, 1859 (original in Notre Dame Archives [NDA]).

86. See Grozier, "Life and Times," 444–45.

87. Memoranda, June 16, 1847. See also June 11, 1847.

88. Memoranda, March 7, 1853.

89. *Pilot*, May 13, 1854.

90. Letter to Boston *Transcript*, reprinted in *Pilot*, February 11, 1854, 3.

91. Lord II, 400, quoting from Fitzpatrick to Eleanor Fitzpatrick, March 4, 1841 (Boland Collection).

92. Grozier, "Life and Times," 32, referring to Lord Acton, "American Diaries," *The Fortnightly Review*, CXI, New Series (January–June 1922), 70–71.

93. Archbishop John Hughes's report to Rome concerning the administration of the Boston Diocese is found in Archbishop Hughes to Cardinal Barnabo, December 18, 1858, De Propaganda Fide Archives, America Centrale Congressi, vol. 18, fol. 483–484, microfilm in NDA, in Latin: "in omnibus, quasi serviliter, insequitur vestigia sui predecessoris." The typed transcript of this report, in English, is in BAA but without the ending, which describes Fitzpatrick as "slavishly" following Fenwick.

94. James F. Connelly, *The Visit of Archbishop Gaetano Bedini to the United States of America: June, 1853–February, 1854* (Roma: Università Gregoriana, 1960). Bedini's final report to Rome after his American visit, July 12, 1854, translation in Connelly, 211.

95. Bedini to Rome, October 8, 1853, translation in Connelly, p. 46.

96. John Lancaster Spalding, *The Life of the Most Reverend M.J. Spalding, D.D., Archbishop of Baltimore* (New York: Catholic Publication Society, 1873), 153, quoting a statement in an undated letter from Archbishop Kenrick to Spalding, to which Spalding replied on February 9, 1852.

97. Sarah Brownson to Sarah Healy, September 4, 1860 (NDA).

98. Memoranda, October 5, 1851.

99. Brownson to Hughes, July 3, 1854 (photocopy in NDA, original in New York Archives).

100. Augustus Thebaud, "Forty Years in the United States of America," *Monograph Series of the United States Catholic Historical Society*, no. 11 (1904), 312, quoted in Grozier, "Life and Times," 36–37.

101. Archbishop Purcell to Archbishop Blanc of New Orleans, May 30, 1859 (BAA copy, original in NDA); quoted in Grozier, "Life and Times," 126.

102. *Memorial to His Holiness Pope Pius IX from John Toland and others*, March 12, 1858, De Propaganda Fide Archives, Congressi America Centrale, Vol 18, fol. 285r, 258v, 259r, 259v, microfilm in NDA.

103. Sacerdos Dei Altissimi to Propaganda Fide, October 6, 1863, fol. 427rv and 428rv, NDA. This letter, written from Albany, also describes Fitzpatrick as "ebriosus" (drunken), which would raise interesting speculation about his stand on the temperance issue. However, since it appears to be the only such reference extant, and since nothing is known about its author's credibility, the matter does not deserve serious consideration.

104. Letter from anonymous priest to an unnamed cardinal in Rome, October 6, 1863, De Propaganda Fide Archives, Scritta. **rif. nei.** Congressi America Centrale, vol. 20, fol. 427rv. Catholic Church. Congregatio de Propaganda Fide Records (PRF), NDA.

105. W. Dunne to Propaganda Fide, October 28, 1865, fol. 1644rv to 1646rv, NDA. Mr. Dunne contended that Fitzpatrick maintained a monopoly on Catholic graveyards, charging $10 to read prayers for the dead there, and refusing to bury Catholics or read prayers at a graveyard established by laypeople where the fee was only $3.

106. According to Whall's recollection more than fifty years later Wiget had actually advised the boys not to recite the Protestant version a week earlier, on March 6, which was what prompted Whall to defy the teacher's order in the first place. Wiget then repeated the advice on the 13th.

107. According to Fitzpatrick's diary, Wiget intended the school to produce vocations to the priesthood. Fitzpatrick, after assisting at an exam there on March 10, 1859, confided to his diary that, while the boys had made "remarkable progress," they could not have done thoroughly all they seemed to know: "There must be more memory than science in the matter." See Memoranda, March 10, 1859.

108. At this time school board or school committee members were still expected to take personal charge of the schools. The members were expected to do onsite visitations of the schools on a regular basis. Therefore, it was not unusual that Mr. Hazelton was present on March 14.

109. *Pilot*, March 26, 1859, letter printed in full.

110. This letter was received by the School Committee on March 21, one week after the Wahl incident, and reprinted in the *Pilot* on March 26, 1859. See also Lord II, 596–9.

111. Memoranda, March 15, 1859.

112. The *Pilot*, which always mirrored the prelate's views but often abandoned his conciliatory public tone, chose to play up the physical punishment side of the Eliot School case, referring to it as "Protestant Torture" and "a case of barbarity." See *Pilot*, March 26, 1859, 4.

113. The Boston press differed considerably in its handling of the matter. The *Daily Traveller* simply recounted the events without comment. The *Atlas and Daily Bee* titled the affair "Roman Catholic Interference in the Public Schools of Boston" and claimed that "Roman Catholic priests in Boston have assumed to take the government and direction of the public schools out of the hands of the teachers and committees." The *Journal* covered the issue on a daily basis. It clearly supported the School Committee, urged the return of the children to school, reported and repeatedly stressed the differences of opinion even among the Catholic clergy, and argued that "Nothing even approaching sectarian teaching had ever been

undertaken at the Eliot School." The *Journal* in particular contrasted the positions of Father Wiget, who counseled the children to "have nothing to do with their [Protestant] religion," and of Father George Haskins, who "expressed himself decidedly opposed to the course which had been taken by the Catholic children," and felt that the grievance should have been taken directly to the School Committee, which he considered intelligent and fair-minded. The *Journal* agreed, and as the controversy dragged on it grew gradually more belligerent. By March 22 it saw a larger plot lurking behind the Eliot case, namely that the Catholic Church would not stop with concessions on the Bible but would next demand a share of the school funds: "Nothing short of a division of the school fund and separate schools will satisfy them." It staunchly opposed any concession whatever, arguing essentially that Catholics in this country are accepted on Protestant terms, since this is a Protestant country: "The use of the English Bible must be preserved in our schools—there must be no hesitation, no compromise in this matter." It reported the sermon of the Rev. A. B. Fuller of the New North Church, Hanover Street, who argued with curious logic that "The Bible, in the recognized Protestant version, should be kept in our schools, because such has always been our policy."

Others, such as the pastor of the City's First Universalist Church, were offended not so much that Catholics objected to Protestantism in the schools as by the fact that they had voiced the objection through rebellion. Perhaps forgetting momentarily the rebellion that the heroes of the Massachusetts commonwealth had so recently engaged in themselves, he argued that "obedience to law is the fundamental feature of our whole American system of government; with it we are safe, without it we are lost."

But the voice of compromise also began to be heard. Even the Rev. Fuller, who wanted the Protestant Bible in the schools simply because it had always been there, though insisting that the School Committee must stick to its rules during the crisis, suggested that "their rules might hereafter be duly revised, but not now."

114. As reported in the *Atlas and Daily Bee*, March 22, 1859. See BSC minutes, March 21, 1859, 32.

115. Lord II, 604, quoting Acts of the State Legislature, 1862, chap. 57. See also *Pilot*, February 1, 1862.

116. *O'Neill's Irish Pictorial*, April 16, 1859.

117. See *Journal*, March 17, 1859.

118. Quoted in the *Boston Traveller*, March 28, 1859.

119. BSC minutes, January 9, 1860, 112, records the protest; January 30, 1860, 117–20, after two evenings of hearing Committee on Elections reports "considerable irregularity in conducting the election in Ward One," but recommends that the vote stand because the majority was large enough to overcome all illegal votes.

120. Amos Lawrence diary, March 18, 1859 (Lawrence papers, MHS).

121. Lord II, 306, 323, 325.

122. Fitzpatrick even lobbied for the Jesuit College when he visited Rome in 1854, where he negotiated with the reluctant Jesuits to see the project through. Lord II, 427–8.

123. *Boston Daily Evening Transcript*, Friday, October 31, 1851, 2.

124. Memoranda, January 10, 1849; March 6, 8, 1849; August 7, 1849. Lord II, 614–6. Harrington portrays the development of parochial schools in St. Mary's parish as Fitzpatrick's doing. In reality, although the bishop fully cooperated and assisted, it was McElroy's initiative. See, for example, McElroy to Purcell, June 22, 1848; July 15, 1859 (NDA).

125. Father John McElroy, S.J., to Bishop John B. Purcell, February 20, 1850 (NDA).

126. *Pilot*, July 30, 1853, 4.

127. Memoranda, June 1, 1852.

128. See, for example, Memoranda, September 17, 20, 1852, regarding their opening a school in Lowell.

129. *Pilot*, April 16, 1853, 8; July 30, 1853, 8.

130. Memoranda, January 8, 1859.

131. Memoranda, May 9, 1859, September 5, 1860.

132. Memoranda, June 26, 1859.

133. Lord II, 619.

134. *Pilot*, December 31, 1864, 4; II, 614–18; Lord II, 616–17.

135. Memoranda, April 27, 1860.

136. McElroy to Archbishop Purcell, July 15, 1859 (NDA).

137. Memoranda, June 23, 1852.

138. Fitzpatrick to Bishop Purcell, September 15, 1849 (NDA).

139. Memoranda, August 12, 1850.

140. Memoranda, March 6, 1852.

141. Ibid.

142. Memoranda, July 16, 1851. See also July 11, 15, 1856; January 8, 1859; May 9, 1859. Fitzpatrick also traveled to other towns in the diocese, apparently simply to attend functions at the parochial schools there. See July 10, 1856, Lowell; July 17, 1856, Salem.

143. Memoranda, July 19, 1853; *Pilot*, July 30, 1853, 4; Memoranda, July 16, 1852.

144. Memoranda, June 1, 1853.

145. Fitzpatrick to the Society for the Propagation of the Faith, Paris, April 26, 1856, microfilm (NDA), in French.

146. Memoranda, September 7, 10, October 12, 1856.

147. Memoranda, April 27, 1860; September 5, 1860.

148. Franz Xaver Weiser, *Holy Trinity Parish, Boston, Mass., 1844–1944* (Boston: Holy Trinity Rectory, 1944), 29; Paul H. Linehan, "Holy Trinity Parish, Boston," *Historical Records and Studies*, vol. VII (New York: The United States Catholic Historical Society, 1914), 132–44.

149. Annual Church Report, Holy Trinity Parish, 1868 (BAA).

150. Memoranda, March 19, 1848; March 25, 1849.

151. Memoranda, March 4, 1851.

152. Lord II, 42–43; 100; 166–9; 171–8; 323–4.

153. *Pilot*, December 29, 1877.

154. *Donahoe's Magazine*, vol. VI, 1881, obituary on p. 453.

155. Memoranda, December 5, 1852; November 17, 1859.

156. *Pilot*, July 24, 1852, 4.

157. *Pilot*, July 24, 1852, 4. The Sisters of Charity school, conducted in conjunction with the cathedral since 1832, closed in 1858 when the cathedral was sold and the sisters moved to the South End. See Lord II, 620.

158. BAA.

159. Grozier essentially makes this argument in "Life and Times."

160. *Pilot*, October 22, 29, 1853. See also Grozier, "Life and Times," 331.

161. *Pilot*, April 23, 1853, 4.

162. Orestes Brownson to James A. McMaster, March 14, 1849 (NDA). McMaster was a prominent American Catholic journalist.

163. Schultz makes this argument in *Culture Factory*.

CHAPTER 4

1. See Lawrence Kennedy, "Power and Prejudice: Boston Political Conflict, 1885–1895" (PhD diss., Boston College, 1987), 111ff.

2. Ibid.

3. Quoted in Lord III, 118ff.

4. See Ibid., 120ff.

5. See Ibid., 120ff.

6. See Thomas Richard Mason, *Reform Politics in Boston* (Cambridge, MA: Harvard University, 1963), 160–4.

7. Actually, Fitzgerald had to overcome not the opposition of Yankee politicians so much as that of other Irish ward bosses, particularly Martin Lomasney, who so disliked Fitzgerald that he actually backed the Republican candidate. See Mason, 160–64.

8. See Mason, *Reform Politics*, 217.

9. *Herald*, December 13, 1905, 6.

10. *Sacred Heart Review*, February 11, 1905, 5; October 20, 1906, 5.

11. *Sacred Heart Review*, November 11, 1905, 5; January 21, 1905, 5.

12. *Sacred Heart Review*, November 18, 1905, 8.

13. Floyd Rodwin, "Middle Income Housing Problems in Boston: An Historical Analysis" (PhD diss., Harvard University, 1949), 13–14.

14. *Pilot*, February 2, 1867, 4.

15. Ibid.

16. *Pilot*, February 17, 1866, 4.

17. *Donahoe's Magazine*, "Notes on Current Topics," vol. ix (May 1883), 406.

18. See, for example, *Sacred Heart Review*, April 27, 1889, 2; February 15, 1890, 5.

19. *Sacred Heart Review*, June 15, 1889, 6.

20. *Sacred Heart Review*, April 27, 1889, 4, 5, 6; May 25, 1889, 5; June 1, 1889, 7.

21. *Sacred Heart Review*, February 9, 1889, 6; June 21, 1890, 6.

22. *Sacred Heart Review*, February 22, 1890, 18–19; March 1, 1890, 6.

23. *Sacred Heart Review*, March 15, 1890, 16; April 5, 1890, 11; August 9, 1890, 14.

24. *Sacred Heart Review*, August 11, 1906, 15–16.

25. *Sacred Heart Review*, November 4, 1905, 15.

26. *Sacred Heart Review*, August 11, 1906, 8.

27. Ibid.

28. Ibid., p. 10.

29. *Sacred Heart Review*, February 25, 1905, 13; March 4, 1905, 13; August 11, 1906, 13.

30. Based on a review of advertisements in the *Sacred Heart Review* from 1900 to 1906.

31. For example, through much of 1891 the *Sacred Heart Review* devoted an unusual amount of space to articles on drink. See, for example, August 1.

32. *Pilot*, July 11, 1891, 4.

33. *Pilot*, March 17, 1894, 4.

34. *Pilot*, June 25, 1892, 4; November 11, 1893, 4; April 4, 1894, 1. The priest, a Paulist named Peter J. O'Callaghan, was a Harvard graduate.

35. *Pilot*, March 31, 1894, 4.

36. See, for example, *Sacred Heart Review*, October 13, 1906, 5.

37. Boston College Archives. Statistics are based on analysis of entrants from the college's founding in 1864 to 1882.

38. Lord III, 6–8.

39. Lord III, 12–13.

40. Lord III, 112–8.

41. Lord III, 8–12.

42. Lord III, 424ff.

43. Bishop Bernard McQuaid to Father Daniel E. Hudson, C.S.C., May 22, 1903 (NDA).

44. Lord III, 334–5. Williams did have assistants, including a Vicar General, a Chancellor, a secretary, and a group of diocesan counselors drawn from the clergy, but he did not seem to make extensive use of them. For example, he, not his secretary, wrote most of his letters. He even kept his own financial records.

45. The quote is taken from p. 79 of a manuscript by Mother Augustine of the Mother of God entitled *Life of Archbishop Williams* that focused on his life as bishop of Boston (BAA). Mother Augustine was a Carmelite nun who was the daughter of Samuel Tuckerman, a prominent Bostonian convert to Roman Catholicism. She was also a godchild of Archbishop Williams and apparently visited him often and even served in some supportive capacity in his administration of the diocese. See Lord III, 443–4.

46. Lord III, 427.

47. Mother Augustine, *Life*, 444.

48. Lord III, 336.

49. Ibid., 185.

50. Mother Augustine, *Life*, 108, 116.

51. Ibid.

52. Donna Merwick, *Boston Priests, 1848–1910: A Study of Social and Intellectual Change* (Cambridge, MA: Harvard University Press, 1973), 3.

53. Mother Augustine, *Life*, 521.

54. Ibid., 72.

55. Ibid., 8.

56. Merwick, *Boston Priests*.

57. Williams to Cardinal Simeoni, Rome, February 18, 1886, in answer to Simeoni's letter of December 18, 1885, regarding the advisability of ethnic parishes in Boston. There are also innumerable instances in his actions that indicate that he never hesitated to accord full equality to ethnic parishes. See, for example, Lord III, 217–9. The implementation of this policy did not always proceed without strife, however. When Italians and Portuguese immigrants began arriving in the North End in the late 1860s and early 1870s, because of their small numbers he first opened a parish for the two groups to share, but this lasted only three years: in 1876 the Italians insisted on splitting off, forming their own parish of St. Leonard. See Lord III, 224. By the early 1880s the Italians had so multiplied that they wanted a second parish. They formed a "San Marco" Society that bought a meeting house. When Williams refused to dedicate it as a church unless they turned over the deed, which was the policy in the Boston diocese, they refused. This precipitated a feud that lasted six years until the Society capitulated, and the Sacred Heart parish was formed in 1890. See Lord III, 225–6.

58. Eduard Hamon, S.J., *Les Canadiens-Français de la Nouvelle-Angleterre*, Quebec, 1891, 391, quoted in Lord III, 196.

59. Lord III, 427.

60. Ibid., 428.

61. Ibid., 138–9, quoting Williams' speech as reprinted in Bernard Corr, ed., *Memorial of the Twenty-Fifth Anniversary of the Consecration of the Most Rev. John J. Williams, D.D., Archbishop of Boston* (Boston, 1891), 105–8.

62. Mother Augustine, *Life*, 86–91.

63. Lord III, 112–15.

64. Mother Augustine, *Life*, 110; Lord III, 385.

65. Mother Augustine, *Life*, 113.

66. Letter of Williams to Sisters of the Good Shepherd, New York, Memoirs, March 1867 (BAA).

67. Memoirs, January 27, 1874. Williams had earlier unsuccessfully solicited the services of the Christian Brothers. See Memoirs, January 22, 1867.

68. Mother Augustine, *Life*, 452.

69. From Williams' Circular Letter of October 5, 1877, quoted in Merwick, *Boston Priests*, 214 n. 63. See Lord III, 388.

70. Mother Augustine, *Life*, 306. She puts the date of the Union's founding as 1873.

71. Lord III, 53–54. See also Memoirs, June 20, 1866.

72. Lord III, 57–62.

73. Quoted in Ibid., 23.

74. Ibid., 79.

75. See Ibid., 90ff.

76. Note in Williams' hand on letter of Cardinal Simeoni to Archbishop Williams, Nov 21, 1891 (BAA), in Lord III, 177, footnote 25. Lord III has a more extensive account of the Bishop Ireland school plan controversy on 172–83.

77. See M. P. Curran, *The Life of Patrick A. Collins* (Boston: privately printed, 1906), 345–46; 374, n. 137.

78. See Lord III, 426–30.

79. Mother Augustine, *Life*, 424.

80. John Bilski, "The Catholic Church and American Imperialism, 1880–1900," *Historical Records and Studies*, vol. xlvii (New York: The United States Catholic Historical Society, 1959), 142.

81. The number of parochial schools includes only schools attached to Catholic parishes. Separate Catholic schools such as the Sisters of Notre Dame Academy and the Jesuits' Boston College are not included in the data. The data on the number of parochial schools is taken from the *Official Catholic Directory*, published each year and listing all parishes, schools, and other institutions for each Roman Catholic diocese in the United States. The directory had several different publishers over the years.

82. See Lord III, 81–85.

83. This notion that the public school movement gained much of its momentum from the belief that the family could no longer be relied on as the primary educational force has been developed in recent years in a variety of historical studies.

84. See Merwick, *Boston Priests*, 76–78, who argues this point.

85. Lord III, 428.

86. This is a point stressed, correctly, by Merwick, *Boston Priests*, 69.

87. Williams' nostalgia for the past seems to have been relatively common among those who were living through the astounding transitions of the late nineteenth century. For example, Edwin P. Seaver, the superintendent of public schools in Boston from 1880 to 1904, had been born in rural western Massachusetts in the 1830s and expressed much the same sentiments, though he seems to have accepted and reacted to the reality more constructively than Williams. See Marvin Lazerson, *Origins of the Urban School, Public Education in Massachusetts 1870–1915* (Cambridge, MA: Harvard University Press, 1971).

88. See Merwick, *Boston Priests*, 171.

89. Ibid., 73.

CHAPTER 5

1. Statistics used in this document are based mostly on the city of Boston and the suburbs within a ten-mile radius, even though the diocese included all of Suffolk, Essex, Middlesex, Plymouth, and Norfolk counties. The reasons for this are several, including the fact that more comparable statistics are available for this more limited area. Perhaps most important, using the towns within the ten-mile radius eliminates the small rural parishes that might have been exceptions to the general rule simply because of their small size and isolation. In fact, parishes outside the ten-mile radius included both rural communities and satellite cities such as Salem.

2. Lord III, 447.

3. James P. Gaffey, "The Changing of the Guard: The Rise of Cardinal O'Connell of Boston," *Catholic Historical Review,* 59 (1973): 225–44.

4. Lord III, from 492; William Henry O'Connell, *Sermons and Addresses of His Eminence William Cardinal O'Connell* (Cambridge, MA: Riverside Press, 1911–1938; 11 vols.), I, 9–17 (BAA).

5. William Henry O'Connell, "In the Beginning," *Sermons and Addresses,* III, 121–39.

6. Ibid.

7. Ibid.

8. See also Robert A. O'Leary, "William Henry O'Connell: A Social and Intellectual Biography" (PhD diss., Tufts University, 1980).

9. Lord III, 570–72.

10. "Address to the Education Association Convention," *Sermons and Addresses,* I, 187.

11. Lord III, 559.

12. Ibid.

13. *Sermons and Addresses,* IV, 234.

14. Ibid.

15. "The Family and the Home," *Sermons and Addresses,* IV, 165–166. See also O'Connell to Mrs. Louise Reggio, October 25, 1930 (O'Connell Papers, BAA); "The Church Essentially a Teaching Body," Address to the religious teachers at Boston College Summer School, June 30, 1924, in *Sermons and Addresses,* VIII, 146–49. See also "The Catholic Parent and the Catholic School," Address to the 20th Annual Catholic Teachers Institute, August 27, 1929, *Sermons and Addresses,* X; Rev. Francis W. Howard, Secretary General to the Catholic Educational Association, thanking O'Connell for inviting the Catholic Education Association to Boston (O'Connell Papers, BAA).

16. O'Connell to Mrs. Louise Reggio, October 25, 1930 (BAA).

17. "The Church Essentially a Teaching Body," *Sermons and Addresses,* VI, 146–49. See also "The Catholic Parent and the Catholic School," *Sermons and Addresses,* X.

18. See Francis W. Howard, Secretary General to the Catholic Educational Association, to O'Connell, July 15, 1908, thanking O'Connell for inviting the Catholic Education Association (BAA).

19. The scandal had to do with his nephew, "Jimmie" O'Connell, whose vocation to the priesthood the cardinal had nurtured, and who had served as the cardinal's influential secretary until he renounced the priesthood for marriage in 1920. The event was a personal disgrace for O'Connell, not only because of the family connection but because of the patronage involved. See O'Leary, "William Henry O'Connell," 94–98, for this and O'Connell's fortunes in Rome.

20. *Sermons and Addresses,* III, 191, 161–2; also, *Sermons and Addresses,* I, 191, for his 1909 address to the Catholic Education Association.

21. *Sermons and Addresses,* I, 161–2.

22. Hugh Francis Blunt, ed., *Readings from Cardinal O'Connell* (New York, D. Appleton-Century Co., 1930), 150, in O'Leary, "William Henry O'Connell," 195.

23. See *Pilot*, August 19, 1908, 4; November 15, 1913, 4; November 4, 1910; pastoral letter of November 30, 1907, *Sermons and Addresses*, I, 73–87.

24. "The Child's Training," pastoral letter of August 15, 1915, *Sermons and Addresses*, V, 35–45.

25. "The Responsibility of Catholic Parents," address at 21st annual Teachers' Institute, August 29, 1930, *Sermons and Addresses*, X, 156–57. This came shortly after Pius XI's encyclical on Christian education, which stated essentially the same thesis.

26. "Moral Training in Education," *Sermons and Addresses*, VIII, 151.

27. *Pilot*, December 20, 1913, 4 [editorial]. O'Connell personally edited the *Pilot* during these years, writing many of the editorials and approving the rest. This is abundantly clear from the *Pilot* file in the archdiocesan archives, so the *Pilot*'s positions are taken here to be O'Connell's own.

28. Address to Catholic Education Association, *Sermons and Addresses*, I.

29. Pastoral letter, "The Family and the Home," *Sermons and Addresses*, IV, 166.

30. *Pilot*, July 17, 1915, 4 [editorial]. See also "Moral Training in Education," *Sermons and Addresses*, VIII, 150–151.

31. "Address to the Catholic Education Association," *Sermons and Addresses*, I, 190. See also "Catholic Education," *Sermons and Addresses*, V, 253–61.

32. See the O'Connell correspondence with the Rev. John O'Brien of the *Review*. O'Connell considered O'Brien "the only troublesome person in the Clergy of the Archdiocese." James O'Connell to Rt. Rev. Sante Tampieri, Rome, January 31, 1913 (BAA).

33. O'Brien to O'Connell, November 8, 1911. According to O'Brien, he was willing to cease publication provided that O'Connell publicly accept responsibility for the paper's demise, which O'Connell was apparently unwilling to do (BAA).

34. Lord III, 523.

35. See Sister Louise, Annals (BAA).

36. See, for example, Annals, Sisters of Notre Dame, St. Augustine's parish, South Boston (Motherhouse archives, Ipswich, MA).

37. O'Connell to the Rev. George A. Lyons, October 3, 1908 (BAA).

38. See, for example, Report of George A. Lyons to O'Connell, December 18, 1908, January 17, 1911, etc. The annals of various convents attest to his diligence in visiting schools. See Annals, Sisters of Notre Dame, St. Augustine Convent, South Boston.

39. Hickey to O'Connell, October 7, 1913 (BAA). See also Augustine F. Hickey, "A Study of the Growth and Development of Catholic Education in the Archdiocese of Boston, 1907–1923" in *A Brief Historical Review of the Archdiocese of Boston* (Boston: Pilot Publishing Company, 1925).

40. See Hickey, *Brief Historical Review*; also Hickey to O'Connell, December 5, 1914; December 3, 1914; December 8, 1914; Sullivan to Hickey, December 4, 1914 (BAA). Some of the communities, notably the Sisters of Notre Dame, the Sisters of St. Joseph, the Sisters of St. Ann, and the Sisters of Providence, already had their own supervisors and merely had to designate these as the liaison with the archdiocese.

41. Hickey to O'Connell, February 1, 1921 (BAA). By 1921 all schools had implemented the music program except for seven French schools and one Polish

school, which gave so much time to foreign-language instruction that they had none left for music.

42. Hickey to O'Connell, April 3, 1919; Haberlin to Hickey, April 5, 1919 (BAA).

43. Quinlan to O'Connell, October 10, 1927; Haberlin to Quinlan, October 11, 1927 (BAA).

44. See Sister Mary of the Holy Angels, *The Quiet Revolution: The Educational Experience of Blessed Julie Billar and the Sisters of Notre Dame de Namur* (Glasgow: Burns, 1966). See also Annals, St. Augustine Parish, Boston.

45. See Sister Magdalena, "Patterns in the Design, A Brief Account of Some Events in the History of the Sisters of St. Joseph of the Archdiocese of Boston," 1965 (mimeographed) (Archives, Sisters of St. Joseph, Brighton, Mass.), 53; *Pilot*, August 1, 1908.

46. The Sisters of St. Joseph were also favored by O'Connell, probably because they were a diocesan congregation directly under his command while others had privileges directly from Rome that exempted them to a degree from control by the local bishop. When pastors wrote asking who to select for a new school, he invariably told them to ask the Sisters of St. Joseph.

47. O'Connell to Lyons, May 10, 1910; Hickey, 21–23.

48. Examples: Lyons to O'Connell, Jan. 16, 1911; Hickey to O'Connell, March 13, 1920.

49. As an example of pettiness, at one point the cardinal refused permission to a speaker from the Providence Diocese, with which he did not get along, stating: "Since when do we take lessons from Providence?" Quinlan to O'Connell, January 23, 1927, with O'Connell's note scribbled in the margin.

50. Hickey to O'Connell, September 25, 1917; O'Connell to Hickey, September 27, 1917 (BAA); Annals, Sisters of Notre Dame, St. Augustine Parish, South Boston, 1917. Some cross-fertilization was already going on an ad hoc basis. See St. Augustine Annals, August 1912, recounting a visit from the Sisters of Charity of Halifax. See also Hickey, "Growth and Development," pp. 21–23; Lord III, 640–1; Quinlan to O'Connell, September 22, 1926. BAA

51. Hickey, *Brief Historical Review*, 21–23; St. Augustine Annals.

52. Lord III, 640–1; Quinlan to O'Connell, September 22, 1926 (BAA).

53. See Hickey, *Brief Historical Review*, 26; St. Augustine Annals, 1912.

54. O'Connell letter to pastors, February 14, 1921. See, for example, Richard J. Quinlan, Supervisor of Schools, to O'Connell, December 8, 1930, a report prepared at O'Connell's command on all the religious activities at Boston College. See also the Rev. Thomas I. Gasson, S.J., President of Boston College, to O'Connell, December 19, 1910, and May 16, 1911, regarding the question of starting schools of law and medicine; and May 23, 1910, regarding O'Connell's refusal of permission for Gasson to speak at the National Education Association convention (BAA).

55. See, for example, Quinlan to O'Connell, December 8, 1930. See also Gasson to O'Connell, December 19, 1910, May 16, 1911, and May 23, 1910.

56. See O'Connell's secretary, Sullivan, to Sister Julia, October 8, 17, 1912, and Sister Julia to O'Connell, October 7, 8, 16, 1912, regarding purchase of property in the Fenway for what was to become Emmanuel College. O'Connell was angry that

the Sisters of Notre Dame had bought the property without consulting him but was delighted with the site and the plan. See also Sr. Rosalia, Superior of Notre Dame to Haberlin, September 12, 1927, and Haberlin to Sr. Rosalia, September 17, 1927 (BAA).

57. "The Catholic High School Movement," *Sermons and Addresses*, VIII, 116–7, a statement made May 17, 1924.

58. Catholics had received only a small fraction of the dollars dispensed over a century. *Pilot*, April 10, 1915, 1.

59. "State Aid," Address to Federation of Catholic Societies, October 8, 1917, *Sermons and Addresses*, V, 267–77.

60. *Pilot*, November 10, 1917, 4.

61. O'Connell to Honorable J. N. Baer, M.C., January 28, 1919 (BAA).

62. *Pilot*, June 28, 1919. See also March 29; and see entire folder in BAA on the Child Labor Amendment.

63. *Pilot*, November 13, 1920. See also January 29, 1921, Haberlin to the Rev. Francis Howard, Secretary General of the Catholic Educational Association, January 19, 1926, and February 4, 1919; Bishop P. J. Muldoon, Rockford, Illinois, to O'Connell, June 13, 1919 and O'Connell to Muldoon, June 16, 1919.

64. C. J. Sullivan, Secretary to Hickey, December 31, 1913. See also Hickey to O'Connell, November 1 and 28, 1913; Hickey to Sullivan, January 1, 1914; Hickey to O'Connell, January 2, 1914; Sullivan to Hickey, January 3, 1914; Hickey to Sullivan, January 5, 1914; March 30, April 21 and 23, 1914; Hickey to O'Connell, April 26, 1919; Hickey to O'Connell April 29, 1919.

65. *Pilot*, November 15, December 13, 1913, 4.

66. See Msgr. M. J. Splaine to Haberlin, November 5, 1919; Splaine, Francis Slattery, and Hickey to Haberlin, November 13, 1919; Splaine to Haberlin, February 18, 1920; Haberlin to Splaine, February 18, 1920; Splaine to Haberlin, February 20 and 23, 1920; Splaine to Haberlin, Mar 28, 1920.

67. *Pilot*, September 4, 1915, 1. The *Pilot* often made such remarks at the beginning and/or end of the school year. See, for example, May 20, 1916, 4; May 27, 1916, 4; June 10, 1916, 4; June 17, 1916, 4; February 10, 1917, 4. See also "The Catholic High School Movement," *Sermons and Addresses*, VIII, 116–7.

68. Riordan to O'Connell, July 2, 1915; Sullivan to Riordan, July 3, 1915; Riordan to O'Connell, July 5, 1915; Sullivan to Riordan, August 14, 1915; Riordan to O'Connell, December 3, 1915 (BAA).

69. Haberlin to the Rev. James H. Flannery, October 29, 1926; October 4, 1927 (BAA).

70. Haberlin to the Rev. Thomas R. McCoy, March 23, 1927 (BAA).

71. Ibid.

72. The period after 1930 is difficult to analyze because of two factors that influenced both parochial and public school enrollments, not always in the same way. The first was the Great Depression, which both drove numbers of children away from schools where they might have to pay and kept larger numbers in school for longer periods because of decreased employment opportunity. The second was a substantial decrease in the school-age population due to the population cycle, and possibly also to the advent of birth control. There is disagreement as to whether and/or how much

the decline in the school-age population affected Catholic families differentially from the general population. To avoid possible pitfalls during this period, comparative enrollment statistics have been limited to the period before 1930, which is a period amply long to establish clearly defined trends.

73. *Pilot*, September 4, 1915.

74. *Pilot*, November 15, December 13, 1913, 4 [editorials].

75. *Sermons and Addresses*, I, 189.

76. Address to Clergy. *Sermons and Addresses*, I, 159.

77. The Rev. John J. Farrell to Father Haberlin, December 11, 1924; see also Farrell to O'Connell, August 22, 1922; O'Connell to Farrell, August 28, 1922; Farrell to the Rev. Francis A. Burke, Secretary, to O'Connell, March 13, 1928 (BAA).

78. See parish file and financial reports. The absence of correspondence regarding building a school in these parishes might not be noteworthy except that in other parish files there is such correspondence. This leads one to conclude that O'Connell was at best inconsistent in his campaign for parochial schools.

79. See the Rev. John H. Harrigan to Haberlin, January 4, 1923; Harrigan and O'Connell correspondence through O'Connell's secretary Burke, January 4, 10, 14, 1928; April 10, 21, 23, 27, 1928; November 16, 1929 (BAA).

80. See Quinlan to O'Connell, September 26, 1927, submitting the list. On this issue of wealthy parishes without schools see also the Rev John H. Harrigan to Haberlin, January 4, 1923; Harrigan to O'Connell and O'Connell correspondence through O'Connell's secretary, Burke, January 4, 10, 14, 1928; April 10, 21, 23, 27, 1928; November 16, 1929. Other examples are abundant in the parish files of parishes with obvious wealth but no school: see the Rev. John J. Farrell of St. Paul's in Dorchester to Haberlin, December 11, 1924; Farrell to O'Connell, August 22, 1922; O'Connell to Farrell, August 28, 1922; Farrell to the Rev. Francis A. Burke, Secretary to O'Connell, March 13, 1928 (all in BAA).

81. At least, there is no record of such sanction.

82. See "The Catholic Parent and the Catholic School," *Sermons and Addresses*, X, 54.

83. See, for example, James W. Sanders, *The Education of an Urban Minority, Catholics in Chicago, 1833–1965* (New York: Oxford University Press, 1977).

84. Lord III, 697. It appears that St. Anne's parish in Boston's Readville section, established in 1919, also began life this way.

85. Lord III, 525, from *Sermons and Addresses*, IV, 58.

86. For details of various academies, see Sister Mary Xaveria Sullivan, *The History of Catholic Secondary Education in the Archdiocese of Boston* (Washington, D.C.: Catholic University of America Press, 1946). For the Walnut Hill Academy, see Sister Mary Borgia, C.S.J. to O'Connell, March 11, 1919 (BAA). See also *Sermons and Addresses*, III, 188–89.

87. For Walnut Hill, see Sister Mary Borgia, C.S.J, to O'Connell, March 11, 1919 (BAA).

88. *Sermons and Addresses*, I, 188–89.

89. See Edward Spiers, *The Central Catholic High School, A Survey of Their History and Status in the United States* (Washington, D.C.: Catholic University of America Press, 1951). See also Sanders, *Education of an Urban Minority*.

90. Haberlin to O'Connell, May 30, 1929; Burke to Haberlin, May 31, 1929 (BAA).

91. See, for example, Sanders, *Education of an Urban Minority.*

92. In all there were twenty-nine French parishes in the entire diocese by 1940, and twenty-four of them (82.8 percent) had schools, far in excess of the overall proportion of parishes with schools in the Boston diocese.

93. Merwick, *Boston Priests.*

CHAPTER 6

1. *Republic,* November 5, 1904, 3.

2. Alice Woodward Karl, "Public School Politics in Boston, 1895–1920" (PhD diss., Harvard University, 1970).

3. *Pilot,* December 15, 1917, 4.

4. *Boston Globe,* July 17, 1963, 24.

5. *Boston Herald,* February 4, 1958, 24.

6. See BSC Proceedings, 1939, 136–42; *Globe,* June 27, 1939, 10; *Herald,* June 27, 1939, 10.

7. *Pilot,* August 3, 1912, 4. See also *Sacred Heart Review,* July 27, 1912, 3. For a general treatment of school politics during this period, see Karl, "Public School Politics."

8. "Report of the Superintendent," BSC document no. 17, 1924, p. 9.

9. "Course in Citizenship," BSC document no. 10, 1924, pp. 89, 73.

10. Based on specific comparison of the 1923 Course of Study for Catholic schools and the 1924 Character Education program implemented by the public schools. Interestingly, though in this case the influence went from the Catholic side into the public, the virtues themselves that were to shape the character of the future Bostonian did not differ much, if at all, from those reached and practiced by generations past of Puritans. Indeed, the self-control and self-respect, honor and reliability, duty, loyalty, and above all love of hard work smacked much more of the so-called Protestant ethic than it did of the allegedly Catholic and Irish virtues. This suggests that although the Irish were now dictating policy for the public schools, they had been so thoroughly "Puritanized" by their past traumatic stay in Boston that the shift in the balance of power made little difference in the running of the schools, except perhaps that the descendants of the Puritans had by this time undergone substantial softening and might have preferred a more progressive change in the schools. The Catholics, though, took smug satisfaction in believing that they had now become the true guardians of that ancient Boston tradition.

11. On this issue see Polly Kaufman, "Boston Women and City School Politics, 1872–1905" (PhD diss., Boston University, 1978).

12. "Children of Immigrants in Schools," vol. I, Part III, table 96, pp. 129–31. A sizeable number of non–French Canadians were listed, for example, many of whom were probably of Irish origin.

13. Attempts to make more dispassionate estimates based on analysis of names have resulted in gross approximations at best. From the names alone, for example, who could have safely concluded that the following were Catholics: Jeremiah Burke,

Frank Thompson, Mary Mellyn, Arthur Gould, Patrick Campbell? Yet every one of these superintendents or assistant superintendents was a Catholic.

14. Interview, Sister Fidelma, C.S.J., with Sister Justin, C.S.J. regarding Sister Mary Loyola Boyle, C.S.J., typewritten transcript in Archives, Sisters of St. Joseph, Brighton, Mass.

15. See Stephen James Clarke, "Two Schools and Two Ideas: A Study of Progressivism and Character Education in the Public Schools of the City of Boston, Massachusetts, and the Parochial Schools of the Roman Catholic Archdiocese of Boston, 1920–1940" (PhD diss., Harvard University, 1965); also Hickey to O'Connell, September 10, 1920; Quinlan to O'Connell, January 1927; Hickey to O'Connell, March 14, 1923; September 13, 1921; September 12, 1922 (BAA); Sister Magdalena, "Patterns in the Design," 53; Sisters of Notre Dame Annals, St. Augustine parish, South Boston, 1920.

16. Thomas I. Gasson, S.J., President, Boston College, to O'Connell, December 3, 1913 (BAA); "Boston College School of Education," document in Boston College Archives, no date but apparently 1919, pp. 72–73.

17. Educational lectures of Rev. James F. Mellyn, S.J. (Boston College Archives). These consist of notes as well as written lectures. *Pilot*, December 16, 1916; also March 21, 1914; December 30, 1916; October 2, 1915; *Republic*, July 23, 1904, 6; also September 10, 1904.

18. Course of Studies, 1923.

19. Course of Studies, Introduction, VII, 132, 145. The suggested readings by no means excluded the classic writers but supplemented these with a generous sprinkling of lesser-known Catholic authors, as indicated.

20. *Course of Studies in the Academies and Parochial Schools of the Sisters of Notre Dame* (Cincinnati: Notre Dame Press, 1895), iv. This plan was still in effect in the Sisters of Notre Dame schools of Boston at least through the 1920s. Interview with Sister Dorothea, S.N.D., Archivist, Ipswich, Mass.

21. "Constitutions of the Sisters of St. Joseph," 91, 10–11, 67 (Archives, Sisters of St. Joseph, Brighton, Mass.); interview of Sr. Fidelma, C.S.J., with Sister Justin McCarthy, C.S.J., October 27, 1977 (transcript in archives).

22. Course of Studies, Introduction, ii–iii.

23. Course of Studies.

24. *Sacred Heart Review* September 3, 1892, 9.

25. Ibid.

26. The French actually had more numerous parishes in the Boston diocese outside of Boston itself, and all of these had schools.

Bibliography

Billington, Ray Allen. *The Protestant Crusade*. New York: Macmillan, 1938.

Burns, Constance Keane. "The Irony of Progressive Reform: Boston, 1898–1910." PhD diss., Boston College, 1985.

Clarke, Stephen James. "Two Schools and Two Ideas: A Study of Progressivism and Character Education in the Public Schools of the City of Boston, Massachusetts, and the Parochial Schools of the roman Catholic Archdiocese of Boston, 1920–1940." PhD diss., Harvard University, 1965.

Cronin, Joseph Marr. *Reforming Boston Schools 1930–2006: Overcoming Corruption and Racial Segregation*. New York: Palgrave-Macmillan, 2008.

Cross, Robert D. "The Origins of Catholic Parochial Schools in America." *American Benedictine Review* 16 (1965): 194–209.

Cullen, James Bernard, ed. *The Story of the Irish in Boston, Together with Biographical Sketches of Representative Men and Noted Women*. Boston: H. A. Plimpton, 1893.

Culver, Raymond. *Horace Mann and Religion in the Massachusetts Public Schools*. New Haven: Yale University Press, 1929.

Curran, M. P. *The Life of Patrick Collins*. Boston: privately printed, 1906.

Dunnigan, David. *A History of Boston College*. Milwaukee: Bruce Publishing, 1947.

Fraser, J. W. "Mayor John F. Fitzgerald and Boston Schools, 1905–1913." *Historical Journal of Massachusetts* 12, no. 2 (1984): 117–30.

Gaffey, James. "The Changing of the Guard: The Rise of Cardinal O'Connell of Boston." *Catholic Historical Review* LIX (1973): 225–44.

Grozier, Richard J. "The Life and Times of John Bernard Fitzpatrick, Third Roman Catholic Bishop of Boston." PhD diss., Boston College, 1966.

Handlin, Oscar. *Boston's Immigrants: A Study in Acculturation 1790–1865*. Rev. and enl. ed. Cambridge, MA: Belknap Press of Harvard University Press, 1991.

Ibson, John Duffy. "Will the World Break Your Heart? A Historical Analysis of the Dimensions and Consequences of Irish-American Assimilation." PhD diss., Brandeis University, 1976.

Johnson, Marilynn S. *The New Bostonians, How Immigrants Have Transformed the Metro Region Since the 1960s.* Amherst: University of Massachusetts Press, 2015.

Kaestle, Carl F., and Maris A. Vinovskis. *Education and Social Change in Nineteenth-Century Massachusetts.* New York: Cambridge University Press, 1980.

Kane, Paula M. *Separatism and Subculture: Boston Catholicism, 1900–1920.* Chapel Hill: University of North Carolina Press, 2001.

Karl, Alice Woodard. "Public School Politics in Boston, 1895–1920." PhD diss., Harvard University, 1970.

Katz, Michael B. *The Irony of Urban School Reform: Educational Innovation in Mid-Nineteenth Century Massachusetts.* Boston: Beacon Press, 1968.

Kaufman, Polly Adams Welts. "Boston Women and City School Politics, 1872–1905: Nurturers and Protectors in Public Education." PhD diss., Boston University, 1978.

Kaufman, Polly Welts. "Julia Harrington Duff, an Irish Woman Confronts the Boston Power Structure, 1900–1905." *Historical Journal of Massachusetts* 18, no. 2 (1990): 113–37.

Kenneally, James J. "The Burning of the Ursuline Convent: A Different View." *Records of the American Catholic Historical Society in Philadelphia* 90 (March–December 1979): 15–21.

Kennedy, Lawrence. "Power and Prejudice: Boston Political Conflict, 1885–1895." PhD diss., Boston College, 1987.

Kinzer, Donald. *An Episode in Anti-Catholicism: The American Protective Association.* Seattle: University of Washington Press, 1964.

Knights, Peter R. *The Plain People of Boston, 1830–1860: A Study in City Growth.* New York: Oxford University Press, 1971.

Lazerson, Marvin. *Origins of the Urban School: Public Education in Massachusetts, 1870–1915.* Cambridge, MA: Harvard University Press, 1971.

Lord, Robert H., John E. Sexton, and Edward T. Harrington. *History of the Archdiocese of Boston in the Various Stages of Its Development, 1604–1943.* 3 vols. Boston: Pilot Publishing Company, 1945.

MacDougall, Isabella. "Transformation of an Ideal: Boston Public Schools, 1888–1891." Honors thesis, Department of History, Radcliffe College, 1967.

Mann, Arthur. *Yankee Reformers in the Urban Age.* Cambridge, MA: Harvard University Press, 1954.

Mason, Thomas Richard. "Reform Politics in Boston." PhD thesis, Harvard University, 1963.

Maynard, Theodore. *Orestes Brownson: Yankee Radical, Catholic.* New York: Macmillan, 1943.

McCaffrey, Lawrence J. *The Irish Diaspora in America.* Bloomington: Indiana University Press, 1976.

Meiring, Bernard J. "Educational Aspects of the Legislation of the Councils of Baltimore, 1829–1884." PhD diss., University of California, Berkeley, 1963.

Merwick, Donna. *Boston Priests, 1848–1910: A Study of Social and Intellectual Change.* Cambridge, MA: Harvard University Press, 1973.

Messerli, Jonathon. *Horace Mann: A Biography.* New York: Alfred A. Knopf, 1972.

Murphy, Francis Stephen Jr. "A History of Teacher Training in the City of Boston and the Role of the Laboratory School as an Integral Part in the Preparation of Teachers." PhD diss., University of Massachusetts, Amherst, 1989.

Nolan, Janet. *Servants of the Poor: Teachers and Mobility in Ireland and Irish America.* Notre Dame, IN: University of Notre Dame Press, 2004.

Oates, Mary J. "Organized Voluntarism: The Catholic Sisters in Massachusetts, 1870–1940." *American Quarterly* 30 (Winter 1978): 652–80.

O'Connell, William Henry. *Sermons and Addresses of His Eminence William Cardinal O'Connell.* 11 vols. Cambridge, MA: Riverside Press, 1911–1938.

O'Connor, Thomas H. *Boston Catholics. A History of the Church and Its People.* Boston: Northeastern University Press, 1984.

O'Connor, Thomas H. *Fitzpatrick's Boston, 1846–1866: John Bernard Fitzpatrick, Third Bishop of Boston.* Boston: Northeastern University Press, 1984.

O'Connor, Thomas H., ed. *Two Centuries of Faith: The Influence of Catholicism on Boston, 1808–2008.* New York: Crossroad Publishing Company, 2009.

O'Leary, Robert A. "William Henry O'Connell: A Social and Intellectual Biography." PhD diss., Tufts University, 1980.

O'Toole, James M. *William Henry O'Connell and the Catholic Church in Boston, 1859–1944.* Notre Dame, IN: University of Notre Dame Press, 1992.

Ryan, Dennis P. *Beyond the Ballot Box: A Social History of the Boston Irish, 1845–1917.* 1983. Reprint, Amherst: University of Massachusetts Press, 1989.

Schreiber, Henry M. "The Working People of Boston in the Middle of the Nineteenth Century." PhD diss., Boston University, 1950.

Schultz, Stanley K. *The Culture Factory, Boston Public Schools, 1789–1860.* New York: Oxford University Press, 1973.

Shattuck, Lemmuel. *Report to the Committee of the City Council Appointed to Obtain the Census of Boston for the Year 1845.* Boston: J. H. Eastburn, 1846.

Solomon, Barbara Miller. *Ancestors and Immigrants: A Changing New England Tradition.* Cambridge, MA: Harvard University Press, 1956.

Thernstrom, Stephan. *The Other Bostonians: Poverty and Progress in the American Metropolis, 1860–1970.* Cambridge, MA: Harvard University Press, 1973.

Tyack, D. B. *Seeking Common Ground: Public Schools in a Diverse Society.* Cambridge, MA: Harvard University Press, 2003.

Vinovskis, Maris A. "Trends in Massachusetts Education, 1826–1860." *History of Education Quarterly* 12 (1972): 501–29.

Walsh, Francis R. "The Boston Pilot: A Newspaper for the Irish Immigrant, 1829–1908." PhD diss., Boston University, 1968.

Walsh, Louis S. *Historical Sketch of the Growth of the Catholic Parochial Schools in the Archdiocese of Boston.* Newton Highlands, MA: Press of St. John's Industrial Training School, 1901.

Walton, Susan Charlotte. "To Preserve the Faith: Catholic Charities in Boston, 1870–1930." PhD diss., Boston University, 1983.

Wilkie, Jane Riblett. "Social Status, Acculturation, and School Attendance in 1850 Boston." *Journal of Social History* 11, no. 2 (Winter 1977): 179–92.

Zolot, Herbert Marshall. "The Issue of Good Government and James Michael Curley: Curley and the Boston Scene from 1897–1918." PhD diss., State University of New York, Stony Brook, 1975.

Index